Latin American Studies

Latin American Studies

An Annotated Bibliography of Core Works

Ana María Cobos
and Ana Lya Sater

McFarland & Company, Inc., Publishers
Jefferson, North Carolina, and London

Library of Congress Cataloguing-in-Publication Data

Cobos, Ana María, 1954–
    Latin American studies : an annotated bibliography of core works /
Ana María Cobos and Ana Lya Sater.
      p.   cm.
    Includes indexes.
    ISBN 0-7864-1256-9 (softcover : 50# alkaline paper)
    1. Latin America—Bibliography.   I. Sater, Ana Lya.   II. Title.

Z1601 .C536 2002
[F1408]
016.98—dc21
                                 2001008123

British Library cataloguing data are available

Cover illustration: ©2002 Artville

Manufactured in the United States of America

McFarland & Company, Inc., Publishers
  Box 611, Jefferson, North Carolina 28640
   www.mcfarlandpub.com

To our families, who have been
so patient throughout this arduous project

Acknowledgments

The authors wish to acknowledge the advice and support received from Iliana Sonntag, Barbara Valk, and Roberto Trujillo. We wish to thank Agustín Espinoza and Melissa Klimowicz for their technical assistance. Debbie Immel, Lucila Soria, and Terri Martin were always willing to verify bibliographic information or provide inter-library loan service. We are grateful to the ALA Publishing Committee Whitney-Carnegie Award for helping us to defray part of the production costs. We thank William F. Sater for the use of his fax machine and personal HAHR collection and John M. Dixon for his editorial advice.

Last, but not least, we thank the staff of the Latin American Studies Association for their initial advice, and our SALALM colleagues for their professional support.

Contents

Preface

Purpose

The purpose of this bibliography is to provide an annotated, recommended, core list of books in the field of Latin American studies. It is aimed primarily at community, junior, four-year college, and large public libraries. It is intended as a selection tool for libraries that do not have a Latin American specialist on staff or whose institutions do not offer degrees in Latin American studies but do offer courses in the field. Besides helping librarians select appropriate materials for their libraries, this bibliography may be used also to evaluate existing collections. Moreover, it will aid teachers, students, and non–Latin Americanist researchers to identify relevant Latin American resources.

Scope

This bibliography surveys books about Latin America for a general readership. It cites more than 1400 sources published in English (or in bilingual editions where one of the languages is English) between 1986 and 2000. These sources span the social sciences, humanities, and natural sciences. An effort has been made to include cross-disciplinary or interdisciplinary works valuable for undergraduate study. In most cases, highly specialized scholarly works and publications resulting from conferences or symposia have been excluded. Books that contain bibliographies or indexes have been given preference. Periodicals, children's literature, and audio-visual resources have been omitted.

For the purposes of this book, Latin America is defined as all geographic areas south of the Rio Grande. While these are chiefly Spanish and Portuguese speaking regions, works about French, English, and Dutch speaking areas also are covered. Literary authors living abroad (e.g., Guillermo Cabrera Infante and Isabel Allende) are included if their work is considered to be "quintessentially Latin American," as defined by Thomas Colchie in the introduction to his *A Hammock Beneath the Mangoes* (Colchie 1991, x). Materials regarding the Hispanic or Latino experience in the United States have been omitted.

In compiling this bibliography, the editors made a conscientious effort to identify items about diverse issues which previous comparable surveys about Latin America have generally ignored, such as works about women, indigenous peoples and other marginalized groups, and the environment. In addition, translations of key works by Latin American authors and scholars have been included.

History

The idea for this project developed from an evaluation of the Latin American collection of the Meyer Library at Stanford University. This activity, using *Books for College Libraries*, 3rd ed. (BCL3), demonstrated the need for a basic, general, core list of Latin American materials. For an undergraduate collection BCL3 was too specialized, uneven, outdated, and incomplete in its coverage of Latin American resources. Further, the sources in BCL3 were often out of print or were in Spanish or Portuguese.

Other surveys of Latin American publications also were unsatisfactory, outdated, or unsuitable, for undergraduate needs. The *SALALM Basic List of Latin American Materials in Spanish, Portuguese, and French* has never been revised and deals only with works in the languages mentioned. *The Handbook of Latin American Studies, The Hispanic American Historical Review, Latin American Studies: A Basic Guide to Sources, Latin America and the Caribbean: A Critical Guide to Research Sources*, and *Latin America in English-Language Reference Books: A Selected, Annotated Bibliography*, while essential for research collections, are too specialized for undergraduates and general users.

This project is supported by a Whitney-Carnegie award from the ALA Publishing Committee.

Methodology

Citations for this work were identified by perusing reviews from a variety of publications, including *Booklist, Choice,*

Hispanic American Historical Review, Library Journal, Los Angeles Times Book Review, New York Review of Books, New York Times Book Review, and *Publishers Weekly*. Catalogs of major university presses that focus on Latin American studies (e.g., University of California, Florida, New Mexico, and Texas at Austin) were also examined. These citations were the core of a master database that was manipulated by author, title, and subject. During the editing process the compilers sought to achieve balance among subjects and to identify key works for each country. Whenever possible, the bibliography lists at least one current, in-print source for each of the nations of the region. Also included are single volumes about Latin America from general multi-volume sets.

Most of the annotations are based on the reviews from the sources mentioned above. Whenever feasible, the compilers examined the recommended titles. The annotations are purposefully brief and focus on description only. Evaluations have been deliberately omitted from the annotations because the authors recommend all works included in this bibliography.

Older titles were checked for availability. Some out-of-print titles have been deleted; whenever available, new editions or similar works have been substituted. A few, valuable out-of-print titles remain in the bibliography because they are available via Internet out-of-print dealers.

Organization

This book is arranged into six chapters, each covering a different broad subject. The chapters are divided into narrower topics, and in some cases, these topics are further subdivided by region or country. These divisions by region or country vary in accordance with the number of citations. For example, when individual Caribbean islands are representd in only a few works, they are grouped under a general Caribbean area heading.

General works appear at the beginning of each chapter or its sections. Multidisciplinary works are assigned to the predominant subject area. Cross-references to other subjects appear in the introductions to the chapters. If several aspects are treated equally in a work, it is assigned to the broadest category. Throughout the work, citations are arranged alphabetically by author or editor's surname, or title if there is no author or editor. English alphabetization rules apply. The index contains entries for authors, titles, geographic regions and countries.

The entries comprise author or editor, title, place of publication, publisher, date, pagination, ISBN, and annotation. "OP" at the end of the annotation indicates the title is out-of-print. Citations also indicate the availability of bibliographies, illustrations, and indices. When available, the URL for the full text is provided. The ISBNs for multi-volume works may be a single number for the set or a unique number for each volume. In the latter case, the initial common digits appear at the end of the citation. The remaining numbers of the ISBN appear in the annotation with the corresponding volume.

The number of citations in each chapter reflects the amount of material published on the subject. However, a selection of representative works by prolific authors has been included in the Literature chapter. Thus, in this bibliography, the majority of citations are found in the Literature and Social Sciences chapters. During the 1990s, for instance, works about Central American politics were a dominant theme while other topics received scant attention. Perhaps in the future, emphasis will be placed on other topics. Meanwhile, this annotated list of books about Latin America is offered as a beginning selection tool for the non-specialist. Plans for an electronic update of the subject are under consideration as a continuation of this effort.

References

American Library Association. Committee on Library Cooperation with Latin America (William C. Haywood, George Finney, Manuel Sánchez, Mary E. Brindley). *Books of Latin American Interest in Public Libraries of the United States.* Chicago: ALA, 1942. (Studies of the A.L.A. Committee on Library cooperation with Latin America; 4).

American Library Association. Committee on Library Cooperation with Latin America (George Finney). *Books of Latin American History: A Study of Collections Available in Colleges and Universities of the United States.* Chicago: ALA, 1942. (Studies of the A.L.A. Committee on Library cooperation with Latin America; 3).

American Library Association. Committee on Library Cooperation with Latin America (Abel Plenn). *List of Latin American Serials: A Survey of Exchanges Available in U.S. Libraries.* Chicago: ALA, 1941. (Studies of the A.L.A. Committee on Library cooperation with Latin America; 1).

Bayitch, S.A. *Latin America and the Caribbean: A Bibliographical Guide to Works in English.* Coral Gables, FL: University of Miami Press, 1967. (Interamerican Legal Studies; 10).

Birkos, Alexander S., and Lewis A. Tambs. *Latin American Studies.* Kent, OH: Kent State University Press, 1971. (Academic Writers Guide to Periodicals; 1).

Books for College Libraries: A Core Collection of 50,000 Titles. 3rd. ed. Chicago: American Library Association, 1988.

Colchie, Thomas, ed. *A Hammock Beneath the Mangoes: Stories from Latin America.* New York: Dutton, 1991.

Covington, Paula. *Latin America and the Caribbean: A Critical Guide to Research Sources.* New York: Greenwood Press, 1992.

Dame, Hartley F., and J. M. Maarum. *Introductory Guide to Latin American Studies: A Bibliographical Essay.* Washington, DC: Center of Research in Social Systems, American University, 1966.

Graham, Ann Hartness. *Latin America in English-Language Reference Books: A Selected, Annotated Bibliography.* New York: Special Libraries Association, 1981.

Griffin, Charles C., and J. Benedict Warren. *Latin America: A Guide to the Historical Literature.* Austin, TX: University of Texas Press, 1971. (Conference on Latin American History; 4).

Handbook of Latin American Studies. Washington, DC: Library of Congress, 1935–

Hawkins, John N. *Teacher's Resource Handbook for Latin American Studies: An Annotated Bibliography of Curriculum Materials Preschool through Grade Twelve.* Los Angeles: UCLA Latin American Center Publications, 1975.

The Hispanic American Historical Review. Washington, DC: Board of Editors of the Hispanic American Historical Review, 1918– .

McNeil, Robert A., ed. *Latin American Studies: A Basic Guide to Sources.* 2nd ed., rev. and enl. Metuchen, NJ: Scarecrow Press, 1990.

REFORMA, Arizona Chapter. *A Core Collection of Print Material for Libraries Serving the Spanish-Speaking of the Southwest.* Tucson, AZ: University of Arizona Libraries, 1978.

Woodbridge, Hensley, and Dan Newberry, co-editors. *Basic List of Latin American Materials in Spanish, Portuguese, and French.* Amherst, MA: SALALM Secretariat, 1975.

I

Reference Works

This section includes reference works such as encyclopedias, dictionaries, and bibliographies on multidisciplinary topics. The majority of citations are from the following three series: "Area Handbook Series," "World Bibliographical Series," and "In Focus." The section is subdivided by region and countries. NB: the URL is provided in the note for out of print titles that are available electronically.

Latin America

1. Adams, Jerome R. *Notable Latin American Women: Twenty-Nine Leaders, Rebels, Poets, Battlers, and Spies, 1500–1900.* Jefferson, NC: McFarland, 1995. 191 p. Bibl., ill., index. ISBN 0786400226.

This work presents the lives and achievements of Latin American women who participated in the conquest, wars of independence, or the arts.

2. Collier, Simon et al., eds. *The Cambridge Encyclopedia of Latin America and the Caribbean.* 2nd ed. New York: Cambridge University Press, 1992. 479 p. Bibl., ill., index. (A Cambridge reference book.) ISBN 0521413222.

This one-volume encyclopedia presents succinct coverage of contemporary issues such as international debt, the environment, and population growth. It also covers the region's extensive cultural and intellectual traditions.

3. Henderson, James D. et al., eds. *A Reference Guide to Latin American History.* Armonk, NY: M.E. Sharpe, 2000. 615 p. Bibl., ill., index. ISBN 1563247445.

This bibliography presents in a chronological, topical, and biographical arrangement, citations covering all aspects of Latin American social, popular, and cultural life from 40,000 BC through 1999. The focus, however, is on twentieth century events.

4. Merrill, Tim, ed. *Guyana and Belize: Country Studies.* 2nd ed. Washington, DC: Library of Congress Research Div., 1993. 408 p. Bibl., ill., index. (Area handbook series; DA Pam 550-82.) ISBN 084440778X.

This series covers cultural, historical, socioeconomic, and political aspects. Research for this edition on Guyana and Belize was completed in January 1992. Full text is available from http://lcweb2.loc.gov/frd/cs/bztoc.html and http://lcweb2.loc.gov/frd/cs/gytoc.html.

5. *South America, Central America and the Caribbean, 2000.* 8th ed. London, England: Europa Publications, 1999. 800 p. Bibl., ill., index. ISBN 1857430670.

This one-volume source includes basic information about most aspects of the forty-eight countries and territories of the region including social issues, economics, finance and industry, government, and culture. It also contains contact information for regional organizations.

6. Tenenbaum, Barbara A., and Georgette M. Dorn et al., eds. *Encyclopedia of Latin American History and Culture.* New York: C. Scribner's Sons, 1996. 5 vols. Bibl., ill., index. ISBN 0684192535.

This 5-volume, award-winning reference set examines Latin American culture. While its focus is social history, politics and economics, other cultural expressions such as anthropology, and archaeology also are examined.

7. Tenenbaum, Barbara A., and Georgette M. Dorn et al., eds. *Latin America: History and Culture.* New York: C. Scribner's Sons, 1999. 4 vols. Bibl., ill., index. ISBN 0684805766.

This 4-volume set is a condensation of the award-winning *Encyclopedia of Latin American History and Culture.*

Argentina

8. Biggins, Alan, comp. *Argentina.* Santa Barbara, CA: Clio Press, 1991. 460 p. Ill., index. (World bibliographical series; 130.) ISBN 1851091092.

Each volume in this series is prepared by a country specialist and provides selected, multidisciplinary references for the generalist.

9. Rudolph, James D., ed. *Argentina: A Country Study.* 3rd ed. Washington, DC: American University Foreign Studies, 1986. 404 p. Bibl., ill., index. (Area handbook series; DA pam 550-73.) ISBN N/A.

See entry 4. Research for this edition was completed in August 1985. (OP)

Belize

10. Wright, Peggy, and Brian E. Coutts, comps. *Belize.* 2nd ed. Santa Barbara, CA: Clio Press, 1993. 307 p. Ill., index. (World

bibliographical series; 21.) ISBN 1851091327. *See* entry 8.

Bolivia

11. Hudson, Rex A., and Dennis M. Hanratty, eds. *Bolivia: A Country Study.* 3rd ed. Washington, DC: Library of Congress Research Div., 1991. 354 p. Bibl., ill., index. (Area handbook series DA pam; 550-66.) ISBN 0160321271.

See entry 4. Research for this edition was completed in December 1989. Full text is available from http://lcweb2.loc.gov/frd/cs/botoc.html. (OP)

12. Yeager, Gertrude, comp. *Bolivia.* Santa Barbara, CA: Clio Press, 1988. 228 p. Index . (World bibliographical series; 89.) ISBN 1851090665. *See* entry 8.

Brazil

13. Dickenson, John P., comp. *Brazil.* Rev. ed. Santa Barbara, CA: Clio Press, 1997. 244 p. Ill., index. (World bibliographical series; 57.) ISBN 1851092595. *See* entry 8.

14. Hudson, Rex A., ed. *Brazil: A Country Study.* 5th ed. Washington, DC: Library of Congress Research Div., 1998. 658 p. Bibl., ill., index. (DA pam; 550-20.) ISBN 0844408549.

See entry 4. Research for this edition was completed in April 1997. Full text is available fromhttp://lcweb2.loc.gov/frd/cs/brtoc.htm.

15. Rocha, Jan. *Brazil: A Guide to the People, Politics, and Culture.* New York: Interlink Books, 1999. 100 p. Bibl., ill. (In focus.) ISBN 1566563283 pbk.

This booklet covers special economic, political, and cultural aspects of the country.

Caribbean Area

16. Berleant-Schiller, Riva, and Susan Lowes, comps. *Antigua and Barbuda.* Santa Barbara, CA: Clio Press, 1995. 210 p. Ill. (World bib-

liographical series; 182.) ISBN 1851092285. *See* entry 8.

17. Boultbee, Paul G., comp. *The Bahamas.* Santa Barbara, CA: Clio Press, 1989. 195 p. Ill., index. (World bibliographical series; 108.) ISBN 1851091025. (OP) *See* entry 8.

18. Crane, Janet, comp. *Martinique.* Santa Barbara, CA: Clio Press, 1995. 174 p. Ill., index. (World bibliographical series; 175.) ISBN 1851091513. *See* entry 8.

19. Haggerty, Richard A., ed. *Dominican Republic and Haiti: Country Studies.* 2nd ed. Washington, DC: Library of Congress Research Div., 1991. 456 p. Bibl., ill., index. (Area handbook series DA pam; 550-36.) ISBN 0844407283.

See entry 4. Research for this edition was completed in December 1989. Full text is available from http://lcweb2.loc.gov/frd/cs/dotoc.html and http://lcweb2.loc.gov/frd/cs/httoc.html. (OP)

20. Meditz, Sandra W., and Dennis M. Hanratty, eds. *Islands of the Commonwealth Caribbean: A Regional Study.* 1st ed. Washington, DC: Library of Congress Research Div., 1989. 771 p. Bibl., ill., index. (Area handbook series DA pam; 550-33).

See entry 4. Research for this edition was completed in September 1987. Full text is available from http://lcweb2.loc.gov/frd/cs/cxtoc.html. (OP)

21. Momsen, Janet Henshall, comp. *St. Lucia.* Santa Barbara, CA: Clio Press, 1996. 179 p. Index. (World bibliographical series; 185.) ISBN 185109136X. *See* entry 8.

22. Myers, Robert A., comp. *Dominica.* Santa Barbara, CA: Clio Press, 1987. 190 p. Bibl., ill., index. (World bibliographical series; 82.) ISBN 1851090312. *See* entry 8.

23. Potter, Robert B., and Graham Dann, comps. *Barbados.* Santa Barbara, CA: Clio Press, 1987. 356 p. Bibl., index. (World bibliographical series; 76.) ISBN 1851090223. *See* entry 8.

24. Schoenhals, Kai P., comp. *Netherlands Antilles, and Aruba.* Santa Barbara, CA: Clio Press, 1993. 160 p. Ill., index. (World biblio-

graphical series; 168.) ISBN 1851092102. (OP) *See* entry 8.

Chile

25. Hudson, Rex A., ed. *Chile: A Country Study.* Washington, DC: Library of Congress Research Div., 1994. 462 p. Bibl., ill., index. (DA pam; 550-77.) ISBN 084440828X.

See entry 4. Research for this edition was completed in March 1994. Full text is available from http://lcweb2.loc.gov/frd/cs/cltoc.html.

Colombia

26. Davis, Robert H., comp. *Colombia.* Santa Barbara, CA: Clio Press, 1990. 204 p. Ill. (World bibliographical series; 112.) ISBN 1851090932. *See* entry 8.

27. Hanratty, Dennis M., and Sandra W. Meditz, eds. *Colombia: A Country Study.* 4th ed. Washington, DC: Library of Congress Research Div., 1990. 364 p. (DA pam; 550-26.) ISBN 0160280184.

See entry 4. Research for this edition was completed in December 1988. Full text is available from http://lcweb2.loc.gov/frd/cs/cotoc.html.

Costa Rica

28. Stansifer, Charles L., comp. *Costa Rica.* Santa Barbara, CA: Clio Press, 1991. 292 p. Ill., index. (World bibliographical series; 126.) ISBN 1851090274. *See* entry 8.

Cuba

29. Hatchwell, Emily, and Simon Calder. *Cuba: A Guide to the People, Politics and Culture.* New York: Interlink Books, 1999. 96 p. Bibl., ill. (In focus.) ISBN 1566562414 pbk. *See* entry 15.

30. Rudolph, James D., ed. *Cuba: A Country Study.* Washington, DC: Headquarters, Dept. of the Army, 1987. 366 p. Bibl., ill., index. (Area handbook series DA pam; 550-152.) *See* entry 4.

31. Stubbs, Jean, Lila, and Meic Haines, comps. *Cuba.* Santa Barbara, CA: Clio Press, 1996. 337 p. Ill., index. (World bibliographical series; 75.) ISBN 1851090215. *See* entry 8.

Dominican Republic

32. Howard, David. *Dominican Republic: A Guide to the People, Politics and Culture.* New York: Interlink Books, 1999. 100 p. Bibl., ill. (In focus.) ISBN 1566562430 pbk. *See* entry 15.

33. Schoenhals, Kai P., comp. *Dominican Republic.* Santa Barbara, CA: Clio Press, 1990. 210 p. Index. (World bibliographical series; 111.) ISBN 1851091106. (OP) *See* entry 8

Ecuador

34. Corkill, David, comp. *Ecuador.* Santa Barbara, CA: Clio Press, 1989. 155 p. Ill. (World bibliographical series; 101). ISBN 185109069X. (OP) *See* entry 8.

35. Hanratty, Dennis M., ed. *Ecuador: A Country Study.* 3rd ed. Washington, DC: Library of Congress Research Div., 1991. 306 p. Bibl., ill., index. (Area handbook series 1057-5294 DA pam; 550-5.) ISBN 0844407305.

See entry 4. Research for this edition was completed in December 1989. Full text is available from http://lcweb2.loc.gov/frd/cs/ectoc.html. (OP)

El Salvador

36. Barry, Tom. *El Salvador: A Country Guide.* 2nd ed. Albuquerque, NM: Inter-

Hemispheric Education Resource Center, 1991. 193 p. Bibl., ill., index. ISBN 0911213309.

This volume is an in-depth reference work on the history, economy, politics, social issues, and U.S. relations of this country.

37. Haggerty, Richard A., ed. *El Salvador: A Country Study.* 2nd ed. Washington, DC: Library of Congress Research Div., 1990. 306 p. Bibl., ill., index. (Area handbook series DA pam; 550-150.) ISBN 0160226082.

See entry 4. Research for this edition was completed in November 1988. Full text is available from http://lcweb2.loc.gov/frd/cs/svtoc.html. (OP)

38. Woodward, Ralph Lee, comp. *El Salvador.* Santa Barbara, CA: Clio Press, 1988. 213 p. (World bibliographical series; 98.) ISBN 1851090738. *See* entry 8.

French Guiana

39. Crane, Janet, comp. *French Guiana.* Santa Barbara, CA: Clio Press, 1998. 160 p. Bibl., index. (World bibliographical series; 210.) ISBN 1851092412. *See* entry 8.

Guatemala

40. O'Kane, Trish. *Guatemala: A Guide to the People, Politics and Culture.* New York: Interlink Books, 1999. 100 p. Bibl., ill. (In focus.) ISBN 1566562422 pbk. *See* entry 15.

41. Woodward, Ralph Lee, comp. *Guatemala.* Rev. and expanded ed. Santa Barbara, CA: Clio Press, 1992. 269 p. Ill., index. (World bibliographical series; 9.) ISBN 1851091882. *See* entry 8.

Guyana

42. Chambers, Frances, comp. *Guyana.* Santa Barbara, CA: Clio Press, 1989. 206 p. Ill. (World bibliographical series; 96.) ISBN 1851090703. (OP) *See* entry 8.

43. Kelly, Robert C. et al., eds. *Country Review, Guyana 1998/1999.* Houston, TX: Country Watchcom, 1998. 60 p. Ill. ISBN 1583100830.

This concise volume presents current political, economic, demographic, and geographic information about Guyana. Regional and country maps also are included.

Haiti

44. Chambers, Frances, comp. *Haiti.* Rev. and expanded ed. Santa Barbara, CA: Clio Press, 1994. 270 p. Ill., index. (World bibliographical series; 39.) ISBN 1851092153. *See* entry 4.

Honduras

45. Howard-Reguindin, Pamela F., comp. *Honduras.* Santa Barbara, CA: Clio Press, 1992. 258 p. Ill., index. (World bibliographical series; 139.) ISBN 1851091378. *See* entry 8.

46. Merrill, Tim L., ed. *Honduras: A Country Study.* 3rd ed. Washington, DC: Library of Congress Research Div., 1995. 318 p. Bibl., ill., index. (Area handbook series 1057-5294 DA pam; 550-151.) ISBN 0844408360.

See entry 4. Research for this edition was completed in December 1993. Full text is available from http://lcweb2.loc.gov/frd/cs/hntoc.html.

Mexico

47. Barry, Tom. *Mexico: A Country Guide.* 1st ed. Albuquerque, NM: Inter-Hemispheric Education Resource Center, 1992. 401 p. Bibl., ill., index. ISBN 091121335X pbk. *See* entry 36.

48. Merrill, Tim L., and Ramón Miró, eds. *Mexico: A Country Study.* 4th ed. Washington, DC: Library of Congress Research Div., 1997. 414 p. Bibl., ill., index. (Area handbook series 1057-5294 DA pam; 550-79.) ISBN 0844408557.

See entry 4. Research for this edition was completed in June 1996. Full text is available from http://lcweb2.loc.gov/frd/cs/mxtoc.html.

49. Philip, George D. E., comp. *Mexico.* Rev. and expanded ed. Santa Barbara, CA: Clio Press, 1993. 195 p. Ill. (World bibliographical series; 48.) ISBN 185109198X. *See* entry 8.

50. Werner, Michael S., ed. *Encyclopedia of Mexico: History, Society & Culture.* Chicago: Fitzroy Dearborn Publishers, 1997. 2 vols. Bibl., ill., index. ISBN 1884964311.

This multi-disciplinary work for the non-specialist treats many topics about Mexico such as literature, politics, history, society, and culture.

Nicaragua

51. Merrill, Tim L., ed. *Nicaragua: A Country Study.* 3rd ed. Washington, DC: Library of Congress Research Div., 1994. 300 p. Bibl., ill., index. (Area handbook series 1057-5294 DA pam; 550-88.) ISBN 084440831X.

See entry 4. Research for this edition was completed in December 1993. Full text is available from http://lcweb2.loc.gov/frd/cs/nitoc.html.

52. Norsworthy, Kent, and Tom Barry. *Nicaragua: A Country Guide.* 2nd ed. Albuquerque, NM: Inter-Hemispheric Education Resource Center, 1990. 226 p. Bibl., ill. ISBN 0911213295 pbk. *See* entry 36.

53. Woodward, Ralph Lee, comp. *Nicaragua.* Rev. and expanded ed. Santa Barbara, CA: Clio Press, 1994. 295 p. Ill., index. (World bibliographical series; 44.) ISBN 1851091890. *See* entry 8.

Panama

54. Barry, Tom. *Panama: A Country Guide.* 1st ed. Albuquerque, NM: Inter-Hemispheric Education Resource Center, 1990. 154 p. Bibl. ill. ISBN 0911213244. *See* entry 36.

55. Meditz, Sandra W., and Dennis M. Hanratty, eds. *Panama: A Country Study.* 4th ed. Washington, DC: Library of Congress Research Div., 1989. 337 p. Bibl., ill., index. (Area handbook series DA pam; 550-46.) ISBN 0160017181.

See entry 4. Research for this edition was completed in December 1987. Full text is available from http://lcweb2.loc.gov/frd/cs/patoc.html.

Paraguay

56. Hanratty, Dennis M., and Sandra W. Meditz, eds. *Paraguay: A Country Study.* 2nd ed. Washington, DC: Library of Congress Research Div., 1990. 288 p. Bibl., ill., index. (Area handbook series DA pam; 550-156.) ISBN 0160191017.

See entry 4. Research for this edition was completed in December 1988. Full text is available from http://lcweb2.loc.gov/cs/pytoc.html.

Peru

57. Fisher, John Robert, comp. *Peru.* Santa Barbara, CA: Clio Press, 1989. 193 p. Ill. (World bibliographical series; 109.) ISBN 1851091009. *See* entry 8.

58. Hudson, Rex A., ed. *Peru: A Country Study.* 4th ed. Washington, DC: Library of Congress Research Div., 1993. 422 p. Bibl., ill., index. (Area handbook series 1057-5294 DA pam; 550-4.) ISBN 0844407747.

See entry 4. Research for this edition was completed in September 1992. Full text is available from http://lcweb2.loc.gov/cs/petoc.html.

Puerto Rico

59. Fernández, Ronald, Serafín Méndez M., and Gail Cueto. *Puerto Rico Past and Present:*

An Encyclopedia. Westport, CT: Greenwood Press, 1998. 375 p. Bibl., ill., index. ISBN 031329822X.

This encyclopedia covers many topics concerning the island's history, its people, biography, politics, and culture, emphasizing the nineteenth and twentieth centuries.

Uruguay

60. Finch, M. H. J., and Alicia Casas de Barrán, comps. *Uruguay.* Santa Barbara, CA: Clio Press, 1989. 232 p. Ill. (World bibliographical series; 102.) ISBN 1851090983. *See* entry 8.

61. Hudson, Rex A., and Sandra W. Meditz, eds. *Uruguay: A Country Study.* 2nd ed. Washington, DC: Library of Congress Research Div., 1992. 302 p. Bibl., ill., index. (Area handbook series DA pam; 550-97.) ISBN 0844407372.

See entry 4. Research for this edition was completed in December 1990. Full text is available from http://lcweb2.loc.gov/frd/cs/uytoc.html.

Venezuela

62. Haggerty, Richard A., ed. *Venezuela: A Country Study.* 4th ed. Washington, DC: Library of Congress Research Div., 1993. 276 p. Bibl., ill., index. (Area handbook series 1057-5294 DA pam; 550-7.) ISBN 084440747X.

See entry 4. Research for this edition was completed in December 1990. Full text is available from http://lcweb2.loc.gov/frd/cs/vetoc.html.

63. Waddell, D. A. G., comp. *Venezuela.* Santa Barbara, CA: Clio Press, 1990. 206 p. Ill., index. (World bibliographical series; 110.) ISBN 1851091068. *See* entry 8.

II

Descriptive Accounts
and Travel Guides

This section includes diaries, journals, chronicles, travel guides, descriptions, and photographs. The section is subdivided by geographic regions.

Caribbean Area

64. Baker, Christopher. *Cuba Handbook.* Chico, CA: Moon Travel, 1997. 714 p. Ill., index. ISBN 1566910951.

This guidebook provides introductory material about Cuban history, its flora and fauna, and other topics of interest to travelers.

65. Harvey, David Alan, and Elizabeth Newhouse. *Cuba.* Washington, DC: National Geographic, 1999. 215 p. Ill. ISBN 0792275012.

This pictorial work of contemporary Cuba includes a brief essay on Cuban history.

66. Mendoza, Tony. *Cuba: Going Back.* 1st ed. Austin, TX: University of Texas Press, 1999. 153 p. Ill. ISBN 0292752334.

This is a personal testimony, told almost exclusively with photographs, of post cold-war Cuba, and its failed attempt to build socialism.

67. Pérez, Louis A., ed. *Slaves, Sugar & Colonial Society: Travel Accounts of Cuba, 1801–1899.* Wilmington, DE: Scholarly Resources, 1992. 259 p. Bibl., index. (Latin American silhouettes.) ISBN 0842023542.

This selection of travel accounts by various authors chronicles Cuban nineteenth century sugar boom, slavery, and rebellion from Spanish rule.

68. Ryan, Alan, ed. *The Reader's Companion to Cuba.* 1st ed. San Diego, CA: Harcourt Brace & Co. 1997. 392 p. ISBN 0156003678 pbk.

This anthology brings together diverse views of Cuba as seen through the eyes of travelers from the mid-nineteenth century through 1992.

Central America

69. Calderwood, Michael, and Gabriel Breña. *Mexico, A Higher Vision: An Aerial Journey from Past to Present.* San Diego, CA: ALTI, 1996. 192 p. Ill. ISBN 1883051061.

This collection of aerial photographs of Mexico, with an introduction by Carlos Fuentes, reveals Mexico's rich and diverse nature and its civilization.

70. Conrad, Jim. *Mexico: A Hiker's Guide to Mexico's Natural History.* Seattle, WA: Mountaineers, 1995. 220 p. Bibl., ill., index. ISBN 0898864240 pbk.

This travel guide presents information about flora, fauna, climate, and peoples that represent the country's diverse landscapes.

71. Frerck, Robert. *Eternal Mexico.* San Francisco: Chronicle Books, 1996. 167 p. Ill. ISBN 0811810240.

This is a colorful presentation of Mexico's natural beauty including its peoples and culture.

72. Kelly, Joyce. *An Archaeological Guide to Mexico's Yucatan Peninsula.* Norman, OK: University of Oklahoma Press, 1993. 364 p. Ill. ISBN 0806124997.

This guidebook provides a description of archaeological sites of the Yucatán peninsula such as Chichen Itza, Tulum, and Uxmal.

73. Ryan, Alan, ed. *The Reader's Companion to Mexico.* 1st ed. San Diego, CA: Harcourt Brace & Co., 1995. 368 p. ISBN 0156760215 pbk.

This compilation brings together diverse views of Mexico as seen through the eyes of familiar and less well-known Mexican and world writers.

74. Schueler, Donald G. *The Temple of the Jaguar: Travels in the Yucatán.* San Francisco: Sierra Club Books, 1993. 253 p. ISBN 0871566516.

This work profiles the Mexican states of the Yucatán peninsula and Belize. It describes the wildlife, environment, people, history, and lifestyle. (OP)

75. Wright, Ronald. *Time Among the Maya: Travels in Belize, Guatemala, and Mexico.* 1st ed. New York: Weidenfeld & Nicolson, 1989. 451 p. Bibl., ill., index. ISBN 1555842917.

This impressionistic travel diary portrays contemporary descendants of the ancient Maya.

South America

76. Bosrock, Mary Murray. *South America: A Fearless Guide to International Communi-*cation and Behavior. St. Paul, MN: International Education Systems, 1997. 384 p. Ill., index. (Put your best foot forward.) ISBN 0963753088.

This is a guide to proper communication etiquette for business travelers.

77. Chatwin, Bruce, and Paul Theroux. *Nowhere Is a Place: Travels in Patagonia.* San Francisco: Yolla Bolly Press book published by Sierra Club Books, 1992. 109 p. Ill. ISBN 0871565005.

This collection of landscape photographs accompanies a description, history and legends of the region.

78. De Roy, Tui. *Galápagos, Islands Born of Fire.* Los Angeles: Warwick Publishing, 1998. 160 p. Ill., index. ISBN 1894020391.

Explanatory notes accompany stunning photography that highlights the natural history of the islands.

79. Kane, Joe. *Running the Amazon.* 1st Vintage departures ed. New York: Vintage Books, 1990. 277 p. Ill. (Vintage departures.) ISBN 067972902X pbk.

This journalistic account of a trip from the source of the Amazon River to the Atlantic Ocean includes insights on environmental effects of development, Shining Path guerrillas, Inca culture, and illegal drug traffic.

80. Kling, Kevin, and Nadia Christensen. *Ecuador, Island of the Andes.* New York: Thames and Hudson, 1988. 170 p. ill. ISBN 050001440X.

This photographic portrait of Ecuador's Indians and their surroundings conveys the strong bond that exists between them and nature. (OP)

81. Leitch, William C. *South America's National Parks: A Visitor's Guide.* Seattle, WA: Mountaineers, 1990. 286 p. Bibl., ill. ISBN 0898862485.

This work describes thirty-two parks accessible to most tourists in Argentina, Brazil, Chile, Colombia, Peru, Venezuela, and Surinam.

82. Lévi-Strauss, Claude. *Saudades do Brasil: A Photographic Memoir.* Translated by Sylvia Modelski. Seattle, WA: University of Washington Press, 1995. 221 p. Ill. ISBN 0295974729.

This is a collection of 180 photographs taken by Lévi-Strauss during his tenure in Brazil, 1935–1939. The photos are of São Paulo and the human and physical landscape of the hinterland.

83. Rambali, Paul. *In the Cities and Jungles of Brazil.* 1st American ed. New York: H. Holt, 1994. 266 p. ISBN 0805030794.

This description of Brazilian society represents its many tiers. It portrays a vivid picture of a vast and complex country including its Indians, the towers and slums of Rio, the sexual and criminal scene, and party-goers. (OP)

III

Humanities

GENERAL WORKS

This section includes works that describe cultural expressions such as literature, music, philosophy, and the arts from multidisciplinary perspectives. Only the first occurrence of a title in the series "Culture and Customs of Latin America and the Caribbean" is described. The section is subdivided by geographic regions.

Latin America

84. Bethell, Leslie, ed. *A Cultural History of Latin America: Literature, Music, and the Visual Arts in the 19th and 20th Centuries.* New York: Cambridge University Press, 1998. Bibl., index. ISBN 0521623278.

These essays examine Latin American cultural production in the nineteenth and twentieth centuries.

85. Henderson, James D. *Conservative Thought in Twentieth Century Latin America: The Ideas of Laureano Gómez.* Athens, OH: Ohio University, Center for International Studies, LAS Program, 1988. 217 p. Bibl., index. (Monographs in international studies. Latin America series; 13.) ISBN 0896801489.

This is an introduction to the conservative thought of the Colombian political philosopher.

86. Mariátegui, José Carlos. *The Heroic and Creative Meaning of Socialism.* Edited and translated by Michael Pearlman. Atlantic Highlands, NJ: Humanities Press, 1996. 208 p. Bibl., index. (Revolutionary studies.) ISBN 1573923818.

Mariátegui is considered to be Latin America's greatest Marxist theoretician. This is a collection of his essays about Marxism, philosophy, literature, art, and culture. Essays about Peruvian and Latin American socioeconomic reality also are included.

87. Rama, Angel. *The Lettered City.* Edited and translated by John Chasteen. Durham, NC: Duke University Press, 1996. 141 p. Bibl., ill., index. (Post-contemporary interventions.) ISBN 0822317575.

Rama is one of Latin America's most important contemporary critics. These essays discuss the influence of Latin American intellectuals on its cultural development.

88. Schutte, Ofelia. *Cultural Identity and Social Liberation in Latin American Thought.* Albany, NY: State University of New York Press, 1993. 313 p. Bibl., index. (SUNY series in Latin American and Iberian thought and culture.) ISBN 0791413179.

This is a brief introduction to Latin American cultural, ethnic, and national identity, including liberation theology.

89. Standish, Peter et al. *Hispanic Culture of Mexico, Central America, and the Caribbean.* Detroit, MI: Gale, 1996. 327 p. Bibl., ill., index. (Dictionary of twentieth-century culture.) ISBN 0810384841.

This title presents background information about art and architecture, cinema and other media, music and dance, and literature of the region.

90. Stavans, Ilan, ed. *The Oxford Book of Latin American Essays.* New York: Oxford University Press, 1997. 518 p. Bibl., index. ISBN 0195092341.

These seventy-seven essays by prominent Latin American authors from Spanish and Portuguese America cover the period 1849–1994. Essay topics vary and include religion, culture, and identity.

Caribbean Area

91. Brown, Isabel Zakrzewski. *Culture and Customs of the Dominican Republic.* Westport, CT: Greenwood Press, 1999. 224 p. Ill., index. (Culture and customs of Latin America and the Caribbean.) ISBN 0313303142.

This series provides an overview of such topics as cinema and other media, literature, religion, and social customs of the contemporary period.

92. Pérez, Louis A. *On Becoming Cuban: Identity, Nationality, and Culture.* Chapel Hill, NC: University of North Carolina Press, 1999. 608 p. Bibl., ill., index. ISBN 0807824879.

This work examines Cuban cultural history from the mid nineteenth century through 1959 and focuses on relations between Cuban and U.S. cultures.

Central America

93. Helmut, Charlene. *Culture and Customs of Costa Rica.* Westport, CT: Greenwood

Press, 2000. 173 p. Ill., index. (Culture and customs of Latin America and the Caribbean.) ISBN 0313304920. See entry 91.

South America

94. Castillo-Feliú, Guillermo I. *Culture and Customs of Chile.* Westport, CT: Greenwood Press, 2000. 168 p. Bibl., ill., index. (Culture and customs of Latin America and the Caribbean.) ISBN 0313307830.

95. Foster, David William, Melisa F., and Darrell B. Lockhart. *Culture and Customs of Argentina.* Westport, CT: Greenwood Press, 1998. 173 p. Ill., index. (Culture and customs of Latin America and the Caribbean.) ISBN 0313303193.

96. Handelsman, Michael. *Culture and Customs of Ecuador.* Westport, CT: Greenwood Press, 2000. 173 p. Ill., index. (Culture and customs of Latin America and the Caribbean.) ISBN 0313302448.

97. Lastarria, José Victorino. *Literary Memoirs.* Edited and translated by R. K. Washbourne et al. New York: Oxford University Press, 2000. 400 p. (Library of Latin America.) ISBN 0195116852.

This work discusses the development of the intellectual life and literary culture of Chile in the colonial period through the nineteenth century.

98. Standish, Peter, ed. *Hispanic Culture of South America.* New York: Gale Research, 1995. 340 p. Bibl., ill., index. (Dictionary of twentieth-century culture.) ISBN 0810384833.

This reference volume focuses on art, cinema, literature, music, and television.

99. Williams, Raymond L., and Kevin G. Guerrieri. *Culture and Customs of Colombia.* Westport, CT: Greenwood Press, 1999. 176 p. Ill., index. (Culture and customs of Latin America and the Caribbean.) ISBN 031330405X.

ART AND ARCHITECTURE

This section includes all forms of fine and folk art, artists and artisans, exhibition catalogs, collections, architecture, and photography. The section is subdivided by geographic regions and countries. For indigenous art see "Anthropology."

Latin America

100. Ades, Dawn. *Art in Latin America: The Modern Era, 1820–1980.* New Haven, CT: Yale University Press, 1989. 361 p. Bibl., ill., index. ISBN 0300045565.

This exhibit catalog from a 1989 London show focuses on painting but also discusses sculpture and mixed media. Biographical information about the artists is included.

101. Braun, Barbara. *Pre-Columbian Art and the Post–Columbian World: Ancient American Sources of Modern Art.* New York: H.N. Abrams, 2000. 339 p. Bibl., ill., index. ISBN 0810929473 pbk.

This study examines the profound influence of pre–Columbian art on twentieth century world artists.

102. Colle, Marie-Pierre. *Latin American Artists in Their Studios.* New York: Vendome Press, 1994. 237 p. Ill. ISBN 0865659575.

Fernando Botero, Rufino Tamayo, Francisco Toledo, Antonio Seguí, Roberto Matta, Carlos Bravo, and Jesús Rafael Soto discuss their views about art and society in Latin America. Full color reproductions accompany the texts.

103. Fane, Diana. *Converging Cultures: Art & Identity in Spanish America.* New York: Harry N. Abrams, 1996. 320 p. Ill. ISBN 0810940302.

This describes the Brooklyn Museum's collection of Spanish-American colonial art. The Viceroyalties of Peru and New Spain are well represented with a variety of items including painting, sculpture, textiles, and furnishings.

104. Fletcher, Valerie J. *Crosscurrents of Modernism: Four Latin American Pioneers; Diego Rivera, Joaquín Torres-García, Wifredo Lam, Matta.* Washington, DC: Hirshhorn Museum and Sculpture Garden in association with the Smithsonian Institution Press, 1992. 295 p. Bibl., ill. ISBN 1560982055.

This volume contains a short account of the life and career of each artist with critical essays. It was written to accompany an exhibit at the Smithsonian Hirshhorn Museum. (OP)

105. Lucie-Smith, Edward. *Latin American Art of the 20th Century.* New York: Thames and Hudson, 1993. 216 p. Bibl., ill., index. (The World of art.) ISBN 0500202605.

This synthesis of twentieth century Latin American visual arts, is arranged by country, includes a chronology, and covers a wide spectrum of artists and movements.

106. Mosquera, Gerardo, ed. *Beyond the Fantastic: Contemporary Art Criticism from Latin America.* 1st MIT Press ed. Cambridge, MA: MIT Press, 1996. 343 p. Bibl., ill. ISBN 0262631725 pbk.

Twenty-two essays by Latin American art critics examine contemporary Latin American art from multicultural, feminist, cultural identity, and folk art perspectives.

107. Oettinger, Marion. *The Folk Art of Latin America: Visiones del Pueblo.* New York: Dutton Studio Books with the Museum of American Folk Art, 1992. 107 p. Bibl., ill. ISBN 0525934359.

This examines the European and Indian roots of Latin American folk art that plays a central role in daily life. This is the exhibition catalog from the Museum of American Folk Art in New York. (OP)

108. Quantrill, Malcolm et al., eds. *Latin American Architecture: Six Voices.* 1st ed. College Station, TX: Texas A&M University Press, 2000. 219 p. Bibl., ill., index. (Studies in architecture and culture; 5.) ISBN 0890969019.

These critical essays analyze the contributions of six contemporary Central and South American architects.

109. Scott, John F. *Latin American Art: Ancient to Modern.* Gainesville, FL: University Press of Florida, 1999. 240 p. Bibl., ill., index. ISBN 0813016452.

This examines Latin American sculpture, pottery, painting, and architecture from pre–Columbian times to the present. Color and black and white illustrations support the text.

110. Sullivan, Edward J., ed. *Latin American Art in the Twentieth Century.* London, England: Phaidon Press, 1996. 352 p. Bibl., ill., index. ISBN 0714832103.

This concise history of twentieth century Latin American art covers well- and lesser-known artists. Latin America's complex diversity is well represented in terms of themes and artistic concepts.

111. Traba, Marta. *Art of Latin America, 1900–1980.* Washington, DC: Inter-American Development Bank, 1994. 178 p. Bibl., ill., index. ISBN 0940602733.

This leading critic uses a chronological-thematic approach to present the complexity and diversity of modern Latin American art within a sociohistorical/cultural context.

112. Turner, Jane Shoaf. *Encyclopedia of Latin American and Caribbean Art.* New York: Grove's Dictionaries, 1999. 782 p. Bibl., ill., index. (Grove encyclopedias of the arts of the Americas.) ISBN 18844466043.

This one-volume encyclopedia covers artists and styles from all countries in the region including women and indigenous groups.

113. Watriss, Wendy, and Lois P. Zamora, eds. *Image and Memory: Photography from Latin America, 1866–1994: FotoFest.* 1st ed. Austin, TX: University of Texas Press, 1998. 450 p. Bibl., ill., index. ISBN 0292791186.

This is the exhibition catalog of the 1992 Houston Fotofest. More than 1,000 images represent ten countries, more than 50 photographers, and span more than 120 years. The accompanying text is in English and Spanish.

Andean Region

114. Le Count, Cynthia Gravelle. *Andean Folk Knitting: Traditions and Techniques from Peru and Bolivia.* Saint Paul, MN: Dos Tejedoras Fiber Arts Publications, 1990. 146 p. Bibl., ill., index. ISBN 0932394078.

This analysis of knitting explores regional styles, design motifs, colors, materials, and techniques. Instructions for ten projects are included. (OP)

Argentina

115. Gradowczyk, Mario H. *Alejandro Xul Solar.* Translated by J. Wilson. New York: Dist. by Abrams, 1996. 255 p. Bibl., ill. ISBN 0810939827.

This first English-language study is about one of Argentina's most influential avant-garde artists.

Caribbean Area

116. Crain, Edward E. *Historic Architecture in the Caribbean Islands.* Gainesville, FL: University of Florida Press, 1994. 256 p. Bibl., ill., index. ISBN 0813012937.

This inclusive work covers the architecture of sixteen islands from English, Spanish, and French influences during the early Amerindian period through World War II.

Colombia

117. Spies, Werner, ed. *Fernando Botero: Paintings and Drawings.* New York: Prestel, 1997. 179 p. Bibl., ill. ISBN 3791318101 pbk.

An in-depth interpretive essay about Botero and six short stories written by him accompany the expanded version of the catalog from the 1986 German exhibition.

118. Sullivan, Edward J. *Fernando Botero: Drawings and Watercolors.* New York: Rizzoli, 1993. 183 p. Bibl., ill. ISBN 0847816656.

This work contains a wide selection of Botero's drawings and watercolors and includes a short biography.

119. Villegas, Benjamín, ed. *Botero Sculptures.* 1st ed. Bogotá, Colombia: Villegas Editores, 1998. 1 vol. unpgd. Bibl., ill. ISBN 9589393640.

This volume showcases Botero's works in small, medium, and large formats.

120. Villegas, Liliana, and Benjamín Villegas Jiménez. *Artefactos: Colombian Crafts from the Andes to the Amazon.* New York: Rizzoli, 1992. 240 p. Bibl., ill., index. ISBN 084781503X.

This presents folk art objects created by Colombian artisans for household use including jewelry, statuary, textiles, and baskets. (OP)

Cuba

121. Balderrama, Maria, ed. *Wifredo Lam and His Contemporaries, 1938–1952.* New York: Studio Museum in Harlem, 1992. 176 p. Bibl., ill. ISBN 0942949080.

This exhibition catalog for the December, 1992, New York retrospective of Lam's work includes several interpretive essays.

122. Camnitzer, Luis. *New Art of Cuba.* 1st ed. Austin, TX: University of Texas Press. 1994. 400 p. Bibl., ill., index. ISBN 0292711492.

These black and white plates illustrate the work of eleven Cuban artists from the 1950s.

123. Lobo Montalvo, María Luisa. *Havana: History and Architecture of a Romantic City.* Translated by Lorna Scott Fox. New York: Monacelli Press, 2000. 320 p. Bibl., ill., index. ISBN 1580930522.

This study of the Cuban capital's development includes its architectural history beginning in the colonial era through the contemporary period.

124. Martínez, Juan A. *Cuban Art and National Identity: The Vanguardia Painters, 1927–1950.* Gainesville, FL: University Press of Florida, 1994. 189 p. Ill. ISBN 0813013062.

This describes the artistic tradition that influenced the new Cuban art.

125. Stout, Nancy, and Jorge Rigau. *Havana = La Habana.* New York: Rizzoli, 1994. 232 p. Ill. ISBN 0847817822.

This volume explores Havana's architectural riches as a context for understanding Cuban history and culture. (OP)

Mexico

126. Albers, Patricia. *Shadows, Fire, Snow: The Life of Tina Modotti.* 1st ed. New York: Clarkson Potter, 1999. 382 p. Bibl., ill., index. ISBN 0609600699.

This is a chronicle of the life of one of Mexico's best known photographers and political activists.

127. Altamirano Piolle, María Elena. *National Homage, José María Velasco, 1840–1912.* Mexico City, Mexico: Amigos del Museo Nacional de Arte, 1995. 2 vols. Bibl., ill., index. ISBN 0826316093 pbk.

This two-volume retrospective set celebrates the life and work of this noteworthy nineteenth century Mexican landscape artist.

128. García Canclini, Néstor. *Transforming Modernity: Popular Culture in Mexico.* Translated by Lidia Lozano. Austin, TX: University of Texas Press, 1993. 128 p. Bibl., ill., index. (Translations from Latin America series.) ISBN 0292727585.

This examines the massification of Mexican folk art as an integral part of the development of the tourism industry.

129. Goldman, Shifra M. *Contemporary Mexican Painting in a Time of Change.* Albuquerque, NM: University of New Mexico Press, 1995. 229 p. Bibl., ill., index. ISBN 0826315623.

This volume studies Mexican painting in the post–World War II era within its historical and sociopolitical contexts.

130. Helms, Cynthia Newman, ed. *Diego Rivera: A Retrospective.* New York: W.W.

Norton, 1998. 372 p. Bibl., ill., index. ISBN 0393046095.

This collection of critical essays was published to accompany the 1986 exhibition to commemorate the artist's birth. The essays trace Rivera's development as an artist within the broader context of twentieth century European artistic movements.

131. Izquierdo, María, and Elizabeth Ferrer, curator. *The True Poetry: The Art of María Izquierdo.* New York: The Americas Society, 1997. 127 p. ISBN 1879128152.

This biographical and critical work of Izquierdo's artistic contributions to Mexican twentieth century art attempts to rediscover the artist, a contemporary of Frida Kahlo, Diego Rivera, and Rufino Tamayo. Reproductions of her major paintings are included and the essays are in English and Spanish.

132. Marnham, Patrick. *Dreaming with His Eyes Open: A Life of Diego Rivera.* 1st ed. New York: Knopf, 1998. 350 p. Bibl., ill., index. ISBN 0679430423.

This biography of the artist's turbulent life includes his personal, political, and artistic adventures.

133. Mauldin, Barbara. *Masks of Mexico: Tigers, Devils, and the Dance of Life.* Santa Fe, NM: Museum of New Mexico Press, 1999. 118 p. Bibl., ill. ISBN 890133298.

This exhibition catalog of the Museum of International Folk Art in Santa Fe provides an introduction to the role of masks in Mexican native rituals and focuses on their role in the celebration of life.

134. McMenamin, Donna. *Popular Arts of Mexico, 1850–1950.* Atglen, PA: Schiffer Pub. 1996. 240 p. Bibl., ill., index. (Schiffer books for collectors.) ISBN 0764300261.

This work presents the history, techniques, and main artisans who produced a variety of Mexican popular art from the mid-nineteenth through the twentieth centuries.

135. Mexican Cultural Institute, and Traveling Exhibition Service, Smithsonian Institution. *Mexico: A Landscape Revisited = Una Visión de Su Paisaje.* New York: Universe Pub., 1995. 128 p. Bibl., ill. ISBN 0876636172.

This bilingual catalog of a traveling exhibition analyzes the importance of Mexican landscape painting.

136. Mutlow, John V., ed. *Ricardo Legorreta: Architects.* New York: Rizzoli, 1997. 240 p. Bibl., ill. ISBN 0847820238.

This work presents twenty-five of Legorreta's most recent and well-known projects in Mexico, Texas, and California.

137. Paz, Octavio. *Essays on Mexican Art.* 1st ed. Translated by Helen Lane. New York: Harcourt Brace, 1993. 303 p. Ill. ISBN 0151290636.

Fourteen essays published between 1960–1986 by the Mexican critic and poet, review Mexican art and politics from the pre–Columbian era to the mid-twentieth century.

138. Peden, Margaret Sayers. *Out of the Volcano: Portraits of Contemporary Mexican Artists.* Washington, DC: Smithsonian Institution Press, 1991. 256 p. Bibl., ill. ISBN 1560980605.

This overview of the arts in contemporary Mexico covers dance, architecture, poetry, and painting. (OP)

139. Rochfort, Desmond. *Mexican Muralists: Orozco, Rivera, Siqueiros.* San Francisco: Chronicle Books, 1998. 239 p. Ill., index. ISBN 0811819280.

This examines the development of the muralist movement and places the work of each artist in its historical, social, and artistic contexts.

140. Tibol, Raquel. *Frida Kahlo: An Open Life.* Albuquerque, NM: University of New Mexico Press, 1993. 230 p. Bibl., ill., index. ISBN 082631418X.

This biography, originally published in Spain in 1983, is based on interviews with Kahlo's friends, her own letters, journals and medical records, and Kahlo's own oral testimony.

141. Williams, Adriana. *Covarrubias.* 1st ed. Edited by Doris Ober. Austin, TX: University of Texas Press, 1994. 318 p. Bibl., ill., index. ISBN 0292790880.

This biography of two of Mexico's most influential cartoonists, Miguel and Rosa Covarrubias, includes a color portfolio of their works.

142. Yampolsky, Mariana, and Chloë Sayer. *The Traditional Architecture of Mexico.* New York: Thames and Hudson, 1993. 208 p. Bibl., ill., index. ISBN 0500341281.

This work examines traditional building practices in Mexico from pre–Columbian times to the present.

South America

143. Bayón, Damián, and Marx Murillo. *History of South American Colonial Art and Architecture: Spanish South America and Brazil.* New York: Rizzoli, 1992. 442 p. Bibl., ill., index. ISBN 0847815552.

This comprehensive overview of colonial South American architecture, painting, and sculpture is organized chronologically and subarranged by country. (OP)

144. Davies, Lucy, and Mo Fini. *Arts & Crafts of South America.* San Francisco: Chronicle Books, 1995. 160 p. Bibl., ill., index. ISBN 0811808122.

This volume covers arts native to South America from the past and present. It also describes artisans, traditional motifs, and techniques.

COMMUNICATIONS AND MASS MEDIA

This section includes journalism, television, radio, and cinema in one alphabetical list.

145. Berg, Charles Ramírez. *Cinema of Solitude: A Critical Study of Mexican Film, 1967–1983.* 1st ed. Austin, TX: University of Texas Press, 1992. 252 p. Bibl., ill., index. (Texas film studies series.) ISBN 0292707916.

This critical study of Mexican cinema analyzes its Golden Age, the 1940s–1950s, as well as the more recent Nuevo Cine (new cinema) of the 1967–83 period.

146. Cole, Richard R., ed. *Communication in Latin America: Journalism, Mass Media, and Society.* Wilmington, DE: Scholarly Resources, 1996. 260 p. Bibl. (Jaguar books on Latin America; 14.) ISBN 0842025588.

The current status of professional journalism in Latin America, its relationship with politics and the mass media, and international propaganda are examined. Case studies for Argentina, Brazil, Chile, and Mexico complete the volume.

147. Foster, David William. *Contemporary Argentine Cinema.* Columbia, MO: University of Missouri Press, 1992. 164 p. Bibl., ill., index. ISBN 0826208606.

This is an analysis of ten major Argentine films produced after the country's return to constitutional democracy in 1983.

148. Hinds, Harold E., and Charles M. Tatum. *Not Just for Children: The Mexican Comic Book in the Late 1960s and 1970s.* New York: Greenwood Press, 1992. 245 p. Bibl., ill., index. (Contributions to the study of popular culture; 30.) ISBN 0313254672.

This volume begins with an overview of the comic book industry and is followed by an analysis of Mexican culture depicted in its comic books.

149. King, John. *Magical Reels: A History of Cinema in Latin America.* New York: Verso, 1990. 266 p. Bibl., ill., index. (Critical studies in Latin American culture.) ISBN 0860912957.

This comprehensive work provides an analysis of Latin American cinema from chronological and geographic perspectives.

150. López Vigil, José Ignacio. *Rebel Radio: The Story of El Salvador's Radio Venceremos.* Translated by Mark Fried. Willimantic, CT: Curbstone Press, 1994. 240 p. Ill. ISBN 1880684217.

This work presents testimonies of the guerrilla underground radio station organizers.

151. Maciel, David R. and Joanne Hershfield, eds. *Mexico's Cinema: A Century of Films & Filmmakers.* Wilmington, DE: SR Books, 1999. 298 p. (Latin American silhouettes.) ISBN 0842026819.

Several essays examine the history and current state of Mexican cinema including its social, economic, and political strife.

152. Menéndez Alarcón, Antonio V. *Power and Television in Latin America: The Dominican Case.* Westport, CT: Praeger, 1992. 199 p. Bibl., ill., index. ISBN 0275942759.

This is an exploration of the relationship between the development and function of television and its use by political and economic elites in the Dominican Republic.

153. Nariman, Heidi Noel. *Soap Operas for Social Change: Toward a Methodology for Entertainment-Education Television.* Westport, CT: Praeger, 1993. 143 p. Bibl., ill., index. (Media and society series.) ISBN 0275943895.

This work examines the successful attempt by the Mexican television network, Televisa, to produce "entertainment-education" soap operas. The themes presented in these programs were women's rights, family planning, responsible parenthood, and sexual education.

154. Pick, Zuzana M. *The New Latin American Cinema: A Continental Project.* 1st ed. Austin, TX: University of Texas Press, 1993. 251 p. Bibl., index. (Texas film studies series.) ISBN 0292765452.

This study of Latin American cinema covers its history, authorship, gender, popular cinema, contemporary critical theories, exile, and ethnicity.

155. Salwen, Michael Brian, and Bruce Garrison. *Latin American Journalism.* Hillsdale, NJ: L. Erlbaum Associates, 1991. 227 p. Bibl., ill., index. ISBN 0805807675.

This volume provides country, theme, and comparative studies of the Latin American press.

156. Schwartz, Ronald. *Latin American Films, 1932–1994: A Critical Filmography.* Jefferson, NC: McFarland, 1997. 294 p. Bibl., ill., index. ISBN.

This introductory volume offers basic information (title, director, language, plot summary) about the film industry of Argentina, Brazil, Cuba, and Mexico.

157. Simpson, Amelia S. *Xuxa: The Mega-Marketing of Gender, Race, and Modernity.* Philadelphia: Temple University Press, 1993. 238 p. Bibl., ill., index. ISBN 1566391016.

This is a study of the Brazilian television performer within the context of Brazil's racial, cultural, and social contradictions.

158. Stock, Ann Marie, ed. *Framing Latin American Cinema: Contemporary Critical Perspectives.* Minneapolis, MN: University of Minnesota Press, 1997. 269 p. Bibl., index. (Hispanic issues; 15.) ISBN 0816629722.

This work gathers analytical perspectives about the cinematic production of several Latin American countries as it tries to answer how a particular view of Latin American cinema has evolved.

MUSIC AND DANCE

This section includes popular, classical, and religious music and dance, interpreters and composers. The section is subdivided by geographic region.

Latin America

159. *Big Book of Latin American Songs: Piano, Vocal, Guitar.* Milwaukee, WI: Hal Leonard Pub., 1992. 320 p. ISBN 0793513839.

This collection of eighty-nine popular favorites includes lyrics in Spanish, Portuguese, and English.

160. Ficher, Miguel et al., comps. and eds. *Latin American Classical Composers: A Biographical Dictionary.* Lanham, MD: Scarecrow Press, 1996. 407 p. Bibl., index. ISBN 0810831856.

This compilation contains biographical information about Latin American past and contemporary classical music composers.

161. Olsen, Dale A., and Daniel E. Sheehy, eds. *The Garland Encyclopedia of World Music, v. 2: South America, Mexico, Central America, and the Caribbean.* New York: Garland Pub., 1998. 1082 p. Bibl., ill., index. ISBN 0824049470.

This volume examines Latin American musical culture from indigenous, folk, popular, and classical traditions through the region's history, ethnology, and mythology. The accompanying CD includes unique recordings.

162. Schechter, John M. et al., eds. *Music in Latin American Culture: Regional Traditions.* New York: Schirmer Books, 1999. 496 p. Bibl., ill., index. ISBN 0028647505.

This comprehensive work covers musical themes and discusses current issues related to tradition, politics, and philosophy. The accompanying CD provides examples of the genres discussed.

Caribbean Area

163. Aparicio, Frances R. *Listening to Salsa: Gender, Latin Popular Music, and Puerto Rican Cultures.* Hanover, NH: University Press of New England, 1998. 290 p. Ill., index. (Music culture.) ISBN 0819553069.

This work explores popular salsa music from race, gender, and class perspectives.

164. Daniel, Yvonne. *Rumba: Dance and Social Change in Contemporary Cuba.* Bloomington: Indiana University Press, 1995. 196 p. Bibl., ill., index. (Blacks in the diaspora.) ISBN 025320948X.

This is an overview of the historical development of rumba in its socioeconomic, political, and religious contexts.

165. Manuel, Peter Lamarche, ed. *Essays on Cuban Music: North American and Cuban Perspectives.* Lanham, MD: University Press of America, 1991. 327 p. Bibl., index. ISBN 0819184306.

Thirteen essays examine sociopolitical issues of Cuban traditional and popular music.

166. Manuel, Peter Lamarche, with K. Bilby and M. Largey. *Caribbean Currents: Caribbean Music from Rumba to Reggae.* Philadelphia: Temple University Press, 1995. 272 p. Ill., index. ISBN 1566393388.

This is a historical, political, and social analysis of Spanish, French, and English Caribbean traditional music.

South America

167. Azzi, María Susana, and Simon Collier. *Le Grand Tango: The Life and Music of Astor Piazzolla.* New York: Oxford University Press, 2000. 326 p. (Bibl., ill., index.) ISBN 0195127773.

This examines the composer's life and his influential work.

168. Béhague, Gerard. *Heitor Villa-Lobos: The Search for Brazil's Musical Soul.* Austin, TX: ILAS, University of Texas at Austin, 1994. 222 p. Bibl., ill., index. (ILAS special publication.) ISBN 0292708238 pbk.

This critical and analytical study of Villa-Lobos' composition, craftsmanship, and ideology also includes biographical information. (OP)

169. Castro, Ruy. *Bossa Nova: The Story of the Brazilian Music That Seduced the World.* 1st Eng. lang. ed. Translated by Lysa Salsbury. Chicago: A. Cappella, 2000. 372 p. Bibl., ill., index. ISBN 1556524099.

This 1990 Brazilian bestseller is a personal narrative of how "street samba" or bossa nova became an international pop/jazz success. Bossa nova's influence in Brazilian culture is an underlying theme.

170. Collier, Simon. *Tango!: The Dance, the Song, the Story.* New York: Thames and Hudson, 1995. 208 p. Bibl., ill., index. ISBN 0500016712.

This volume presents the history of the dance including its singers and dancers.

171. Guillermoprieto, Alma. *Samba.* 1st ed. New York: Knopf, 1990. 244 p. ISBN 0394571894.

This description of Rio de Janeiro's carnival includes an interpretation of Afro-Brazilian history and culture.

172. Lewis, John Lowell. *Ring of Liberation: Deceptive Discourse in Brazilian Capoeira.* Chicago: University of Chicago Press, 1992. 263 p. Bibl. discography, ill., index. ISBN 0226476820.

This volume examines the origin of *capoeira,* the Brazilian martial arts, through diverse perspectives such as anthropology, linguistics, dance, and music.

173. McGowan, Chris, and Ricardo Pessanha. *The Brazilian Sound: Samba, Bossa Nova, and the Popular Music of Brazil.* New ed. Philadelphia: Temple University Press, 1998. 248 p. Bibl., ill., index. ISBN 1566395445.

This survey of Brazilian popular music is written by expert writers from *Billboard* magazine.

174. Perrone, Charles A. *Masters of Contemporary Brazilian Song: MPB, 1965–1985.* 1st ed. Austin, TX: University of Texas Press, 1989. 253 p. Bibl., index. ISBN 0292751028.

This study of contemporary Brazilian popular music includes six major songwriters and performers: Chico Buarque, Caetano Veloso, Gilberto Gil, Milton Nascimento, João Bosco, and Aldir Blanc.

175. Schreiner, Claus. *Música Brasileira: A History of Popular Music and the People of Brazil.* Translated by Mark Weinstein. New York: Marion Boyars, 1993. 306 p. Bibl., ill. ISBN 071452946X.

This is a history of Brazil's popular music from its pre-colonial roots through the twentieth century.

176. Tarasti, Eero. *Heitor Villa-Lobos: The Life and Works, 1887–1959.* Jefferson, NC: McFarland, 1995. 438 p. Bibl., ill., index. (Oxford studies of composers.) ISBN 0786400137.

This work examines Villa-Lobos' diverse works within the context of Brazilian and Latin American classical music history.

177. Taylor, Julie M. *Paper Tangos.* Durham, NC: Duke University Press, 1998. 124 p. Bibl., ill. (Public planet books.) ISBN 0822321750.

This is a sociopolitical study of the tango as an expression of Argentine culture.

178. Vianna, Hermano. *The Mystery of Samba: Popular Music and National Identity in Brazil.* Edited and translated by John C. Chasteen. Chapel Hill, NC: University of North Carolina Press, 1999. 147 p. Bibl., index. (Latin America in translation/en traducción/em tradução.) ISBN 080782464X.

Samba, Brazil's national dance, is examined as a sociocultural phenomenon within the context of Brazilian nation-building.

RELIGION

This section includes Catholicism, Protestantism, Afro-Caribbean religions and other syncretic experiences, liberation theology, religious figures, ceremonies, and festivals. The section is subdivided by geographic regions and countries. For indigenous religions see "Anthropology."

Latin America

179. Berryman, Phillip. *Liberation Theology: Essential Facts About the Revolutionary Movement in Latin America— and Beyond.* Philadelphia: Temple University Press, 1987. 231 p. Bibl., index. ISBN 087722479X.

This overview of the controversial and influential movement is written by a strong proponent. It also provides responses to the major issues raised in the debate.

180. Berryman, Phillip. *Religion in the Megacity: Catholic and Protestant Portraits from Latin America.* Maryknoll, NY: Orbis Books, 1996. 210 p. ISBN 1570750831.

This presents the historical development of Catholic, Protestant, and Pentecostal communities in Brazil and Venezuela and suggests that the region is rapidly becoming religiously pluralistic.

181. Boff, Leonardo. *Introducing Liberation Theology.* Translated by Clodovis Boff and Paul Burns. Maryknoll, NY: Orbis Books, 1987. 99 p. Bibl. ISBN 0883445751.

This concise history and thematic introduction outlines the theological method of liberation theology and its fundamental themes.

182. Brown, Robert McAfee. *Gustavo Gutiérrez: An Introduction to Liberation Theology.* Maryknoll, NY: Orbis Books, 1990. 224 p. Bibl., index. ISBN 0883445972.

This is an overview of Gutiérrez's groundbreaking theology whose impact has been felt throughout Latin America and beyond. (OP)

183. Cleary, Edward L., and Hannah W. Stewart-Gambino. *Power, Politics, and Pentecostals in Latin America.* Boulder, CO: Westview Press, 1997. 261 p. Index. ISBN 081332128X.

This work describes the phenomenal growth of Pentecostalism in Latin America and examines its influence in traditional social structures, local institutions, and workplace relations.

184. Cleary, Edward L., and Hannah W. Stewart-Gambino, eds. *Conflict and Competition: The Latin American Church in a Changing Environment.* Boulder, CO: L. Rienner Publishers, 1993. 234 p. ISBN 1555872514.

The essays in this volume discuss how socially active sectors of the Catholic Church in the region have had to change their strategies as the political situation has shifted. (OP)

185. Cook, Guillermo. *New Face of the Church in Latin America: Between Tradition and Change.* Maryknoll, NY: Orbis Books, 1994. 289 p. Bibl. (American Society of Missiology series; 18.) ISBN 0883449374 pbk.

This is an analysis of the religious life of Latin Americans and the evolving sociopolitical dynamics of the region.

186. Domínguez, Jorge I., ed. *The Roman Catholic Church in Latin America.* New York: Garland, 1994. 412 p. Bibl. (Essays on Mexico, Central and South America; 3.) ISBN 0815314876.

Volume three of this series provides a summary of scholarly debates by Latin American experts in religion who cover a wide variety of topics ranging from liberation theology, the Catholic Church's role in development, to the growth of Protestantism in the region.

187. Dussel, Enrique D., ed. *The Church in Latin America, 1492–1992.* Maryknoll, NY: Orbis Books, 1992. 501 p. Bibl., ill. (A history of the Church in the Third World; 1.) ISBN 0883448203.

This three-part tome provides a chronology of the church from the conquest to the present and its history from a geographic perspective. Selected issues such as Protestantism, liberation theology, base Christian communities, and other related topics also are examined.

188. Garrard-Burnett, Virginia, ed. *On Earth as It Is in Heaven: Religion in Modern Latin America.* Wilmington, DE: SR Books, 2000. 251 p. Bibl. (Jaguar books on Latin America; 18.) ISBN 0842025847.

This text examines various religious expressions including Catholicism, popular Indian and African religions, to the more recent developments in the Protestant and Mormon churches.

189. González-Wippler, Migene. *Santería: The Religion, Faith, Rites, Magic.* 2nd ed. St. Paul, MN: Llewellyn Pub., 1994. 346 p. Bibl., ill., index. (Llewellyn's world religion & magic series.) ISBN 1567183298 pbk.

This volume focuses on the Yoruba pantheon of gods and goddesses (orishas), Santería hierarchy, spirit possession, and animal sacrifice as practiced in the Caribbean and Brazil.

190. Goodpasture, H. McKennie, ed. *Cross and Sword: An Eyewitness History of Christianity in Latin America.* Maryknoll, NY: Orbis Books, 1989. 314 p. Bibl., ill., index. ISBN 0883445905.

This examines liberation theology within its historical context and includes a discussion of the role of Christianity in the region.

191. Gutiérrez, Gustavo. *Las Casas: In Search of the Poor of Jesus Christ.* Translated by Robert R. Barr. Maryknoll, NY: Orbis Books, 1993. 682 p. Bibl., index. ISBN 0883448386.

Not unlike the current theological debates in liberation theology, in the sixteenth century Father Las Casas struggled with the legitimacy of colonialism and evangelization. This is an examination of Las Casas' contemporary theological significance.

192. Lehmann, David. *Struggle for the Spirit: Religious Transformation and Popular Culture in Brazil and Latin America.* Cambridge, MA: Blackwell, 1996. 244 p. Bibl., index. ISBN 0745617840.

This study of the phenomenal growth of Pentecostalism in Brazil and Latin America suggests that Pentecostalism, unlike the established Catholic Church, confronts societal values and behaviors, is conservative, and politically aggressive.

193. Levine, Daniel H. *Religion and Political Conflict in Latin America.* Chapel Hill, NC: University of North Carolina Press, 1986. 266 p. Bibl., index. ISBN 0807816892.

This is a study of the evolution of Latin American Catholicism since 1968. Base Christian communities and pressure for change in the social order are among the concerns of grassroots religious movements.

194. Miller, Daniel R., ed. *Coming of Age: Protestantism in Contemporary Latin America.* Lanham, MD: University Press of America, 1994. 234 p. Bibl. (Calvin Center series; 1.) ISBN 0819194069.

This is an assessment of the growth of Protestantism and its role in the future of the region's religious development.

195. Min, Anselm Kyongsuk. *Dialectic of Salvation: Issues in Theology of Liberation.* Albany, NY: State University of New York Press, 1989. 207 p. Bibl., index. ISBN 0887069088.

This volume discusses liberation theology issues in the Latin American context.

196. Schwaller, John F., ed. *The Church in Colonial Latin America.* Wilmington, DE: SR Books, 2000. 252 p. Bibl. (Jaguar books on Latin America; 21.) ISBN 0842027033.

This is a descriptive history of the development and sociopolitical influence of the Church during the colonial period.

197. Sigmund, Paul E., ed. *Religious Freedom and Evangelization in Latin America: The Challenge of Religious Pluralism.* Maryknoll, NY: Orbis Books, 1999. 358 p. Bibl., index. ISBN 157075263X pbk.

This examines the evolution of greater religious freedom as an outgrowth of political changes in the late twentieth century. The evolving role of the Catholic Church is presented within the context of Protestant growth and evangelization.

198. Stoll, David. *Is Latin America Turning Protestant?: The Politics of Evangelical Growth.* Berkeley, CA: University of California Press, 1990. 424 p. ISBN 0520064992.

This volume explores possible social and political consequences of Protestant religious influence and is based on case studies of Nicaragua, Guatemala, and Ecuador.

Brazil

199. Adriance, Madeleine Cousineau. *Promised Land: Base Christian Communities and the Struggle for the Amazon.* Albany, NY: State University of New York Press, 1995. 202 p. Bibl., ill., index. (SUNY series in religion, culture, and society.) ISBN 0791426491.

This overview of base Christian communities in Brazil's Amazon region examines the relationship between religion and social change, the role of women, and the complex role of the Catholic Church in the communities.

200. Hess, David J. *Samba in the Night: Spiritism in Brazil.* New York: Columbia University Press, 1994. 214 p. Bibl., index. ISBN 0231084323.

This is an ethnography of the author's own journey through spiritism and other alternative religions in Brazil.

201. Voeks, Robert A. *Sacred Leaves of Candomblé: African Magic, Medicine, and Religion in Brazil.* 1st ed. Austin, TX: University of Texas Press, 1997. 236 p. Bibl., ill., index. ISBN 0292787308.

This work summarizes candomblé's origin, diffusion, spiritual practices, and medicinal use of plants.

Caribbean Area

202. Castro, Fidel, with Frei Betto. *Fidel and Religion: Castro Talks on Revolution and Religion with Frei Betto.* New York: Simon & Schuster, 1987. 314 p. ISBN 067164114X.

These interviews between a Dominican priest and Fidel Castro explore the Cuban leader's attitudes towards religion and Christianity. (OP)

203. Fernández Olmos, Margarite, and Lizabeth Paravisini-Gebert, eds. *Sacred Possessions: Vodou, Santería, Obeah, and the Caribbean.* New Brunswick, NJ: Rutgers University Press, 1997. 312 p. Ill. ISBN 0813523605.

This is an examination of Afro-Caribbean religions including colonial experiences that influenced its development.

204. Galembo, Phyllis. *Vodou: Visions and Voices of Haiti.* Berkeley, CA: Ten Speed Press, 1998. 113 p. ISBN 089815989X.

This is an introduction to the historical development of African religions in Haiti.

Mexico

205. Brading, D. A. *Church and State in Bourbon Mexico: The Diocese of Michoacán, 1749–1810.* New York: Cambridge Uni-

versity Press, 1994. 300 p. Bibl., index. ISBN 0521460921.

This description of religious life in Michoacán during the eighteenth century includes the involvement of the clergy in the independence movement. The work's focus is the clash between baroque Catholicism and enlightened despotism.

206. Carmichael, Elizabeth, and Chloë Sayer. *The Skeleton at the Feast: The Day of the Dead in Mexico.* 1st University of Texas Press ed. Austin, TX: University of Texas Press, 1992. 160 p. Bibl., ill., index. ISBN 0292776586.

This is a study of the religious festival from popular culture and folk art perspectives. (OP)

207. Castillo, Ana, ed. *Goddess of the Americas = La Diosa de las Américas: Writings on the Virgin of Guadalupe.* New York: Riverhead Books, 1996. 231 p. ISBN 1573220299.

This work includes essays, fiction, drama, poetry, and historical pieces by renowned writers who examine the centuries-long impact of the Virgin on Mexican society and beyond.

208. Gruzinski, Serge. *The Conquest of Mexico: The Incorporation of Indian Societies into the Western World, 16th–18th Centuries.* Translated by Eileen Corrigan. New York: Cambridge University Press, 1993. 336 p. Bibl., ill., index. ISBN 0745608736.

This is an examination of Mexican indigenous nobles and commoners responses to Europeanization and acculturation demands made by Spanish colonial authorities.

209. MacEaoin, Gary. *The People's Church: Bishop Samuel Ruiz of Mexico and Why He Matters.* New York: Crossroad, 1996. 174 p. Index. ISBN 0824515765.

The life and work of Samuel Ruiz, bishop of Chiapas since the 1960s, is the focus of this volume. Ruiz's work is exemplary of the transformation and democratization of the Catholic Church in Mexico.

210. Poole, Stafford. *Our Lady of Guadalupe: The Origins and Sources of a Mexican*

National Symbol, 1531–1797. Tucson, AZ: University of Arizona Press, 1995. 325 p. Bibl., index. ISBN 0816515263.

This is a detailed study of the Mexican Guadalupan tradition including its devotion and apparition stories.

211. Porter, Eliot, and Ellen Auerbach. *Mexican Celebrations.* 1st ed. Albuquerque, NM: University of New Mexico Press, 1990. 115 p. Ill. ISBN 0826312098.

These color photographs of religious fiestas date back to the mid–1950s and present church interiors, festival decorations, costumed performers and dancers, and scenes from Indian church celebrations. (OP)

212. Tavard, George H. *Juana Inés de la Cruz and the Theology of Beauty: The First Mexican Theology.* Notre Dame, IN: University of Notre Dame Press, 1991. 239 p. Bibl., index. ISBN 0268012067.

This is a theological analysis of the life and work of Sor Juana Inés de la Cruz.

Peru

213. Klaiber, Jeffrey L. *The Catholic Church in Peru, 1821–1985: a social history.* Washington, DC: Catholic University of America Press, 1992. 417 p. ISBN 0813207479.

While the focus of this work is the growth and development of the Catholic Church in the contemporary period (1955–75), it also provides an overview of the institution since independence.

214. Sallnow, Michael J. *Pilgrims of the Andes: Regional Cults in Cusco.* Washington, DC: Smithsonian Institution Press, 1987. 351 p. Bibl., ill., index. (Smithsonian series in ethnographic inquiry.) ISBN 0874748267.

This is a study of the role of pilgrimage in the life of Andean peasants of southern Cusco. These pilgrimages blend Christian and native semiotic systems. (OP)

IV

Languages and Literature

LANGUAGES

This section contains dictionaries and language studies in one alphabetical list. For indigenous languages see "Anthropology."

215. Gold, David L., ed. *Random House Latin-American Spanish Dictionary: Spanish-English, English-Spanish.* 2nd ed. New York: Random House, 2000. 680 p. ISBN 0375407200.

This dictionary contains more than 60,000 entries, 10,000 of which are Latin American terms, and includes a pronunciation guide.

216. Lipski, John M. *Latin American Spanish.* New York: Longman, 1994. 426 p. Bibl., index. ISBN 0582087619.

This work presents a synthesis of studies of American varieties of Spanish. Part I focuses on the evolution of Spanish in Latin America; Part II examines individual Latin American dialects.

217. McElroy, Onyria Herrera, and Lola L. Grabb. *Spanish-English, English-Spanish Medical Dictionary = Diccionario Médico, Español-Inglés, Inglés-Español.* 2nd ed. Boston: Little, Brown and Co. 1996. 513 p. ISBN 0316554480.

This dictionary contains more than 20,000 entries, and includes basic English and Spanish grammars, and a key to pronunciation.

218. Olivares, Rafael A. *NTC's Dictionary of Latin American Spanish.* Lincolnwood, IL: NTC Pub. Group, 1997. 375 p. Index. ISBN 0844279633.

This dictionary contains more than 6,000 words from nineteen Latin American countries.

219. Steiner, Roger, ed. *Simon & Schuster's International Dictionary: English/Spanish, Spanish/English.* 2nd ed. New York: Macmillan, 1997. 1597 p. ISBN 0028620135.

This dictionary contains more than 200,000 entries, includes technical and scientific terms, regionalisms, and idiomatic expressions.

220. Stephens, Thomas M. *Dictionary of Latin American Racial and Ethnic Terminology.* 2nd ed. Gainesville, FL: University Press of Florida, 1999. 1072 p. Bibl., index. ISBN 081301705X.

This is a comprehensive compilation of racial and ethnic terms in Part I, Spanish; Part II, Portuguese; and Part III, French.

221. Seção Lexicográfica das Edições Melhoramentos. *Michaelis Dicionário Ilustrado = Michaelis Illustrated Dictionary.* ed. 61. São Paulo, SP, Brazil: Melhoramentos, 1997. 2 v. Ill. ISBN 85060159-.

More than 4,000 entries include idiomatic expressions and key to pronunciation, V. I, inglês-português (-95); V. II, português-inglês (-87).

LITERATURE

This section includes anthologies and original works (usually without annotations) by one or more authors followed by works of literary criticism. Due to the extensive availability of Latin American literature and literary criticism materials, the section is subdivided by these subtopics: "Anthologies and Original Works" and "Literary Criticism." The section is subdivided by geographic regions and countries. Guadeloupe, Haiti, and Martinique are listed under "Caribbean Area."

Latin America

Anthologies and Original Works

222. Agosín, Marjorie, ed. *The House of Memory: Stories by Jewish Women Writers of Latin America.* Translated by Elizabeth Rosa Horan. New York: CUNY Feminist Press, 1999. 246 p. Bibl. ISBN 1558612084 pbk.

This anthology of contemporary Latin American Jewish women writers includes Clarice Lispector, Margo Glantz, Alicia Kozameh, among others.

223. Agosín, Marjorie, ed. *Landscapes of a New Land: Fiction by Latin American Women.* Fredonia, NY: White Pine Press, 1989. 194 p. ISBN 0934834962.

This collection of twenty-two stories is arranged by themes that reflect social, moral, and ethical concerns.

224. Benner, Susan E., and Kathy S. Leonard, eds. and trans. *Fire from the Andes: Short Fiction by Women from Bolivia, Ecuador, and Peru.* 1st ed. Albuquerque, NM: University of New Mexico Press, 1998. 189 p. Bibl., ill. ISBN 082631824X.

This anthology includes stories by twenty-four contemporary women writers.

225. Cajiao Salas, Teresa, and Margarita Vargas, eds. *Women Writing Women: An Anthology of Spanish-American Theater of the 1980s.* Albany, NY: State University of New York Press, 1997. 468 p. Bibl., ill., index. (SUNY series in Latin American and Iberian thought.) ISBN 079143205X.

This collection includes well known women dramatists from Chile, Puerto Rico, Mexico, Venezuela, and Argentina.

226. Canfield, Cass, Jr., ed. *Masterworks of Latin American Short Fiction: Eight Novellas.* 1st ed. New York: Icon Editions, 1996. 385 p. ISBN 0064315029.

The selections are written by G. García Márquez, Ana Lydia Vega, G. Cabrera Infante, Alvaro Mutis, Alejo Carpentier, Julio Cortázar, João Guimarães Rosa, and Felisberto Hernández.

227. Colchie, Thomas, ed. *A Hammock Beneath the Mangoes: Stories from Latin America.* New York: Dutton, 1991. 430 p. ISBN 0525933670.

This collection of mid-nineteenth and twentieth century authors from Brazil, Chile, Mexico, the Caribbean, and the River Plate regions includes a brief biobibliography of each writer.

228. Correas de Zapata, Celia, ed. *Short Stories by Latin American Women: The Magic and the Real.* Houston, TX: Arte Público Press, 1990. 224 p. ISBN 1558850023 pbk.

This anthology contains stories by well-established Latin American women writers. Among them are: I. Allende, R. Castellanos, A. Dávila, R. Ferré, C. Lispector, E. Poniatowska, and L. Valenzuela.

229. Doggart, Sebastian. *Latin American Plays: New Drama from Argentina, Cuba, Mexico and Peru.* London, England: N. Hern, 1996. 230 p. Bibl. (The International collection.) ISBN 1854592491.

The selections are: *Rappaccini's Daughter* by Octavio Paz; *Night of the Assassins* by José Triana; *Saying Yes* by Griselda Gambaro; *Orchids in the Moonlight* by Carlos Fuentes; and *Mistress of Desires* by Mario Vargas Llosa.

230. Erro-Peralta, Nora, and Caridad Silva, eds. *Beyond the Border: A New Age in Latin American Women's Fiction.* 1st U. Press of Florida ed. Gainesville, FL: University Press of Florida, 2000. 283 p. Bibl. ISBN 0813017858.

These stories reflect the growing importance and development of Latin American women writers (from Argentina, Brazil, Chile, Cuba, and Mexico) as they experiment with non-traditional forms of expression. Each story includes a bibliography.

231. Fernández Olmos, Margarite, and Lizabeth Paravisini-Gebert, eds. *Pleasure in the Word: Erotic Writings by Latin American Women.* Fredonia, NY: White Pine Press, 1993. 284 p. ISBN 1877727318.

This collection of thirty-two pieces includes Pía Barros, Alejandra Pizarnik, and Rosario Ferré.

232. González Echevarría, Roberto, ed. *The Oxford Book of Latin American Short Stories.* New York: Oxford University Press, 1997. 481 p. Bibl., index. ISBN 0195095901.

This diverse collection of widely read short stories from Spanish- and Portuguese-speaking countries is organized chronologically and includes a few stories by contemporary women writers.

233. Herrera, Andrea O'Reilly, ed. *A Secret Weavers Anthology: Selections from the White Pine Press Secret Weavers Series.* Fredonia, NY: White Pine Press, 1998. 225 p. ISBN 1877727822 pbk.

This anthology includes well-known authors such as A. Storni, C. Peri Rossi. L. Valenzuela, G. Mistral, and M. Agosín. The stories address topics ranging from identity to gender and politics.

234. Leonard, Kathy S. ed., and trans. *Cruel Fictions, Cruel Realities: Short Stories by Latin American Women Writers.* Pittsburgh, PA: Latin American Literary Review Press, 1997. 131 p. Bibl. ISBN 0935480870.

While the themes of these stories are diverse, they all deal with cruelty. This collection represents twelve women writers

from Argentina, Bolivia, Chile, Colombia, Ecuador, and Peru.

235. Poey, Delia, ed. *Out of the Mirrored Garden: New Fiction by Latin American Women.* 1st ed. New York: Anchor Books, 1996. 222 p. Bibl., index. ISBN 0385475942 pbk.

This anthology gathers the work of fifteen emerging women writers. The themes include politics, sexuality, and family.

236. Stavans, Ilan, ed. *Prospero's Mirror: A Translators' Portfolio of Latin American Short Fiction.* 1st ed. Willimantic, CT: Curbstone Press, 1998. 323 p. Bibl. ISBN 1880684497 pbk.

This compilation includes favorite selections of mostly obscure Latin American authors by well-known translators of Latin American fiction.

237. Stavans, Ilan, ed. *Tropical Synagogues: Short Stories.* New York: Holmes & Meier, 1994. 239 p. Bibl. ISBN 0841913404.

This collection, organized geographically, presents twenty stories by Latin American Jewish authors from 1910 to the present and includes three stories by J. L. Borges with Jewish themes.

238. Tapscott, Stephen, ed. *Twentieth-Century Latin American Poetry: A Bilingual Anthology.* 1st ed. Austin, TX: University of Texas Press, 1996. 418 p. Bibl., index. (The Texas Pan American series.) ISBN 0292781385.

This bilingual anthology includes well-established and lesser-known poets. The selections are lyric and not epic or narrative in style with brief biographical statements.

Literary Criticism

239. Cussen, Antonio. *Bello and Bolívar: Poetry and Politics in the Spanish American Revolution.* New York: Cambridge University Press, 1992. 208 p. Bibl., index. (Cambridge studies in Latin American and Iberian literature; 6.) ISBN 052141248X.

This analysis of Bello's literary production includes one chapter about Bolívar's politics and poetics.

240. Flores, Angel. *Spanish American Authors: The Twentieth Century.* New York: Wilson, 1992. 915 p. ISBN 0824208064.

This biobibliographical resource includes more than 300 novelists and poets from Spanish America with literary analysis by prominent scholars.

241. Foster, David William. *Cultural Diversity in Latin American Literature.* 1st ed. Albuquerque, NM: University of New Mexico Press, 1994. 178 p. Bibl., index. ISBN 0826314902.

This critical work addresses a variety of themes such as Brazilian writers, gay literature, the role of the feminine voice, and Argentine-Jewish authors.

242. Foster, David William. *Gay and Lesbian Themes in Latin American Writing.* 1st ed. Austin, TX: University of Texas Press, 1991. 178 p. Bibl., index. (The Texas Pan American series.) ISBN 0292776462.

This volume examines approximately two dozen Latin American gay and lesbian literary works published between 1895 and 1989 from Argentina, Brazil, Chile, Cuba, Mexico, Nicaragua, Colombia, Peru, and Venezuela.

243. Foster, David William, and Daniel Altamiranda, eds. *Spanish American Literature: A Collection of Essays.* New York: Garland, 1997. 5 vols. ISBN 0815326777 series.

These essays cover colonial, nineteenth, and twentieth century authors and texts. V. 1: Theoretical debates in Spanish American literature; V. 2: Writers of the Spanish colonial period; V. 3: From Romanticism to *Modernismo* in Latin America; V. 4: Twentieth century Spanish American literature to 1960; V. 5: Twentieth century Spanish American literature since 1960.

244. García Pinto, Magdalena. *Women Writers of Latin America: Intimate Histories.* 1st ed. Translated by Trudy Balch and M. García Pinto. Austin, TX: University of Texas

Press, 1991. 258 p. Bibl., ill., index. (The Texas Pan American series.) ISBN 0292738625.

This collection of interviews with Isabel Allende, Rosario Ferré, Sylvia Molloy, Albalucía Angel, Margo Glantz, Elvira Orphée, Elena Poniatowska, Marta Traba, Luisa Valenzuela, and Ida Vitale discusses obstacles overcome by the writers, their motivation, and personal and social experiences as writers. (OP)

245. Gazarian-Gautier, Marie-Lise. *Interviews with Latin American Writers.* 1st ed. Elmwood, IL: Dalkey Archive Press, 1989. 359 p. Bibl., ill. ISBN 0916583325.

Widely translated authors such as Guillermo Cabrera Infante, Elena Poniatowska, Carlos Fuentes, Isabel Allende, Mario Vargas Llosa, and several lesser known fiction writers present their views about Latin American literature.

246. González, Aníbal. *Journalism and the Development of Spanish American Narrative.* New York: Cambridge University Press, 1993. 165 p. Bibl., index. (Cambridge studies in Latin American and Iberian literature; 8.) ISBN 0521414253.

This work studies the influence of journalistic discourse on selected Latin American texts. Among the authors examined are Lizardi, Sarmiento, Palma, Borges, García Márquez, and Poniatowska.

247. González Echevarría, Roberto. *The Voice of the Masters: Writing and Authority in Modern Latin American Literature.* First pbk print ed. Austin, TX: University of Texas Press, 1988. 195 p. Bibl., index. (Latin American monographs / ILAS, the University of Texas at Austin; 64.) ISBN 0292787162.

This is an analysis of the power structure behind such cultural masters as Rodó and Sarmiento. The author concludes that these classic works have been used by the governing elite to justify their advantageous positions in an oppressive system. (OP)

248. González Echevarría, Roberto, and Enrique Pupo-Walker, eds. *The Cambridge History of Latin American Literature.* New

York: Cambridge University Press, 1996. 3 v. Bibl., index. ISBN 0521482402.

This compilation discusses Latin American literary production from pre–Columbian times to the present. V. 1: discovery to modernism; V. 2: The twentieth century; V. 3: Brazilian literature.

249. González, Mike, and David Treece. *The Gathering of Voices: The Twentieth-Century Poetry of Latin America.* New York: Verso, 1992. 403 p. Bibl., index. (Critical studies in Latin American culture.) ISBN 0860913694.

This work examines poetry in relation to *modernismo*, avant-garde, socioeconomic, and political issues. Rubén Darío, Pablo Neruda, Octavio Paz, Nicolás Guillén, César Vallejo, and Ernesto Cardenal are the poets whose works are analyzed.

250. Jackson, Richard L. *Black Literature and Humanism in Latin America.* Athens, GA: University of Georgia Press, 1988. 166 p. Bibl., index. ISBN 0820309796.

This is a survey of contributions by some of Spanish America's most important living writers. As background to the formation of the Afro-Hispanic literary canon, the author also examines major writers like Nicolás Guillén. (OP)

251. Jackson, Richard L. *Black Writers and the Hispanic Canon.* New York: Twayne Publishers, 1997. 139 p. Bibl., index. (Twayne's world authors series; TWAS 867.) ISBN 0805778012.

This is an analysis of the prose and poetic works by Manuel Zapata Olivella, Pilar Barrios, Pablo Sojo, and others.

252. Jrade, Cathy Login. *Modernismo, Modernity, and the Development of Spanish American Literature.* 1st ed. Austin, TX: University of Texas Press, 1998. 193 p. Bibl., index. (The Texas Pan American series.) ISBN 0292740492.

This work explores the *modernista* period as the basic foundation of contemporary Latin American literature.

253. Kaminsky, Amy K. *Reading the Body Politic: Feminist Criticism and Latin American Women Writers.* Minneapolis, MN: University of Minnesota Press, 1993. 160 p. Index. ISBN 0816619476.

Anglo-American and continental feminist literary criticism is applied to Latin American authors Alicia Portnoy, Elena Garro, Cristina Peri Rossi, Sylvia Molloy, and Gaby Brimmer.

254. Lindstrom, Naomi. *The Social Conscience of Latin American Writing.* 1st University of Texas Press ed. Austin, TX: University of Texas Press, 1998. 187 p. Bibl., index. (The Texas Pan American series.) ISBN 0292746989.

This work employs the vocabulary and methodology of the social sciences to analyze concepts (postmodernism, testimonial and women's writing, gender issues) in selected texts.

255. Lindstrom, Naomi. *Twentieth-Century Spanish American Fiction.* 1st ed. Austin, TX: University of Texas Press, 1994. 246 p. Bibl., ill., index. (The Texas Pan American series.) ISBN 0292781199.

This comprehensive survey of Spanish American literary production of the twentieth century begins with Rodo's *Ariel* and ends with Rigoberta Menchú's Nobel Peace Prize award. (OP)

256. Luis, William, ed. *Modern Latin-American Fiction writers, First Series.* Detroit: Gale Research, 1992. 404 p. Bibl., ill., index. (Dictionary of literary biography; 11.) ISBN 0810375907.

This work provides biocritical information about twentieth century authors.

257. Luis, William, and Ann González, eds. *Modern Latin-American Fiction Writers, Second Series.* Detroit: Gale Research, 1995. 413 p. Bibl., ill., index. (Dictionary of literary biography; 145.) ISBN 0810355590.

See previous citation.

258. Martínez, Elena M. *Lesbian Voices from Latin America: Breaking Ground.* New York: Garland Pub. 1996. 223 p. (Latin American studies; 7.) ISBN 0815313497.

This volume traces the themes and literary techniques employed by five Latin American lesbian writers. The writers are Magaly Alabau, Sylvia Molloy, Rosa María Roffiel, Nancy Cárdenas, and Luz María Umpierre.

259. Marting, Diane E., ed. *Spanish American Women Writers: A Bio-Bibliographical Source Book.* New York: Greenwood Press, 1990. 645 p. Bibl., index. ISBN 0313251940.

This volume is a guide to the life and work of fifty women writers from the colonial period to the present. It includes essays about Indian women authors of Spanish America and a few Latinas from the U.S.

260. Menton, Seymour. *Latin America's New Historical Novel.* 1st ed. Austin, TX: University of Texas Press, 1993. 228 p. Bibl., index. (The Texas Pan American series.) ISBN 0292751575.

This volume defines the Latin American new historical novel since 1979 and concludes with an examination of some characteristic examples.

261. Meyer, Doris, ed. *Reinterpreting the Spanish American Essay: Women Writers of the 19th and 20th Centuries.* 1st ed. Austin, TX: University of Texas Press, 1994. 246 p. (The Texas Pan American series.) ISBN 0292751672.

Twenty-one studies by Latin American literature specialists examine essays by Flora Tristán, Gertrudis Gómez de Avellaneda, Clorinda Matto de Turner, Victoria Ocampo, Alfonsina Storni, Rosario Ferré, Cristina Peri Rossi, and Elena Poniatowska.

262. Moss, Joyce, and Lorraine Valestuk. *Latin American Literature and Its Times.* Detroit, MI: Gale, 1999. 562 p. Bibl., ill., index. (World literature and its times; 1.) ISBN 0787637262.

Classic and contemporary writings are included in this volume that also presents a discussion of the works themselves within their historical and social contexts.

263. Rowe, William. *Poets of Contemporary Latin America: History and the Inner Life.* New York: Oxford University Press, 2000. 370 p. (Oxford Hispanic studies.) ISBN 0198158920.

Poets active since the 1950s are the focus of this volume. They are: Nicanor Parra, Ernesto Cardenal, Gonzalo Rojas, Jorge E. Eielson, Juan L. Ortiz, Ana Enriqueta Terán, Raúl Zurita, and Carmen Ollé.

264. Running, Thorpe. *The Critical Poem: Borges, Paz, and Other Language-Centered Poets in Latin America.* Lewisburg, PA: Bucknell University Press, 1996. 194 p. Bibl., index. ISBN 0838753191.

This volume analyzes contributions by eight poets from Mexico, Argentina, and Chile, active in the 1960s–1980s, whose works ponder meaning through philosophy of language.

265. Sefamí, Jacobo, comp. *Contemporary Spanish American Poets: A Bibliography of Primary and Secondary Sources.* New York: Greenwood Press, 1992. 245 p. (Bibliographies and indexes in world literature; 33.) ISBN 0313278806.

This bibliography covers poets born between 1910 and 1952.

266. Smith, Verity, ed. *Encyclopedia of Latin American literature.* Chicago: Fitzroy Dearborn, 1997. 926 p. Bibl., ill., index. ISBN 1884964184.

This one-volume encyclopedia contains survey essays about literature, all genres and time periods, for each Latin American country. Substantive essays about individual writers and significant works with bibliographies complete the volume.

267. Solé, Carlos A., and Maria Isabel Abreu, eds. *Latin American Writers.* New York: Scribner's, 1989. 3 vols. Bibl., index. ISBN 068418463X.

This reference set includes bibliographic/critical essays for 176 major writers from all nineteen countries of Spanish America and Brazil and covers all genres and time periods.

268. Swanson, Philip. *The New Novel in Latin America: Politics and Popular Culture After the Boom.* New York: Manchester University Press, 1996. 186 p. Bibl., index. ISBN 0719040388.

This volume analyzes and characterizes

Latin American literary movements (boom, post boom, postmodernism) of the latter half of the twentieth century and examines several of its exemplary texts.

269. Versenyi, Adam. *Theatre in Latin America: Religion, Politics, and Culture from Cortés to the 1980s.* New York: Cambridge University Press, 1993. 229 p. Bibl., index. ISBN 0521419387.

This work traces the religious origins of Latin American drama including the relationship between the Catholic Church and popular theater. (OP)

270. Weiss, Judith A. et al. *Latin American Popular Theatre: The First Five Centuries.* 1st ed. Albuquerque, NM: University of New Mexico Press, 1993. 269 p. Bibl., ill., index. ISBN 0826314015.

This introduction to the evolution of Latin American theater, from pre–Columbian times to the present, also includes an overview of popular theater activity during the second half of the twentieth century. (OP)

271. Williams, Raymond L. *The Modern Latin American Novel.* New York: Twayne Publishers, 1998. 177 p. Bibl., index. (Twayne's critical history of the novel.) ISBN 0805716556.

This analysis of the development of twentieth century long fiction covers works by major authors such as García Márquez, Vargas Llosa, and other lesser known writers.

272. Williams, Raymond L. *The Postmodern Novel in Latin America: Politics, Culture, and the Crisis of Truth.* 1st ed. New York: St. Martin's Press, 1995. 150 p. Bibl., index. ISBN 0312164580.

This surveys the development of Latin American postmodern fiction ("resolutely historical and inescapably political") in its political and cultural contexts. The examples are from Mexico, the Andean region, Southern Cone, and Caribbean.

273. Zamora, Lois Parkinson, and Wendy B. Faris, eds. *Magical Realism: Theory, History, Community.* Durham, NC: Duke University Press, 1995. 581 p. Bibl., index. ISBN 0822316110.

This work provides a thorough introduction and discussion of Latin America's most important contemporary literary movement.

Argentina

Anthologies and Original Works

274. Bioy Casares, Adolfo. *Selected Stories.* Translated by Suzanne Jill Levine. New York: New Directions, 1994. 176 p. ISBN 0811212750.

275. Borges, Jorge Luis. *Collected Fictions.* Translated by Andrew Hurley. New York: Viking, 1998. 565 p. ISBN 0670849707.

276. Borges, Jorge Luis. *Selected Non-Fictions.* Translated by Esther Allen et al. New York: Viking, 1998. 559 p. ISBN 0670849472.

277. Borges, Jorge Luis. *Selected Poems.* Edited by Alexander Coleman. New York: Viking, 1999. 477 p. ISBN 0670849413.

Bilingual edition.

278. Borinsky, Alicia. *Dreams of the Abandoned Seducer.* Translated by Cola Franzen. Lincoln, NE: University of Nebraska Press, 1998. 192 p. ISBN 0803261446.

279. Bullrich, Silvina. *Tomorrow I'll say, Enough.* Translated by Julia Shirek Smith. Pittsburgh, PA: Latin American Literary Review Press, 1996. 189 p. (Discoveries.) ISBN 0935480706.

280. Cortázar, Julio. *62: A Model Kit.* Translated by Gregory Rabassa. New York: New Directions, 2000. 288 p. ISBN 0811214370 pbk.

281. Cortázar, Julio. *Hopscotch.* Translated by Gregory Rabassa. New York: Pantheon Books, 1987. 574 p. ISBN 0394752848 pbk.

282. Fares, Gustavo, and E. Cazaubón Hermann, eds. *Contemporary Argentinean Women Writers: A Critical Anthology.* Translated by L. Britt. Gainesville, FL: University

Press of Florida, 1998. 250 p. Bibl., ill., index. ISBN 0813015537.

This anthology includes short biographies, interviews, and selections by fourteen contemporary Argentine women authors. The stories provide a different perspective about Argentina's political and socioeconomic upheaval in the twentieth century.

283. Gambaro, Griselda. *The Impenetrable Madam X*. Translated by Evelyn Picón Garfield. Detroit: Wayne State University Press, 1991. 149 p. (Latin American literature and culture series.) ISBN 0814321267.

284. Gelman, Juan. *Unthinkable Tenderness: Selected Poems*. Edited and translated by Joan Lindgren. Berkeley, CA: University of California Press, 1997. 191 p. ISBN 0520205863.

285. Gerchunoff, Alberto. *The Jewish Gauchos of the Pampas*. Translated by Prudencio de Pereda. Albuquerque, NM: University of New Mexico Press, 1998. 149 p. Ill. (Jewish Latin America.) ISBN 0826317677 pbk.

286. Giardinelli, Mempo. *Sultry Moon*. Translated by P. J. Duncan. Pittsburgh, PA: Latin American Literary Review Press, 1998. 111 p. (Discoveries.) ISBN 0935480927.

This is the first time a non–Mexican author received Mexico's National Book Award.

287. Glickman, Nora, and Gloria F. Waldman, eds. and trans. *Argentine Jewish Theatre: A Critical Anthology*. Lewisburg, PA: Bucknell University Press, 1996. 346 p. Bibl., ill. ISBN 083875287X.

The theme of these plays is the historical Jewish migration to Argentina.

288. Güiraldes, Ricardo. *Don Segundo Sombra*. Critical ed. Translated by P. Owen Steiner. Pittsburgh, PA: University of Pittsburgh Press, 1995. 302 p. Bibl. (The Pittsburgh editions of Latin American literature.) ISBN 0822938510.

289. Levinson, Luisa Mercedes. *The Two Siblings and Other Stories*. Translated by S. E.

Lipp. Pittsburgh, PA: Latin American Literary Review Press, 1996. 1995. (Discoveries.) ISBN 0935480781.

290. Mármol, José. *Amalia*. Edited by Doris Sommer and translated by Helen Lane. New York: Oxford University Press, 2000. 752 p. (Library of Latin America.) ISBN 0195122763.

291. Martínez, Tomás Eloy. *The Perón Novel*. 1st Vintage int. ed. Translated by Helen Lane. New York: Vintage International, 1999. 435 p. ISBN 0679768017 pbk.

292. Martínez, Tomás Eloy. *Santa Evita*. 1st American ed. Translated by Helen Lane. New York: Knopf, 1996. 371 p. ISBN 0679447040.

293. Martínez Estrada, Ezequiel. *Holy Saturday and Other Stories*. Translated by Leland H. Chambers. Pittsburgh, PA: Latin American Literary Review Press, 1988. 159 p. (Discoveries.) ISBN 0935480307.

294. Medina, Enrique. *Las Tumbas = The Tombs*. Translated by David William Foster. New York: Garland, 1993. 319 p. (World literature in translation.) ISBN 082407436X.

295. Puig, Manuel. *Heartbreak Tango: A Serial*. Translated by Carolyn and John Brushwood. New York: Penguin Books, 1991. 224 p. ISBN 0140153462.

296. Puig, Manuel. *Kiss of the Spider Woman and Two Other Plays*. Translated by Allan Baker and Ronald Christ. New York: W.W. Norton, 1994. 192 p. ISBN 0393311481 pbk.

297. Puig, Manuel. *Pubis Angelical*. 1st U. of Minnesota Press ed. Translated by Elena Brunet. Minneapolis, MN: University of Minnesota Press, 2000. 236 p. ISBN 0816636818 pbk.

298. Sábato, Ernesto R. *The Tunnel*. Translated by Margaret Sayers Peden. New York: Ballantine Books, 1991. 231 p. ISBN 0345373774 pbk.

Bilingual edition.

299. Sarmiento, Domingo Faustino. *Facundo, or, Civilization and Barbarism.* Translated by Mary Mann. New York: Penguin Books, 1998. 240 p. (Penguin classics.) ISBN 0140436774.

300. Shua, Ana María. *The Book of Memories.* 1st ed. Translated by Dick Gerdes. Albuquerque, NM: University of New Mexico Press, 1998. 178 p. (Jewish Latin America.) ISBN 0826319483.

301. Soriano, Osvaldo. *A Funny Dirty Little War.* Translated by Nick Caistor. New York: Readers International, 1989. 108 p. ISBN 0930523180 pbk.

302. Soriano, Osvaldo. *Winter Quarters: A Novel of Argentina.* Translated by Nick Caistor. New York: Readers International, 1989. 192 p. ISBN 0930523695.

303. Sorrentino, Fernando. *Sanitary Centennial and Selected Short Stories.* 1st ed. Translated by Thomas C. Meehan. Austin, TX: University of Texas Press. 1988. 186 p. (The Texas Pan American series.) ISBN 029277608X.

304. Steimberg, Alicia. *Musicians & Watchmakers.* Translated by Andrea G. Labinger. Pittsburgh, PA: Latin American Literary Review Press, 1998. 127 p. (Discoveries.) ISBN 093548096X.

305. Traba, Marta. *Mothers and Shadows.* Revised ed. Translated by Jo Labanyi. New York: Readers International, 1989. 178 p. ISBN 0930523156.

306. Valenzuela, Luisa. *Bedside Manners.* Translated by Margaret Jull Costa. New York: High Risk Books/Serpent's Tail, 1988. 121 p. ISBN 1852423137.

307. Valenzuela, Luisa. *Clara.* Translated by Andrea Labinger. Pittsburgh, PA: Latin American Literary Review Press, 1999. 182 p. ISBN 1891270095.

308. Valenzuela, Luisa. *Symmetries.* Translated by Margaret Jull Costa. New York: Serpent's Tail, 1998. 167 p. (Serpent's Tail high risk books.) ISBN 1852425431.

309. Vázquez Rial, Horacio. *Triste's History.* Translated by Jo Labanyi. New York: Readers International, 1990. 216 p. ISBN 0930523717.

Literary Criticism

310. Bell-Villada, Gene H. *Borges and His Fiction: A Guide to His Mind and Art.* 1st ed. Austin, TX: University of Texas Press, 1999. 325 p. Bibl., index. (The Texas Pan American series.) ISBN 0292708777.

This introduces the life and work of the Argentine master and includes political and personal experiences that contribute to a more thorough understanding of Borges' national and international influence.

311. Levine, Suzanne Jill. *Manuel Puig and the Spider Woman.* 1st ed. New York: Farrar, Straus, Giroux, 2000. 448 p. Bibl., ill., index. ISBN 0374281904.

This is a critical biography of the late Argentine author whose works explore the effect of film on human life and culture.

312. Lindstrom, Naomi. *Jorge Luis Borges: A Study of the Short Fiction.* New York: Twayne, 1990. 174 p. Bibl., index. (Twayne's studies in short fiction; 16.) ISBN 080578327X.

A three-part study of Borges' short fiction includes an overview of the evolution of his work in the 1960s and 1970s, a translated extract from an interview with Borges, and two critical studies. (OP)

313. Ocampo, Victoria. *Victoria Ocampo: Writer, Feminist, Woman of the World.* 1st ed. Edited and translated by P. Owen Steiner. Albuquerque, NM: University of New Mexico Press, 1999. 190 p. Bibl., ill., index. ISBN 0826320031.

This work examines the complex life of Ocampo, one of the twentieth century's most influential writers and feminists.

314. Peavler, Terry J. *Julio Cortázar.* New York: Twayne, 1990. 154 p. Bibl., ill., index. (Twayne's world authors series; TWAS 816.) ISBN 0805782575.

This critical work examines Cortazar's short stories and some of his novels.

315. Rodríguez-Luis, Julio. *The Contemporary Praxis of the Fantastic: Borges and Cortázar.* New York: Garland, 1991. 131 p. Bibl., index. (Garland reference library of the humanities. LAS; 1435.) ISBN 0815301014.

This study proposes a definition of fantastic literature that can be applied to contemporary Latin American texts. It is also useful for understanding the difference between "magical realism" and fantastic literature. (OP)

316. Stabb, Martin S. *Borges Revisited.* New York: Twayne, 1991. 151 p. Bibl., ill., index. (Twayne's world authors series; TWAS 819.) ISBN 080578263X.

This work examines Borges' life and works including his influence on U.S. and Latin American letters and his contributions to New Criticism. (OP)

317. Tittler, Jonathan. *Manuel Puig.* New York: Twayne, 1993. 152 p. Bibl., ill., index. (Twayne's world authors series; TWAS 836.) ISBN 0805782893.

This is a critical analysis of Puig's novels, plays, stories, and screenplays. (OP)

Bolivia

318. Aguirre, Nataniel. *Juan de la Rosa: Memoirs of the Last Soldier of the Independence Movement; A Novel.* Edited by A. M. Paz Soldán and translated by Sergio G. Waisman. New York: Oxford University Press, 1998. 329 p. Bibl. (Library of Latin America.) ISBN 0195113276.

319. Reyes, Sandra, ed. *Oblivion and Stone: A Selection of Contemporary Bolivian Poetry and Fiction.* Translated by John DuVal et al. Fayetteville, AR: University of Arkansas Press, 1998. 273 p. ISBN 1557285128.

This anthology of poems and short stories reflects the socioeconomic and political repression of daily life.

320. Santos, Rosario, ed. *The Fat Man from La Paz: Contemporary Fiction from Bolivia.* 1st ed. New York: Seven Stories Press, 2000. 314 p. ISBN 1583220305.

These twenty stories, available in English for the first time, represent social, political, and cultural themes that cover the last 75 years of Bolivian fiction.

Brazil

Anthologies and Original Works

321. Alencar, José Martiniano de. *Iracema: A Novel.* Edited by Naomi Lindstrom and translated by Clifford E. Landers. New York: Oxford University Press, 2000. 148 p. (Library of Latin America.) ISBN 0195115473.

322. Alencar, José Martiniano de. *Senhora: Profile of a Woman.* 1st ed. Translated by Catarina F. Edinger. Austin, TX: University of Texas Press, 1994. 198 p. (The Texas Pan American series.) ISBN 0292704496.

323. Almeida, Manuel Antônio de. *Memoirs of a Militia Sergeant.* Translated by Ronald W. Sousa. New York: Oxford University Press, 1999. 224 p. (Library of Latin America.) ISBN 019511549X pbk.

324. Alves, Antônio de Castro. *The Major Abolitionist Poems.* Translated by Amy A. Peterson. New York: Garland, 1990. 169 p. (World literature in translation; 5.) ISBN 0824029917. (OP)

325. Alves, Miriam, ed. *Finally Us … : Contemporary Black Brazilian Women Writers.* 1st ed. Translated by Carolyn R. Durham. Colorado Springs, CO: Three Continents Press, 1995. 258 p. Bibl., ill. ISBN 0894107895.

Bilingual edition.

326. Amado, Jorge. *Doña Flor and Her Two Husbands: A Moral and Amorous Tale.* New York: Avon Books, 1998. 624 p. ISBN 0380354020.

327. Amado, Jorge. *Gabriela, Clove, and Cinnamon.* New York: Avon Books, 1988. 425 p. ISBN 0380754703.

328. Andrade, Carlos Drummond de. *Travelling in the Family: Selected Poems.* 1st ed.

Edited by T. Colchie, translated by E. Bishop and G. Rabassa. New York: Random House, 1986. 134 p. ISBN 0394747518 pbk. (OP)

329. Azevedo, Aluísio. *Mulatto.* Translated by Murray G. MacNicoll. Rutherford, NJ: Fairleigh Dickinson University Press, 1990. 298 p. ISBN 0838633803.

330. Azevedo, Aluísio. *The Slum: A Novel.* Translated by David H. Rosenthal. New York: Oxford University Press, 2000. 222 p. Bibl. (Library of Latin America.) ISBN 0195121872.

This is the first English language translation of Azevedo's classic work that portrays late nineteenth century Brazil.

331. Cunha, Helena Parente. *Woman Between Mirrors.* Translated by F. P. Ellison and N. Lindstrom. Austin, TX: University of Texas Press, 1989. 132 p. (The Texas Pan American series.) ISBN 0292790457.

332. Fonseca, Rubem. *Bufo & Spallanzani.* Translated by Clifford E. Landers. New York: Dutton, 1990. 249 p. ISBN 0525248722. (OP)

333. Fonseca, Rubem. *Vast Emotions and Imperfect Thoughts.* 1st ed. Translated by Clifford Landers. Hopewell, NJ: Ecco Press, 1998. 312 p. ISBN 0880015837.

334. França Júnior, Oswaldo. *Beneath the Waters.* 1st American ed. Translated by Margaret A. Neves. New York: Ballantine Books, 1990. 165 p. ISBN 0345364619. (OP)

335. Hollanda, Chico Buarque de. *Turbulence: A Novel.* 1st American ed. Translated by Peter Bush. New York: Pantheon Books, 1992. 164 p. ISBN 0679412646. (OP)

336. Lins, Osman. *Avalovara.* Rep. ed. Translated by Gregory Rabassa. Austin, TX: University of Texas Press, 1990. 344 p. (The Texas Pan American series.) ISBN 029270416X pbk.

337. Lispector, Clarice. *The Apple in the Dark.* 1st University of Texas Press ed. Translated by Gregory Rabassa. Austin, TX: University of Texas Press, 1986. 361 p. (The Texas Pan American series.) ISBN 0292703929 pbk. (OP)

338. Lispector, Clarice. *The hour of the star.* Translated by Giovanni Pontiero. New York: New Directions, 1992. 96 p. ISBN 0811211908 pbk.

339. Lispector, Clarice. *Selected Crônicas.* Translated by Giovanni Pontiero. New York: New Directions, 1996. 212 p. (A New Directions paperbook; 834.) ISBN 0811213404 pbk.

340. Machado de Assis, Joaquim Maria. *Dom Casmurro: A Novel.* Translated by John Gledson. New York: Oxford University Press, 1997. 258 p. (Library of Latin America.) ISBN 0195103084.

341. Machado de Assis, Joaquim Maria. *The Posthumous Memoirs of Brás Cubas: A Novel.* Translated by Gregory Rabassa. New York: Oxford University Press, 1997. 219 p. (Library of Latin America.) ISBN 0195101693.

342. Machado de Assis, Joaquim Maria. *Quincas Borba.* Translated by Gregory Rabassa. New York: Oxford University Press, 1998. 290 p. Bibl. (Library of Latin America.) ISBN 0195106814.

343. Melo Neto, João Cabral de. *Selected Poetry, 1937–1990.* Edited by Djelal Kadid. Hanover, NH: University Press of New England, 1994. 200 p. Bibl. (Wesleyan poetry.) ISBN 0819522171.

344. Melo, Patricia. *The Killer.* 1st ed. Translated by Clifford E. Landers. Hopewell, NJ: Ecco Press, 1997. 217 p. ISBN 088015748.

345. Palmer, Michael et al., eds. *Nothing the Sun Could Not Explain: 20 Contemporary Brazilian Poets.* Los Angeles: Sun & Moon Press, 1997. 312 p. (Sun & Moon classics; 82.) ISBN 1557133662.

This bilingual anthology of contemporary Brazilian poets represents the modernist and concrete literary movements.

346. Piñon, Nélida. *The Republic of Dreams: A Novel.* 1st American ed. Translated by Helen Lane. New York: Knopf, 1989. 663 p. ISBN 0394555252.

347. Rawet, Samuel. *The Prophet and Other Stories.* Translated by Nelson Vieira. Albuquerque, NM: University of New Mexico Press, 1998. 86 p. Bibl. (Jewish Latin America.) ISBN 0826318371.

348. Ribeiro, Edgard Telles. *I Would Have Loved Him If I Had Not Killed Him.* 1st U.S. ed. Translated by Margaret A. Neves. New York: St. Martin's Press, 1994. 199 p. ISBN 0312110022. (OP)

349. Ribeiro, João Ubaldo. *The Lizard's Smile.* Translated by Clifford E. Landers. New York: Atheneum, 1994. 355 p. ISBN 0689121253. (OP)

350. Sadlier, Darlene J., ed. and trans. *One Hundred Years After Tomorrow: Brazilian Women's Fiction in the 20th Century.* Bloomington, IN: Indiana University Press, 1992. 241 p. Bibl., ill. ISBN 025335045X.

Clarice and Elisa Lispector, Dinah Silveira de Queiroz, Rachel de Queiroz, and Lya Luft are among the twenty Brazilian authors in this collection. The stories relate women's struggles with government, society, men, and other women.

351. Scliar, Moacyr. *The Collected Stories of Moacyr Scliar.* 1st ed. Translated by Eloah F. Giacomelli. Albuquerque, NM: University of New Mexico Press, 1998. 475 p. (Jewish Latin America.) ISBN 0826319114.

352. Scliar, Moacyr. *The Strange Nation of Rafael Mendes.* 1st hardcover ed. Translated by Eloah F. Giacomelli. New York: Harmony Books, 1987. 309 p. ISBN 0517567768. (OP)

353. Soares, Jô. *A Samba for Sherlock.* 1st ed. Translated by Clifford E. Landers. New York: Pantheon, 1997. 271 p. Bibl. ISBN 0679400656.

354. Steen, Edla van. *Early Mourning.* Translated by David S. George. Pittsburgh, PA: Latin American Literary Review Press, 1997. 142 p. (Discoveries.) ISBN 0935480846 pbk.

This work received the Brazilian Academy of Letters Prize for best novel and the Pen Club of Brazil Best Book Prize in 1993.

355. Steen, Edla van. *Village of the Ghost Bells: A Novel.* 1st ed. Translated by David S. George. Austin, TX: University of Texas Press, 1991. 197 p. (The Texas Pan American series.) ISBN 0292730632 pbk.

Literary Criticism

356. Chamberlain, Bobby J. *Jorge Amado.* New York: Twayne, 1990. 132 p. ill. (Twayne's world authors series; TWAS 767.) ISBN 0805782613.

This brief biography includes an analysis of Amado's most famous works.

357. DiAntonio, Robert E. *Brazilian Fiction: Aspects and Evolution of the Contemporary Narrative.* Fayetteville, AR: University of Arkansas Press, 1989. 221 p. ISBN 1557280568.

This volume analyzes noteworthy contemporary works. (OP)

358. Fitz, Earl E. *Machado de Assis.* New York: Twayne, 1989. 149 p. Bibl., ill., index, (Twayne's world authors series; TWAS 809.) ISBN 0805782443.

This introduces the life and work of the influential nineteenth century Brazilian author.

359. Graham, Richard, ed. *Machado de Assis: Reflections on a Brazilian Master Writer.* Austin, TX: University of Texas Press, 1999. 134 p. Bibl., index. (Critical reflections on Latin America series.) ISBN 0292728212.

This is an overview of the works of the nineteenth century master.

360. Quinlan, Susan Canty. *The Female Voice in Contemporary Brazilian Narrative.* New York: P. Lang, 1991. 205 p. Bibl., ill., index. (American university studies. Series XXII, Latin American university studies; 7.) ISBN 0820412813.

This volume documents the development of Brazilian women's fiction from its beginning to the late twentieth century.

361. Stern, Irwin, ed. *Dictionary of Brazilian Literature.* New York: Greenwood Press, 1988. 402 p. Bibl., index. ISBN 0313249326.

This overview of Brazilian literature is arranged alphabetically by topics and authors.

Caribbean Area

Anthologies and Original Works

362. Breton, Marcela, ed. *Rhythm & Revolt: Tales of the Antilles.* New York: Plume, 1995. 278 p. ISBN.

Twenty-five noteworthy short stories represent the region's duality from the 1920s to the late twentieth century.

363. Brown, Stuart, and John Wickham, eds. *The Oxford Book of Caribbean Short Stories.* New York: Oxford University Press, 1999. 476 p. Bibl. ISBN 0192832417 pbk.

This collection contains fifty-one short stories by twentieth century Caribbean writers of former Dutch, English, French, and Spanish colonies.

364. Campbell, Elaine, and Pierrette Frickey, eds. *The Whistling Bird: Women Writers of the Caribbean.* Boulder, CO: Lynne Rienner Publishers, 1998. 274 p. ISBN 0894104098.

This work includes selections of short stories, poetry, drama, and novel excerpts by little known women authors from the French-, Spanish-, and English-speaking Caribbean.

365. Chamoiseau, Patrick. *Creole Folktales.* Translated by Linda Coverdale. New York: New Press, 1994. 113 p. ISBN 1565841859.

366. Chamoiseau, Patrick. *Texaco.* Translated by Rose-Myriam Réjouis. New York: Pantheon Books, 1997. 401 p. ISBN 0679432353.

This work was awarded the Prix Goncourt.

367. Condé, Maryse. *Desirada.* Translated by Richard Philcox. New York: Soho Press, 2000. 272 p. ISBN 1569472157.

368. Donnell, Alison, and Sarah Lawson Welsh, eds. *The Routledge Reader in Caribbean Literature.* New York: Routledge, 1996. 540 p. Bibl., index. ISBN 0415120489.

This collection of twentieth century works includes non-fiction, poetry, and short prose from a representative sample of Aglophone and West Indian authors. An effort was made to include famous and less well-known works as well as addressing issues of nationality, gender, and ethnicity.

369. Esteves, Carmen C., and Lizabeth Paravisini-Gebert, eds. *Green Cane and Juicy Flotsam: Short Stories by Caribbean Women.* New Brunswick, NJ: Rutgers University Press, 1991. 273 p. Bibl., ill. ISBN 0813517370.

This is a collection of twenty-seven short stories written by women authors from eleven Caribbean countries from Dutch, English, French, and Hispanic Caribbean.

370. Fernández Olmos, Margarite, and Lizabeth Paravisini-Gebert, eds. *Remaking a Lost Harmony: Stories from the Hispanic Caribbean.* Fredonia, NY: White Pine Press, 1995. 249 p. Bibl. (Dispatches.) ISBN 1877727369 pbk.

These twenty-five short stories from Puerto Rico, Cuba, and the Dominican Republic are available in English for the first time.

371. Laferrière, Dany. *Dining with the Dictator.* Translated by David Homel. Toronto, Canada: Coach House Press, 1994. 207 p. ISBN 0889104808 pbk. (OP)

372. Nunez, Elizabeth. *Bruised Hibiscus: A Novel.* Seattle, WA: Seal Press, 2000. 286 p. ISBN 1580050360.

This work won the 1999 Independent Award for Multicultural Fiction.

Literary Criticism

373. Benítez Rojo, Antonio. *The Repeating Island: The Caribbean and the Postmodern Perspective.* 2nd ed. Translated by James Maraniss. Durham, NC: Duke University Press, 1996. 350 p. Bibl., index. (Post-contemporary interventions.) ISBN 0822318601.

This collection of essays examines Caribbean society emphasizing the African influence. The writers whose works are considered are: Bartolomé de las Casas, Nicolás Guillén, Fanny Buitrago, and Alejo Carpentier, among others.

374. Cartey, Wilfred G. *Whispers from the Caribbean: I Going Away, I Going Home.* Los Angeles: Center for Afro-American Studies, University of California, 1991. 503 p. (Afro-American culture and society series; 11.) ISBN 0934934355.

This is a detailed study of nearly seventy works by twenty-six, mostly male, Caribbean novelists.

375. Conde, Mary, and Thorunn Lonsdale, eds. *Caribbean Women Writers: Fiction in English.* New York: St. Martin's Press, 1999. 233 p. Bibl., index. ISBN 0312218613.

This collection of essays addresses common themes such as cultural identity, marginalization, and migration.

376. Dance, Daryl Cumber. *Fifty Caribbean Writers: A Bio-Bbibliographical Critical Sourcebook.* New York: Greenwood Press, 1986. 530 p. ISBN 0313239398.

This collection presents and analyzes the works of fifty Anglophone Caribbean authors.

377. Davis, Gregson. *Aimé Césaire.* New York: Cambridge University Press, 1997. 208 p. Bibl., index. (Cambridge studies in African and Caribbean literature.) ISBN 0521390729.

This critical biography of Césaire, considered to be a founder of the *négritude* movement, also provides details of his political and intellectual activities in his native Martinique.

378. Gikandi, Simon. *Writing in Limbo: Modernism and Caribbean Literature.* Ithaca, NY: Cornell University Press, 1992. 260 p. Index. ISBN 0801425751.

This is an analysis of the gap between colonial traditionalism and the discourse of national identity, European modernism, and postcolonial revisionism.

379. James, Louis. *Caribbean Literature in English.* New York: Longman, 1999. 232 p. Bibl., ill., index. (Longman literature in English series.) ISBN 0582493552.

This concise, interdisciplinary introduction to Caribbean literature examines the interplay between locale, history, and language.

380. Pfaff, Françoise. *Conversations with Maryse Condé.* Lincoln, NE: University of Nebraska Press, 1996. 178 p. Bibl., index. ISBN 0803237138.

This is a biographical and critical introduction to the author's works.

Central America

Anthologies and Original Works

381. Beverley, John, and Marc Zimmerman. *Literature and Politics in the Central American Revolutions.* 1st ed. Austin, TX: University of Texas Press, 1990. 252 p. (New interpretations of Latin America series.) ISBN 0292746660.

This work examines themes and types of contemporary Central American literature. The feminization of literature, revolutionary and testimonial poetry, are examples of political literature that flourished in a context of national liberation. (OP)

382. Jaramillo Levi, Enrique, ed. *When New Flowers Bloomed: Short Stories by Women Writers from Costa Rica and Panama.* Pittsburgh, PA: Latin American Literary Review Press, 1991. 208 p. (Discoveries.) ISBN 0935480471 pbk.

This anthology includes writings by authors previously unavailable to English language readers.

383. Jaramillo Levi, Enrique, and Leland H. Chambers, eds. *Contemporary Short Stories from Central America.* 1st ed. Austin, TX: University of Texas Press, 1994. 275 p. (Translations from Latin America series.) ISBN 0292740301.

This anthology represents outstanding examples of Central American short stories from the last twenty-five years with a brief and critical introduction to the genre.

384. Santos, Rosario, ed. *And We Sold the Rain: Contemporary Fiction from Central America.* 2nd ed. New York: Seven Stories Press, 1996. 257 p. ISBN 1888363037.

This collection of contemporary fiction represents twenty Central American authors. The main theme of the stories is the overwhelming need to exist with dignity while confronting daily violence.

Chile

Anthologies and Original Works

385. Alegría, Fernando. *Allende: A Novel.* Translated by Frank Janney. Stanford, CA: Stanford University Press, 1993. 303 p. Bibl., ill. ISBN 0804719985.

386. Allende, Isabel. *The House of the Spirits.* Translated by Magda Bogin. New York: Bantam Books, 1986. 433 p. ISBN 0553273914.

387. Allende, Isabel. *Paula.* 1st ed. Translated by Margaret Sayers Peden. New York: Harper Collins, 1995. 330 p. ISBN 0060172533.

388. Allende, Isabel. *The Stories of Eva Luna.* Translated by Margaret Sayers Peden. New York: Atheneum, 1991. 330 p. ISBN 0689121024.

389. Blest Gana, Alberto. *Martín Rivas.* Edited by Jaime Concha and translated by Tess O'Dwyer. New York: Oxford University Press, 1999. 389 p. (Library of Latin America.) ISBN 0195107144.

390. Bombal, María Luisa. *House of Mist; and, The Shrouded Woman: Two Novels.* 1st U. of Texas Press ed. Austin, TX: University of Texas Press, 1995. 259 p. ISBN 029270836X.

391. Cerda, Luis. *To Die in Berlin.* Translated by Andrea G. Labinger. Pittsburgh, PA: Latin American Literary Review Press, 1999. 176 p. ISBN 1891270028.

392. Donoso, José. *Curfew: A Novel.* Translated by Alfred MacAdam. New York: Grove Press, 1994. 310 p. ISBN 0802133819 pbk.

393. Donoso, José. *The Obscene Bird of Night: A Novel.* 1st Verba Mundi ed. Translated by Hardie St. Martin and Leonard Mades. Boston: David R. Godine Pub., 1995. 438 p. ISBN 1567920462 pbk.

394. Dorfman, Ariel. *Death and the Maiden.* New York: Penguin Books, 1992. 79 p. ISBN 0140482385.

395. Eltit, Diamela. *E. Luminata.* Translated by Ronald Christ. Santa Fe, NM: Lumen, 1997. 240 p. ISBN 0930829409.

396. Fuguet, Alberto. *Bad Vibes.* 1st ed. Translated by Kristina Cordero. New York: St. Martin's Press, 1997. 308 p. ISBN 0312150598.

397. Huidobro, Vicente. *Altazor, or, A Voyage in a Parachute (1919): A Poem in VII Cantos.* Translated by Eliot Weinberger. Saint Paul, MN: Graywolf Press, 1988. 167 p. (Palabra sur.) ISBN.

Bilingual edition.

398. Lihn, Enrique. *Figures of Speech: Poems by Enrique Lihn.* Translated by David Oliphant. Austin, TX: Host Pub. 1999. 187 p. ISBN 0924047178 pbk.

Bilingual edition.

399. Mistral, Gabriela. *A Gabriela Mistral Reader.* Edited by M. Agosín, translated by M. Giachetti. Fredonia, NY: White Pine Press, 1993. 227 p. ISBN 1877727180 pbk.

400. Mistral, Gabriela. *Poemas de las Madres = The Mothers' Poems.* Translated by Christiane J. Kyle. Cheney, WA: EWU Press, 1996. 39 p. ISBN 0910055297.

401. Neruda, Pablo. *Canto General.* 50th Anniversary ed. Translated by Jack Schmitt. Berkeley, CA: University of California Press,

2000. 407 p. Bibl., ill. (Latin American literature and culture; 7.) ISBN 0520227093.

402. Neruda, Pablo. *Memoirs.* Translated by Hardie St. Martin. New York: Viking Press, 1992. 350 p. ISBN 014018628X.

403. Neruda, Pablo. *Neruda's Garden: An Anthology of Odes.* Translated by Maria Jacketti. Pittsburgh, PA: Latin American Literary Review Press, 1995. 253 p. ISBN 0935480803 pbk.
   Bilingual edition.

404. Neruda, Pablo. *One Hundred Love Sonnets = Cien Sonetos de Amor.* 1st ed. Translated by Stephen Tapscott. Austin, TX: University of Texas Press, 1986. 222 p. Ill. ISBN 0292760299.

405. Neruda, Pablo. *Twenty Love Poems and a Song of Despair.* Translated by W.S. Merwin. San Francisco: Chronicle Books, 1993. 79 p. Ill. ISBN 0811803201.
   Bilingual edition

406. Parra, Marco Antonio de la. *The Secret Holy War of Santiago de Chile: A Novel.* Translated by Charles P. Thomas. New York: Interlink Books, 1994. 319 p. (Emerging voices.) ISBN 1566561272.

407. Reyes, Sandra, ed. and trans. *One More Stripe to the Tiger: A Selection of Contemporary Chilean Poetry and Fiction.* Fayetteville, AR: University of Arkansas Press, 1989. 311 p. ISBN 1557280347.
   This is a selection of twenty-one contemporary poets and ten short story writers. (OP)

408. Sepúlveda, Luis. *The Old Man Who Read Love Stories.* 1st Harvest ed. Translated by Peter Bush. New York: Harcourt Brace, 1994. 131 p. (Harvest in translation. A Harvest book.) ISBN 0156002728.

409. Skármeta, Antonio. *Burning Patience.* 1st English language ed. New York: Pantheon Books, 1987. 118 p. (A Pantheon modern writers original.) ISBN 0394555767. (OP)

410. Teillier, Jorge. *In Order to Talk with the Dead: Selected Poems of Jorge Teillier.* 1st ed.

Translated by Carolyne Wright. Austin, TX: University of Texas Press, 1993. 129 p. (The Texas Pan American series.) ISBN 0292738676.
   Bilingual edition.

411. White, Steven F., ed. and trans. *Poets of Chile: A Bilingual Anthology, 1965–1985.* Greensboro, NC: Unicorn Press, 1986. 283 p. Bibl., ill. ISBN 087775179X.
   This work samples the work of twenty young poets.

412. Zurita, Raúl. *Anteparadise.* Translated by Jack Schmitt. Berkeley, CA: University of California Press, 1986. 217 p. Ill. ISBN 0520054342.
   Bilingual edition.

Literary Criticism

413. Agosín, Marjorie. *Pablo Neruda.* Translated by Lorraine Roses. New York: Twayne, 1986. 157 p. Bibl., ill., index. (Twayne's world authors series. TWAS; 769.) ISBN 0805766200.
   This work includes a biography of the Nobel laureate and a critical reading of his poetry and prose. (OP)

414. Allende, Isabel. *Conversations with Isabel Allende.* 1st ed. Edited by John Rodden. Austin, TX: University of Texas Press, 1999. 477 p. Bibl., ill., index. (The Texas Pan American series.) ISBN 0292770928.
   This collection of interviews from the 1980s and 1990s covers topics such as feminism, family history, and the writing process.

415. Riquelme Rojas, Sonia, and Edna Aguirre Rehbein, eds. *Critical Approaches to Isabel Allende's Novels.* New York: P. Lang, 1991. 201 p. Bibl., ill. (American university studies. Series XXII, Latin American literature; 14.) ISBN 0820414956.
   This volume presents critical perspectives for interpreting Allende's works. (OP)

416. Teitelboim, Volodia. *Neruda: An Intimate Biography.* 1st ed. Translated by Beverly DeLong-Tonelli. Austin, TX: University of

Texas Press, 1991. 506 p. Bibl., ill., index. (The Texas Pan American series.) ISBN 0292755481.

This critical biography is written by a personal friend of the poet.

Colombia

Anthologies and Original Works

417. Buitrago, Fanny. *Señora Honeycomb: A Novel.* 1st ed. Translated by Margaret Sayers Peden. New York: HarperCollins, 1996. 232 p. ISBN 0060173653.

Buitrago has received several literary prizes. This is her first English translation.

418. Cepeda Samudio, Alvaro. *La Casa Grande: A Novel.* 1st ed. Translated by Seymour Menton. Austin, TX: University of Texas Press, 1991. 109 p. (The Texas Pan American series.) ISBN 0292746679. (OP)

419. García Márquez, Gabriel. *The Autumn of the Patriarch.* 1st HarperPerennial ed. Translated by Gregory Rabassa. New York: HarperPerennial, 1991. 269 p. ISBN 0060919639.

420. García Márquez, Gabriel. *Collected Stories.* 1st Perennial classics ed. Translated by Gregory Rabassa. New York: HarperCollins Pub., 1999. 343 p. (Perennial classics.) ISBN 0060932686.

This collection contains *Leaf Storm and Other Stories*; *No One Writes to the Colonel*; *Innocent Eréndira and Other Stories*.

421. García Márquez, Gabriel. *Love in the Time of Cholera.* 1st American ed. Translated by Edith Grossman. New York: Knopf, 1988. 348 p. ISBN 0394561619.

422. García Márquez, Gabriel. *One Hundred Years of Solitude.* Translated by Gregory Rabassa. New York: HarperCollins, 1998. 416 p. ISBN 0060929790.

423. Mutis, Alvaro. *The Adventures of Maqroll: Four Novellas.* 1st ed. Translated by Edith Grossman. New York: Harper Collins, 1995. 369 p. ISBN 0060170042. (OP)

424. Restrepo, Laura. *The Angel of Galilea.* 1st ed. Translated by Dolores M. Koch. New York: Crown Publishers, 1998. 193 p. ISBN 0609603264.

This novel was an international best-seller.

425. Restrepo, Laura. *Leopard in the Sun: A Novel.* 1st American ed. Translated by Stephen A. Lytle. New York: Crown Publishers, 1999. 242 p. ISBN 0609603868.

426. Zapata Olivella, Manuel. *Chambacu, Black Slum.* Translated by Jonathan Tittler. Pittsburgh, PA: Latin American Literary Review Press, 1989. 128 p. (Discoveries.) ISBN 0935480390.

Literary Criticism

427. Bell-Villada, Gene H. *García Márquez: The Man and His Work.* Chapel Hill, NC: University of North Carolina Press, 1990. 247 p. ISBN 0807818755.

This thorough examination of themes, structures, and characters in García Márquez's main works also includes observations about his world, life, politics, and literary training.

428. Janes, Regina. *One Hundred Years of Solitude: Modes of Reading.* New York: Twayne, 1991. 160 p. Bibl., ill., index. (Twayne's masterworks studies; 70.) ISBN 0805779892.

This work examines the novel in its literary and historical contexts.

429. McNerney, Kathleen. *Understanding Gabriel García Márquez.* Columbia, SC: University of South Carolina Press, 1989. 180 p. Bibl., index. (Understanding contemporary European and Latin American literature.) ISBN 0872495639.

This concise introduction to the life and works of García Márquez includes his journalistic essays. The sociohistorical approach emphasizes the link between the content of his works and the society in which they were written. (OP)

Costa Rica

430. Lobo, Tatiana. *Assault on Paradise: A Novel.* 1st ed. Translated by Asa Zatz. Willimantic, CT: Curbstone Press, 1998. 297 p. ISBN 1880684462 pbk.

This work received the Sor Juana Inés de la Cruz prize in 1995.

Cuba

Anthologies and Original Works

431. Arenas, Reinaldo. *The Assault.* Translated by Andrew Hurley. New York: Viking, 1994. 145 p. ISBN 0670840661.

432. Arenas, Reinaldo. *Farewell to the Sea: A Novel of Cuba.* Translated by Andrew Hurley. New York: Penguin, 1994. 413 p. ISBN 0140066365 pbk.

433. Barnet, Miguel. *Rachel's Song: A Novel.* 1st ed. Translated by W. Nick Hill. Willimantic, CT: Curbstone Press, 1991. 125 p. ISBN 0915306875 pbk.

434. Behar, Ruth, ed. *Bridges to Cuba = Puentes a Cuba.* Ann Arbor, MI: University of Michigan Press, 1995. 421 p. ISBN 0472096117.

This anthology of poems, short stories, and essays represents the Cuban diaspora. Authors who still live on the island and authors who left it explore issues of reconciliation, rupture, and memories.

435. Benítez Rojo, Antonio. *Sea of Lentils.* Translated by James Maraniss. Amherst, MA: University of Massachusetts Press, 1990. 201 p. Ill. ISBN 0870237233.

436. Benítez Rojo, Antonio. *A View from the Mangrove.* Translated by James Maraniss. Amherst, MA: University of Massachusetts Press, 1998. 243 p. ISBN 1558491368.

437. Bush, Peter, ed. *The Voice of the Turtle: An Anthology of Cuban Stories.* 1st Grove Press ed. New York: Grove Press, 1998. 383 p. ISBN 0802135552 pbk.

438. Cabrera Infante, Guillermo. *Infante's Inferno.* Translated by Suzanne J. Levine. New York: Marlowe & Co., 1998. 416 p. ISBN 1569247072 pbk.

439. Cabrera Infante, Guillermo. *Three Trapped Tigers.* Translated by D. Gardner and Suzanne J. Levine. New York: Marlowe & Co., 1997. 487 p. ISBN 1569247137 pbk.

440. Carpentier, Alejo. *The Chase.* 1st ed. Translated by Alfred MacAdam. New York: Farrar, Straus, Giroux, 1989. 121 p. ISBN 0374120838.

441. Carpentier, Alejo. *The Harp and the Shadow: A Novel.* Translated by Thomas and Carol Christensen. San Francisco: Mercury House, 1990. 159 p. ISBN 0916515710.

442. Carpentier, Alejo. *The Kingdom of This World.* Translated by Harriet de Onís. New York: Noonday Press, 1989. 186 p. ISBN 0374521972.

443. Estévez, Abilio. *Thine Is the Kingdom: A Novel.* 1st ed. Translated by David Frye. New York: Arcade, 1999. 327 p. ISBN 1559704519.

444. Gómez de Avellaneda y Arteaga, Gertrudis. *Sab; and, Autobiography.* 1st ed. Translated by Nina M. Scott. Austin, TX: University of Texas Press, 1993. 157 p. Bibl. (The Texas Pan American series.) ISBN 0292776551.

445. Guillén, Nicolás. *New Love Poetry: In Some Springtime Place: Elegy.* Edited and translated by Keith Ellis. Toronto, Canada: University of Toronto Press, 1994. 159 p. Bibl., ill., index. ISBN 080200427X.

Bilingual edition.

446. Lezama Lima, José. *Paradiso.* 1st ed. Translated by Gregory Rabassa. Austin, TX: University of Texas Press, 1988. 466 p. (The Texas Pan American series.) ISBN 029276507X pbk.

447. Martí, José. *Versos Sencillos = Simple Verses.* Translated by Manuel A. Tellechea. Houston, TX: Arte Público Press, 1997. 123 p. (Recovering the U.S. Hispanic literary heritage.) ISBN 1558852182.

These poems constitute Martí's autobiography.

448. Montero, Mayra. *In the Palm of Darkness: A Novel.* 1st ed. Translated by Edith Grossman. New York: HarperCollins, 1997. 181 p. ISBN 0060187034.

449. Montero, Mayra. *The Messenger: A Novel.* 1st ed. Translated by Edith Grossman. New York: HarperFlamingo, 1999. 218 p. ISBN 0060192232.

450. Padilla, Heberto. *A Fountain, a House of Stone: Poems.* 1st ed. Translated by Alastair Reid and Alexander Coleman. New York: Farrar, Straus, Giroux, 1991. 109 p. ISBN 0374157812.

Bilingual edition.

451. Piñera, Virgilio. *Cold Tales.* Translated by Mark Schafer. Hygiene, CO: Eridanos Press, 1988. 282 p. (The Eridanos library; 8.) ISBN 0941419185.

452. Ponte, Antonio José. *In the Cold of the Malecón & Other Stories.* Translated by Cola Franzen and Dick Cluster. San Francisco: City Lights, 2000. 127 p. ISBN 0872863743 pbk.

453. Rivera, Esteban, and Juana Ponce de León, eds. *Dream with No Name: Contemporary Fiction from Cuba.* A Seven Stories Press 1st ed. New York: Seven Stories Press, 1998. 303 p. ISBN 188836372X.

This anthology covers well-known and new writers (both expatriates and island-dwellers) whose work appears in English for the first time. The stories cover the period before and after the revolution. The themes are varied and include many topics previously censored.

454. Sarduy, Severo. *Cobra; and, Maitreya.* 1st ed. Translated by Suzanne Jill Levine. Normal, IL: Dalkey Archive Press, 1995. 273 p. ISBN 1564780767 pbk.

455. Valdés, Zoé. *I Gave You All I Had.* Translated by Nadia Benabid. New York: Arcade Pub., 1999. 256 p. ISBN 1559704772.

This work received the Planeta Prize.

456. Valdés, Zoé. *Yocandra in the Paradise of Nada: A Novel of Cuba.* 1st ed. Translated by Sabina Cienfuegos. New York: Arcade Pub. 1997. 157 p. Bibl. ISBN 1559703628.

457. Yáñez, Mirta, ed. *Cubana: Contemporary Fiction by Cuban Women.* Translated by Dick Cluster and Cindy Schuster. Boston: Beacon Press, 1998. 213 p. ISBN 0807083364.

This anthology gathers short fiction by contemporary women authors who examine Cuba's crisis.

Literary Criticism

458. Cuadra, Angel. *Angel Cuadra: The Poet in Socialist Cuba.* Edited by Warren Hampton. Gainesville, FL: University of Florida Press, 1994. 158 p. Ill. ISBN 0813012619.

Bilingual edition.

459. González Echevarría, Roberto. *Alejo Carpentier, the Pilgrim at Home.* 1st University of Texas Press ed. Austin, TX: University of Texas Press, 1990. 334 p. Bibl., index. (The Texas Pan American series.) ISBN 0292704178.

This examination of Carpentier's main works includes biographical background.

460. Martínez, Julio A., ed. *Dictionary of Twentieth-Century Cuban Literature.* New York: Greenwood Press, 1990. 537 p. ISBN 0313251851.

This volume contains biobibliographical essays for more than one hundred Cuban authors, active since 1900, who have an international following.

461. Pellón, Gustavo. *José Lezama Lima's Joyful Vision: A Study of Paradiso and Other Prose Works.* 1st ed. Austin, TX: University of Texas Press, 1989. 151 p. Bibl., ill., index. (The Texas Pan American series.) ISBN 0292740204.

This work distinguishes Lezama Lima's work from that of his disciple Severo Sarduy and compares Lezama Lima with other Latin American contemporary authors.

462. Roses, Lorraine Elena. *Voices of the Storyteller: Cuba's Lino Novás Calvo.* New

York: Greenwood Press, 1986. 155 p. Bibl., index. (Contributions to the study of world literature; 14.) ISBN 0313250774.

This is an analysis of Novás Calvo's main short stories.

463. Souza, Raymond D. *Guillermo Cabrera Infante: Two Islands, Many Worlds.* 1st ed. Austin, TX: University of Texas Press, 1996. 195 p. Bibl., index. (The Texas Pan American series.) ISBN 0292776950.

This biographical work contains some critical information about Cabrera Infante's writings, his film scripts, and the creative process.

464. West, Alan. *Tropics of History: Cuba Imagined.* Westport, CT: Bergin & Garvey, 1997. 214 p. Bibl., index. ISBN 0897893387.

Cuba's major writers explore its cultural politics.

Dominican Republic

465. Alvarez, Julia. *How the García Girls Lost Their Accents.* 1st ed. Chapel Hill, NC: Algonquin Books of Chapel Hill, 1991. 290 p. ISBN 0945575572.

466. Alvarez, Julia. *In the Time of the Butterflies.* 1st ed. Chapel Hill, NC: Algonquin Books of Chapel Hill, 1994. 325 p. ISBN 1565120388.

467. Sención, Viriato. *They Forged the Signature of God.* Translated by Asa Zatz. Willimantic, CT: Curbstone Press, 1995. 250 p. ISBN 1880684330 pbk.

This work received the Dominican Republic's National Novel Award in 1993, which later was denied to the author given the political scandal that ensued. The novel is a depiction of the Trujillo-Balaguer regime.

Ecuador

468. Ortiz, Adalberto. *Juyungo.* Rep. ed. Translated by Jonathan Tittler and Susan

Hill. Boulder, CO: L. Rienner, 1991. 226 p. ISBN 0894100912 pbk.

469. Yáñez Cossío, Alicia. *Bruna and Her Sisters in the Sleeping City.* Translated by Kenneth J. A. Wishnia. Evanston, IL: Northwestern University Press, 1999. 240 p. ISBN 0810114089.

El Salvador

470. Alegría, Claribel. *Luisa in Realityland.* Translated by Darwin J. Flakoll. Willimantic, CT: Curbstone Press, 1987. 152 p. ISBN 0915306700.

471. Alegría, Claribel, ed. *On the Front Line: Guerrilla Poems of El Salvador.* 1st ed. Translated by Darwin J. Flakoll. Willimantic, CT: Curbstone Press, 1989. 89 p. ISBN 0915306867.

This is a bilingual edition of poetry written by Salvadoran revolutionaries representing the Farabundo Martí Liberation Front.

472. Alegría, Claribel. *Umbrales = Thresholds: Poems.* 1st ed. Translated by Darwin J. Flakoll. Willimantic, CT: Curbstone Press, 1996. 69 p. ISBN 1880684365.

Bilingual edition.

473. Argueta, Manlio. *Little Red Riding Hood in the Red Light District: A Novel.* Translated by Edward Waters Hood. Willimantic, CT: Curbstone Press, 1998. 237 p. ISBN 1880684322.

474. Bencastro, Mario. *A Shot in the Cathedral.* Translated by Susan Giersbach Rascón. Houston, TX: Arte Público Press, 1996. 215 p. ISBN 155885164X pbk.

475. Bencastro, Mario. *The Tree of Life: Stories of Civil War.* Translated by Susan Giersbach Rascón. Houston: Arte Público Press, 1997. 112 p. ISBN 1558851860 pbk.

476. Benítez, Sandra. *Bitter Grounds.* New York: Hyperion, 1997. 445 p. ISBN 0786861576.

477. Dalton, Roque. *El Salvador at War: A Collage Epic.* Edited by Marc Zimmerman. Minneapolis, MN: MEP Publications, 1988. 306 p. Ill. (Studies in Marxism; 23.) ISBN 0930656539.

478. Dalton, Roque. *Small Hours of the Night: Selected Poems of Roque Dalton.* 1st ed. Edited by Hardie St. Martin, translated by J. Cohen. Willimantic, CT: Curbstone Press, 1996. 201 p. ISBN 1880684357.

479. Lindo, Hugo. *The Ways of Rain = Maneras de Llover; and Other Poems.* Translated by Elizabeth Gamble Miller. Pittsburgh, PA: Latin American Literary Review Press, 1986. 160 p. (Discoveries.) ISBN 0935480242.

These twenty-eight cantos are inspired by the *Popol Vuh.*

Guatemala

480. Arias, Arturo. *After the Bombs: A Novel.* Translated by Asa Zatz. Willimantic, CT: Curbstone Press, 1990. 221 p. ISBN 0915306883.

481. Asturias, Miguel Angel. *Men of Maize.* Critical ed. Translated by Gerald Martin. Pittsburgh, PA: University of Pittsburgh Press, 1993. 466 p. Bibl., ill. (The Pittsburgh editions of Latin American literature.) ISBN 0822937670.

482. Asturias, Miguel Angel. *The Mirror of Lida Sal: Tales Based on Mayan Myths and Guatemalan Legends.* Translated by G. Alter-Gilbert. Pittsburgh, PA: Latin American Literary Review Press, 1997. 126 p. (Discoveries.) ISBN 0935480838.

Asturias weaves Maya and other Guatemalan folk myths into tales of contemporary transcendence.

483. Asturias, Miguel Angel. *The President.* Translated by Frances Partridge. Prospect Heights, IL: Waveland Press, 1997. 286 p. ISBN 0881339512.

484. Esquivel, Julia. *The Certainty of Spring: Poems by a Guatemalan in Exile.* Translated by Anne Woehrle. Washington, DC: Ecumenical Program in Central America and the Caribbean, 1993. 1 vol. Ill. ISBN 0918346118. Bilingual edition.

485. Goldman, Francisco. *The Long Night of White Chickens.* 1st ed. New York: Atlantic Monthly Press, 1992. 450 p. ISBN 0871135094.

486. Montejo, Víctor. *Sculpted Stones = Piedras Labradas.* 1st ed. Translated by Víctor Perera. Willimantic, CT: Curbstone Press, 1995. 107 p. ISBN 1880684144 pbk. Bilingual edition.

487. Monterroso, Augusto. *Complete Works & Other Stories.* 1st ed. Translated by Edith Grossman. Austin, TX: University of Texas Press, 1995. 152 p. (The Texas Pan American series.) ISBN 0292751834.

Guyana

488. Kempadoo, Oonya. *Buxton Spice.* 1st American ed. New York: Dutton, 1999. 169 p. ISBN 0525945067.

Honduras

489. Gold, Janet N. *Clementina Suárez: Her Life and Poetry.* Gainesville, FL: University of Florida Press, 1995. 305 p. Bibl., ill., index. ISBN 0813013372.

This is a portrait of the Honduran poet and promoter of the arts.

Mexico

Anthologies and Original Works

490. Acosta Hernández, Juvenal, ed. *Light from a Nearby Window: Contemporary Mexican Poetry.* San Francisco: City Lights Books, 1994. 231 p. ISBN 087286281X.

This bilingual anthology of twenty-one writers, born since 1945, represents different regions of Mexico.

491. Arredondo, Inés. *Underground River and Other Stories.* Translated by Cynthia Steele. Lincoln, NE: University of Nebraska Press, 1996. 128 p. (Latin American women writers.) ISBN 0803210345.

492. Azuela, Mariano. *The Underdogs.* Crit. ed. Translated by Frederick H. Fornoff. Pittsburgh, PA: University of Pittsburgh Press, 1992. 165 p. (The Pittsburgh editions of Latin American literature.) ISBN 082293728X.

493. Boullosa, Carmen. *They're Cows, We're Pigs.* 1st ed. Translated by Leland H. Chambers. New York: Grove Press, 1997. 180 p. ISBN 0802116108.

494. Bowen, J. David, and Juan A. Ascencio, eds. *Pyramids of Glass: Short Fiction from Modern Mexico.* San Antonio, TX: Corona Pub. Co., 1994. 244 p. ISBN 0931722993.

This anthology about contemporary life in Mexico includes twenty-seven short stories by well-known Mexican authors.

495. Campobello, Nellie. *Cartucho; and, My Mother's Hands.* 1st ed. Translated by D. Meyer and I. Matthews. Austin, TX: University of Texas Press, 1988. 129 p. (The Texas Pan American series.) ISBN 0292711115. (OP)

496. Campos, Julieta. *Celina or the Cats.* Translated by Leland H. Chambers. Pittsburgh, PA: Latin American Literary Review Press, 1995. 140 p. (Discoveries.) ISBN 0935480722.

497. Campos, Julieta. *The Fear of Losing Eurydice: A Novel.* 1st American ed. Translated by Leland H. Chambers. Elmwood, IL: Dalkey Archive Press, 1993. 121 p. ISBN 1564780201.

498. Castellanos, Rosario. *Another Way to Be: Selected Works of Rosario Castellanos.* Translated by Myralyn Frizzelle Allgood. Athens, GA: University of Georgia Press, 1990. 146 p. ISBN 0820312223.

This collection contains approximately two dozen items from Castellanos' prose and poetry. The last section is in bilingual format. (OP)

499. Castellanos, Rosario. *City of Kings.* Translated by Robert S. Rudder. Pittsburgh, PA: Latin American Literary Review Press, 1993. 143 p. (Discoveries.) ISBN 0935480633.

500. Castellanos, Rosario. *Meditation on the Threshold: A Bilingual Anthology of Poetry.* Translated by Julian Palley. Tempe, AZ: Bilingual Press/Editorial Bilingüe, 1988. 176 p. ISBN 0916950808.

501. Castellanos, Rosario. *A Rosario Castellanos Reader: An Anthology of Her Poetry, Short Fiction, Essays, and Drama.* 1st ed. Translated by Maureen Ahern. Austin, TX: University of Texas Press, 1988. 378 p. (The Texas Pan American series.) ISBN 0292770391.

502. Cerda, Martha. *Señora Rodríguez and Other Worlds.* Translated by Sylvia Jiménez-Andersen. Durham, NC: Duke University Press, 1997. 133 p. (Latin America in translation/en traducción/em tradução.) ISBN 0822318865.

503. Cuéllar, José Tomás de. *The Magic Lantern: A Novel and Novella.* Edited by Margo Glantz and translated by Margaret Carson. New York: Oxford University Press, 2000. 166 p. (Library of Latin America.) ISBN 0195115023.

504. Esquivel, Laura. *Like Water for Chocolate: A Novel in Monthly Installments, with Recipes, Romances, and Home Remedies.* 1st ed. Translated by Carol and Thomas Christenson. New York: Doubleday, 1992. 245 p. ISBN 0385420161.

505. Fuentes, Carlos. *Christopher Unborn.* 1st American ed. Translated by Alfred MacAdam. New York: Farrar, Straus, Giroux, 1989. 531 p. ISBN 0374123349.

506. Fuentes, Carlos. *The Crystal Frontier: A Novel in Nine Stories.* 1st Farrar, Straus, and Giroux ed. Translated by Alfred MacAdam. New York: Farrar, Straus, and Giroux, 1997. 266 p. ISBN 0374132771.

507. Fuentes, Carlos. *The Death of Artemio Cruz.* 1st ed. Translated by Alfred MacAdam. New York: Farrar, Straus, Giroux, 1991. 307 p. ISBN 0374135592.

508. Fuentes, Carlos. *The Years with Laura Díaz.* Translated by Alfred MacAdam. New York: Farrar, Straus, Giroux, 2000. 544 p. ISBN 0374293414.

509. Galindo, Sergio. *Otilia's Body: A Novel.* 1st ed. Translated by Carolyn and John Brushwood. Austin, TX: University of Texas Press, 1994. 225 p. Ill. (The Texas Pan American series.) ISBN 0292727690.

510. Gander, Forrest, ed. *Mouth to Mouth: Poems by Twelve Contemporary Mexican Women.* 1st ed. Translated by Zoe Anglesey. Minneapolis, MN: Milkweed Editions, 1993. 233 p. ISBN 0915943719.

511. Garro, Elena. *First Love; & Look for My Obituary: Two Novellas.* 1st ed. Translated by David Unger. Willimantic, CT: Curbstone Press, 1997. 112 p. ISBN 1880684519 pbk.

These works received the Sor Juana Inés de la Cruz Prize.

512. Garro, Elena. *Recollections of Things to Come.* Reprint ed. Translated by Ruth L.C. Simms. Austin, TX: University of Texas Press, 1986. 289 p. Ill. (The Texas Pan American series.) ISBN 0292770324 pbk. (OP)

513. Juana Inés de la Cruz. *The Answer = La Respuesta.* Edited and translated by Electa Arenal and Amanda Powell. New York: CUNY Feminist Press, 1994. 196 p. Bibl., index. ISBN 1558610766.

This new translation and thorough introduction draw upon the social, cultural, female and spiritual contexts of Sor Juana's reply to the bishop of Puebla in which she argues for a literary space for women in the world of letters.

514. Juana Inés de la Cruz. *Poems, Protest, and a Dream: Selected Writings.* Translated by Margaret Sayers Peden. New York: Penguin Books, 1997. 254 p. ISBN 0140447032 pbk.

This is a bilingual edition of Mexico's highly acclaimed and influential seventeenth century poet.

515. Juana Inés de la Cruz. *A Woman of Genius: The Intellectual Autobiography of Sor Juana Inés de la Cruz.* 2nd ed. Translated by Margaret Sayers Peden. Salisbury, CT: Lime Rock Press, 1987. 104 p. Bibl., ill. ISBN 0915998157 pbk.

516. León Portilla, Miguel, ed. *Fifteen Poets of the Aztec World.* 1st ed. Norman, OK: University of Oklahoma Press, 1992. 307 p. Bibl., ill., index. ISBN 0806124415.

This anthology of Nahuatl texts and their English translations includes an introduction to historical, intellectual, and thematic problems associated with this poetry.

517. López Portillo y Pacheco, José. *They Are Coming … : The Conquest of Mexico.* Translated by Beatrice Berler. Denton, TX: University of North Texas Press, 1992. 375 p. Bibl., ill., index. ISBN 0929398351.

518. López Velarde, Ramón. *Song of the Heart: Selected Poems.* 1st ed. Translated by Margaret Sayers Peden. Austin, TX: University of Texas Press, 1995. 104 p. Ill. ISBN 0292746857.

519. López y Fuentes, Gregorio. *El Indio.* Translated by Anita Brenner. New York: Continuum, 1988. 256 p. ISBN 0804464294 pbk.

This novel received the Mexican National Award in Literature. Engravings by Diego Rivera illustrate the work.

520. Mastretta, Angeles. *Lovesick.* Translated by Margaret Sayers Peden. New York: Riverhead Books, 1997. 292 p. ISBN 1573220620.

521. Mastretta, Angeles. *Tear This Heart Out.* 1st ed. Translated by Margaret Sayers Peden. New York: Riverhead Books, 1997. 293 p. ISBN 1573226025 pbk.

522. Molina, Silvia. *The Love You Promised Me.* Translated by David Unger. Willimantic, CT: Curbstone Press, 1999. 160 p. ISBN 1880684624 pbk.

This work received the Sor Juana Inés de la Cruz Prize.

523. Montemayor, Carlos. *Blood Relations: A Novel.* Translated by Dale Carter and Alfonso González. Kaneohe, HI: Plover Press, 1995. 112 p. (Plover contemporary

Latin-American classics in English translation series.) ISBN 0917635167.

This novel received the Xavier Villaurrutia Prize and garnered First Prize for the Novel in *El Nacional*'s fiftieth anniversary contest.

524. Montemayor, Carlos. *Gambusino: A Novel.* Translated by John Copeland. Kaneohe, HI: Plover Press, 1997. 113 p. (Plover contemporary Latin-American classics in English translation series.) ISBN 0917635213.

525. Muñiz-Huberman, Angelina. *Enclosed Garden.* Translated by Lois Parkinson Zamora. Pittsburgh, PA: Latin American Literary Review Press, 1988. 103 p. (Discoveries.) ISBN 0935480293.

This work received the 1985 Xavier Villaurrutia Prize.

526. Novo, Salvador. *The War of the Fatties and Other Stories from Aztec History.* 1st ed. Translated by Michael Alderson. Austin, TX: University of Texas Press, 1994. 232 p. Bibl. (The Texas Pan American series.) ISBN 0292790597.

527. Pacheco, José Emilio. *Battles in the Desert & Other Stories.* Translated by Katherine Silver. New York: New Directions, 1987. 117 p. ISBN 0811210197.

528. Pacheco, José Emilio. *City of Memory and Other Poems.* 1st ed. Translated by Cynthia Steele and David Lauer. San Francisco: City Lights, 1997. 193 p. ISBN 0872863247 pbk.

529. Paso, Fernando del. *Palinuro of Mexico.* 1st American ed. Translated by Elisabeth Plaister. Normal, IL: Dalkey Archive Press, 1996. 557 p. ISBN 1564780953 pbk.

This work received the Premio Novela México.

530. Paz, Octavio. *The Collected Poems of Octavio Paz, 1957–1987.* Edited and translated by Eliot Weinberger. New York: New Directions, 1987. 669 p. Bibl., ill., index. ISBN 0811210375.

Bilingual edition.

531. Revueltas, José. *Human Mourning.* Minneapolis, MN: University of Minnesota Press, 1990. 208 p. (Emergent literatures.) ISBN 0816618097.

532. Reyes, Luis Eduardo. *Modelo Antiguo: A Novel of Mexico City.* 1st ed. Translated by Sharon Franco and Joe Hayes. El Paso, TX: Cinco Puntos Press, 1997. 184 p. ISBN 0938317326 pbk.

533. Rojas, Emilio. *Little Friend.* Translated by Delbert Riddle. Rockport, MA: Element, 1992. 125 p. Ill. ISBN 185230281X.

534. Rulfo, Juan. *The Burning Plain, and Other Stories.* Translated by George D. Schade. Austin, TX: University of Texas Press, 1990. 175 p. Ill. (The Texas Pan American series.) ISBN 0292701322 pbk.

535. Rulfo, Juan. *Pedro Páramo.* 1st ed. Translated by Margaret Sayers Peden. New York: Grove Press, 1994. ISBN 0802133908.

536. Sabines, Jaime. *Pieces of Shadow: Selected Poems of Jaime Sabines.* Translated by W. S. Merwin. Mexico, D.F. Mexico: Papeles Privados, 1996. 205 p. ISBN 1568860234.

Bilingual edition.

537. Samperio, Guillermo. *Beatle Dreams and Other Stories.* Translated by R. Cluff and L.H. Quackenbush. Pittsburgh, PA: Latin American Literary Review Press, 1995. 169 p. (Discoveries.) ISBN 0935480609.

538. Solares, Ignacio. *Lost in the City: Two Novels.* 1st ed. Translated by C. and J. Brushwood. Austin, TX: University of Texas Press, 1998. 144 p. (The Texas Pan American series.) ISBN 0292777310.

539. Stavans, Ilan. *The One-Handed Pianist and Other Stories.* 1st ed. Albuquerque, NM: University of New Mexico Press, 1996. 196 p. ISBN 082631645X.

540. Taibo, Paco Ignacio. *Four Hands.* 1st ed. Translated by Laura C. Dail. New York: St. Martin's Press, 1994. 378 p. ISBN 0312109873.

541. Varela, Félix. *Xicoténcatl: An Anonymous Historical Novel About the Events Leading Up to the Conquest of the Aztec Empire.*

Translated by Guillermo I. Castillo-Feliú. Austin, TX: University of Texas Press, 1999. 156 p. ISBN 0292712138.

542. Villaurrutia, Xavier. *Nostalgia for Death: Poetry.* Translated by Eliot Weinberger. Port Townsend, WA: Copper Canyon Press, 1993. 148 p. ISBN 1556590539.

This collection contains an essay by Octavio Paz entitled "A Critical Study of Villaurrutia."

Literary Criticism

543. Burgess, Ronald D. *The New Dramatists of Mexico, 1967–1985.* Lexington, KY: University Press of Kentucky, 1991. 166 p. Bibl., index. ISBN 0813117275.

This introduction to works by recent Mexican dramatists includes biographical information, plot summaries, and critical commentary.

544. Cortés, Eladio, ed. *Dictionary of Mexican Literature.* New York: Greenwood Press, 1992. 768 p. ISBN 0313262713.

This comprehensive biobibliographical and critical reference work covers all time periods but focuses on the twentieth century.

545. Cypess, Sandra Messinger. *La Malinche in Mexican Literature: From History to Myth.* 1st ed. Austin, TX: University of Texas Press, 1991. 239 p. Bibl., index. (The Texas Pan American series.) ISBN 0292751311.

This provides new perspectives on the influence of the Mexican mythological figure on art, thought, and culture.

546. De Beer, Gabriella. *Contemporary Mexican Women Writers: Five Voices.* 1st ed. Austin, TX: University of Texas Press, 1996. 266 p. Bibl., ill. (The Texas Pan American series.) ISBN 0292715854.

This examines works by Carmen Boullosa, Brianda Domecq, Angeles Mastretta, María Luisa Puga, and Silvia Molina.

547. Duncan, J. Ann. *Voices, Visions, and a New Reality: Mexican Fiction Since 1970.* Pittsburgh, PA: University of Pittsburgh Press, 1986. 263 p. Bibl., index. (Pitt Latin American series.) ISBN 0822938154.

This studies the narrative technique, recurrent imagery, and themes of contemporary fiction. (OP)

548. Foster, David William, ed. *Mexican Literature: A History.* 1st ed. Austin, TX: University of Texas Press, 1994. 458 p. Bibl. (The Texas Pan American series.) ISBN 0292724829.

These twelve essays examine significant Mexican literary production from pre–Columbian through contemporary times.

549. Jorgensen, Beth Ellen. *The Writing of Elena Poniatowska: Engaging Dialogues.* 1st ed. Austin, TX: University of Texas Press, 1994. 172 p. ill. (The Texas Pan American series.) ISBN 0292740328.

This work analyzes four of Poniatowska's most influential works.

550. Kirk, Pamela. *Sor Juana Inés de la Cruz: Religion, Art, and Feminism.* New York: Continuum, 1998. 180 p. ISBN 082641043X.

In the seventeenth century Sor Juana defended women's right to education and made important contributions to feminist theology and literature.

551. O'Connell, Joanna. *Prospero's Daughter: The Prose of Rosario Castellanos.* 1st ed. Austin, TX: University of Texas Press, 1995. 263 p. Bibl., index. (The Texas Pan American series.) ISBN 0292760418.

This work examines Castellanos' prose writings that focus on gender issues in the context of *indigenismo*.

552. Paz, Octavio. *Sor Juana, or, The Traps of Faith.* Translated by Margaret Sayers Peden. New York: Cambridge University Press, 1988. 547 p. Bibl., ill., index. ISBN 067482105X.

This extensive, in-depth biography of the seventeenth century nun and poet, examines her works in their historical context.

553. Schaefer, Claudia. *Danger Zones: Homosexuality, National Identity, and Mexican Culture.* Tucson, AZ: University of Arizona Press, 1996. 159 p. Bibl., index. ISBN 0816516667.

This volume analyzes representative works by Mexican gay and lesbian authors and argues that their work has contributed to broadening the definition of Mexican national identity.

554. Schaefer, Claudia. *Textured Lives: Women Art and Representation in Modern Mexico.* Rep. ed. Tucson, AZ: University of Arizona Press, 1994. 163 p. Bibl., index. ISBN 0816514747 pbk.

This is an analysis of the contributions of Frida Kahlo, Rosario Castellanos, Elena Poniatowska, and Angeles Mastretta to Mexican literature and the arts.

555. Steele, Cynthia. *Politics, Gender, and the Mexican Novel, 1968–1988: Beyond the Pyramid.* 1st ed. Austin, TX: University of Texas Press, 1992. 209 p. Bibl., ill., index. (The Texas Pan American series.) ISBN 0292765304.

This work studies how Mexican writers (E. Poniatowska, F. del Paso and J. E. Pacheco) have responded to the 1968 Mexico City student massacre and other social crises.

556. Taylor, Kathy. *The New Narrative of Mexico: Sub-Versions of History in Mexican Fiction.* Lewisburg, PA: Bucknell University Press, 1994. 185 p. Bibl., index. ISBN 0838752667.

This is an analysis of the interdependence of literary fiction and history in four contemporary novels by E. Poniatowska, E. Garro, J. E. Pacheco and F. Campbell.

557. Valdés, María Elena de. *The Shattered Mirror: Representations of Women in Mexican Literature.* 1st University of Texas Press ed. Austin, TX: University of Texas Press, 1998. 278 p. Bibl., index. (The Texas Pan American series.) ISBN 0292715919.

This work presents the evolution of the representation of Mexican women in literary works. Among the authors whose work is examined are Carlos Fuentes, Juana Inés de la Cruz, Octavio Paz, Rosario Castellanos, Luisa J. Hernández, María Luisa Puga, Elena Poniatowska, Laura Esquivel, and Sandra Cisneros.

558. Van Delden, Maarten. *Carlos Fuentes, Mexico and Modernity.* 1st ed. Nashville, TN: Vanderbilt University Press, 1998. 262 p. Bibl., index. ISBN.

This examines the literary and political evolution of Mexico's premier novelist.

559. Williams, Raymond L. *The Writings of Carlos Fuentes.* 1st ed. Austin, TX: University of Texas Press, 1996. 185 p. Bibl., index. (The Texas Pan American series.) ISBN 029279097X.

This volume contains biographical information and an interview with Fuentes. It examines the themes of history, culture, and identity in his work with particular emphasis on his novel, *Terra Nostra.*

560. Wilson, Jason. *Octavio Paz.* New York: Twayne, 1986. 165 p. Bibl., index. (Twayne's world authors series; TWAS 783.) ISBN 0805766308.

This analysis of Paz's writing (poetry and essays) discusses his preoccupation with the role of poetry in human liberation from solitude and alienation. (OP)

Nicaragua

Anthologies and Original Works

561. Aguilar, Rosario. *The Lost Chronicles of Terra Firma.* Translated by Edward Waters Hood. Fredonia, NY: White Pine Press, 1997. 186 p. (Secret weavers series; 10.) ISBN 1877727628.

562. Belli, Gioconda. *The Inhabited Woman.* 1st Eng. lang. ed. Translated by Kathleen N. March. Willimantic, CT: Curbstone Press, 1994. 412 p. ISBN 1880684179.

563. Borge Martínez, Tomás. *Have You Seen A Red Curtain in My Weary Chamber?: Poems, Stories and Essays.* Edited and translated by Russell Bartley et al. Willimantic, CT: Curbstone Press, 1989. 160 p. Bibl., ill. ISBN 0915306816.

This work includes an interview, poetry, and essays by T. Borge, one of the founders of the Sandinista National Liberation Front.

564. Cardenal, Ernesto. *Cosmic Canticle.* Translated by Jonathan Lyons. Willimantic,

CT: Curbstone Press, 1993. 490 p. ISBN 1880684071.

565. Cardenal, Ernesto. *The Doubtful Strait = El Estrecho Dudoso.* Translated by John Lyons. Bloomington, IN: Indiana University Press, 1995. 189 p. ISBN 025331318X.
  Bilingual edition.

566. Cuadra, Pablo Antonio. *The Birth of the Sun: Selected Poems, 1935–1985.* Translated by Steven F. White. Greensboro, NC: Unicorn Press, 1988. 178 p. Bibl. (A Series of translations of poetries; 3.) ISBN 0877752044.

567. Gullette, David, trans. *Nicaraguan Peasant Poetry from Solentiname.* Albuquerque, NM: West End Press, 1988. 209 p. Bibl., ill. ISBN 0931122481.
  Bilingual edition.

568. Ramírez, Sergio. *Stories.* Translated by Nick Caistor. New York: Readers International, 1986. 118 p. ISBN 0930523288.

Literary Criticism

569. Dawes, Greg. *Aesthetics and Revolution: Nicaraguan Poetry, 1979–1990.* Minneapolis, MN: University of Minnesota Press, 1993. 217 p. Bibl., index. ISBN 0816621462.
  This work examines poetic expression during Nicaragua's revolutionary period.

Paraguay

570. Roa Bastos, Augusto Antonio. *I, the Supreme.* 1st ed. Translated by Helen Lane. New York: Knopf, 1986. 433 p. ISBN 0394535359. (OP)

Peru

Anthologies and Original Works

571. Bryce Echenique, Alfredo. *A World for Julius: A Novel.* 1st ed. Translated by Dick

Gerdes. Austin, TX: University of Texas Press, 1992. 430 p. (The Texas Pan American series.) ISBN 0292790716 pbk.

572. De Ferrari, Gabriella. *Gringa Latina: A Woman of Two Worlds.* Boston: Houghton Mifflin Co., 1995. 176 p. ISBN 0305709342.

573. Goldemberg, Isaac. *The Fragmented Life of Don Jacobo Lerner.* Translated by Robert S. Picciotto. Albuquerque, NM: University of New Mexico Press, 1999. 213 p. (Jewish Latin America.) ISBN 0826320740.

574. Matto de Turner, Clorinda. *Torn from the Nest.* Edited by A. Cornejo Polar and translated by J. H. R. Polt. New York: Oxford University Press, 1998. 174 p. Bibl., index. (Library of Latin America.) ISBN 0195110056.

575. Ortega, Julio. *Ayacucho, Goodbye; Moscow's Gold.* Translated by Edith Grossman and Alita Kelley. Pittsburgh, PA: Latin American Literary Review Press, 1994. 103 p. (Discoveries.) ISBN 0935480668 pbk.

576. Ramos-García, Luis, and Luis Fernando Vidal, eds. *From the Threshold: Contemporary Peruvian Fiction in Translation.* Austin, TX: Studia Hispanica Editors, Prickly Pear Press, 1987. 313 p. Bibl., ill. (Colección Poiesis; 6.) ISBN 0934840075.
  This bilingual edition of short stories was published between 1970 and 1980 as an alternative to the "boom" writers. Biographical notes about the authors are included. (OP)

577. Ribeyro, Julio Ramón. *Marginal Voices: Selected Stories.* 1st ed. Translated by Dianne Douglas. Austin, TX: University of Texas Press, 1993. 137 p. (The Texas Pan American series.) ISBN 029277057X.
  This author received the Juan Rulfo International Latin American and Caribbean Prize for Literature.

578. Riesco, Laura. *Ximena at the Crossroads.* Translated by Mary G. Berg. Fredonia, NY: White Pine Press, 1998. 269 p. (Secret weavers series; 12.) ISBN 1877727806 pbk.
  This work received Peru's Best Novel Prize of 1994.

579. Vallejo, César. *The Black Heralds = Los Heraldos Negros.* Translated by R. Schaaf and K. Ross. Pittsburgh, PA: Latin American Literary Review Press, 1990. 174 p. (Discoveries.) ISBN 0935480439.
Bilingual edition. (OP)

580. Vallejo, César. *Trilce.* Translated by Clayton Eshleman. New York: Marsilio, 1992. 276 p. Bibl., ill. ISBN 0941419509.
Bilingual edition.

581. Vallejo, César. *Tungsten: A Novel.* Translated by Robert Mezey. Syracuse, NY: Syracuse University Press, 1988. 133 p. ISBN 081560226X.

582. Vargas Llosa, Mario. *Captain Pantoja and the Special Service.* Translated by Gregory Kolovakos. New York: Noonday Press, 1990. 244 p. ISBN 0374522367 pbk. (OP)

583. Vargas Llosa, Mario. *The Cubs and Other Stories.* Translated by Gregory Kolovakos and R. Christ. New York: Noonday Press, 1989. ISBN 0374521948 pbk. (OP)

584. Vargas Llosa, Mario. *The Green House.* reprint ed. Translated by Gregory Rabassa. New York: Noonday Press, 1986. 405 p. ISBN 0374518882 pbk.

585. Vargas Llosa, Mario. *Making Waves.* 1st FSG ed. Edited and translated by John King. New York: Farrar, Straus and Giroux, 1997. 338 p. Bibl., index. ISBN 0374200386.
This work presents Vargas Llosa's personal views on government, society and culture, and the role of the writer in society.

586. Vargas Llosa, Mario. *The Time of the Hero.* Reissue ed. Translated by Lysander Kemp. New York: Farrar, Strauss and Giroux, 1986. 409 p. ISBN 0374520216 pbk.

Literary Criticism

587. Booker, M. Keith. *Vargas Llosa among the Postmodernists.* Gainesville, FL: University of Florida Press, 1994. 239 p. Bibl., index. ISBN 0813012481.
This work seeks to distinguish modernism from postmodernism as exemplified by M. Vargas Llosa's literary production.

588. Castro-Klarén, Sara. *Understanding Mario Vargas Llosa.* Columbia, SC: University of South Carolina Press, 1990. 247 p. (Understanding modern European and Latin American literature.) ISBN 0872496686.
These critical essays examine Vargas Llosa's fiction tracing the development of his craft, its themes, and literary theory.

589. Kristal, Efraín. *Temptation of the Word: The Novels of Mario Vargas Llosa.* 1st ed. Nashville, TN: Vanderbilt University Press, 1998. 256 p. Bibl., index. ISBN 0826513018.
This detailed examination of Vargas Llosa's literary works discusses the authors who have influenced his creative genius.

Puerto Rico

590. Blanco, Evangeline. *Caribe: A Novel of Puerto Rico.* 1st ed. New York: Doubleday, 1998. 302 p. ISBN 0385486502.
This novel won the University of California, Irvine's 21st Annual Chicano/Latino Literary Contest.

591. Burgos, Julia de. *Song of the Simple Truth: Obra Completa Poética: The Complete Poems.* 1st ed. Translated by Jack Agüeros. Willimantic, CT: Curbstone Press, 1997. 523 p. ISBN 1880684241.
Bilingual edition

592. Ferré, Rosario. *Eccentric Neighborhoods.* 1st. ed. New York: Farrar, Straus, and Giroux, 1998. 340 p. Ill. ISBN 0374924902.

593. Ferré, Rosario. *The House on the Lagoon.* 1st ed. New York: Farrar, Straus and Giroux, 1995. 407 p. ill. ISBN 0374173117.

594. Laguerre, Enrique A. *Benevolent Masters.* Translated by Gino Parisi. Maplewood, NJ: Waterfront Press, 1986. 237 p. Bibl., ill. ISBN 0943862094. (OP)

595. Marzán, Julio. *The Numinous Site: The Poetry of Luis Palés Matos.* Madison, NJ: Fairleigh Dickinson University Press, 1995. 199 p. Bibl., index. ISBN 0838635814.

596. Santos Febres, Mayra. *Urban Oracles: Stories.* Translated by N. Budoff and L. Platón Lázaro. Cambridge, MA: Lumen Editions, 1997. ISBN 1571290346 pbk.

597. Soto Vélez, Clemente. *The Blood That Keeps Singing = La Sangre que Sigue Cantando: Selected Poems.* Translated by Martín Espada. Willimantic, CT: Curbstone Press, 1991. 125 p. ISBN 0915306786 pbk.

Bilingual edition.

Uruguay

598. Benedetti, Mario. *Blood Pact & Other Stories.* 1st ed. Translated by Daniel Balderston. Willimantic, CT: Curbstone Press, 1997. 213 p. ISBN 188068439X pbk.

599. Galeano, Eduardo H. *The Book of Embraces.* 1st ed. Translated by Cedric Belfrage and Mark Schafer. New York: W.W. Norton, 1991. 281 p. ill. ISBN 0393029603.

600. Hernández, Felisberto. *Piano Stories.* Translated by Luis Harss. New York: Marsilio Publishers, 1993. 260 p. (The Eridanos library.) ISBN 094141955X.

601. Onetti, Juan Carlos. *A Brief Life.* Translated by Hortense Carpentier. New York: Serpent's Tail, 1994. 292 p. (Extraordinary classics.) ISBN 1852423013 pbk.

602. Onetti, Juan Carlos. *Goodbyes and Stories.* 1st ed. Translated by Daniel Balderston. Austin, TX: University of Texas Press, 1990. 174 p. (The Texas Pan American series.) ISBN 0292727437. (OP)

603. Onetti, Juan Carlos. *The Shipyard.* Translated by Nick Caistor. New York: Serpent's Tail, 1992. 186 p. (Extraordinary classics series.) ISBN 1852421916.

604. Ponce de León, Napoleón Baccino. *Five Black Ships: A Novel of the Discoverers.* 1st U.S. ed. Translated by Nick Caistor. New York: Harcourt Brace, 1994. 347 p. ISBN 0151562962. (OP)

605. Quiroga, Horacio. *The Exiles and Other Stories.* 1st ed. Translated by J. David Danielson. Austin, TX: University of Texas Press, 1987. 156 p. (The Texas Pan American series.) ISBN 0292720505. (OP)

606. Rodó, José Enrique. *Ariel.* 1st ed. Translated by Margaret Sayers Peden. Austin, TX: University of Texas Press, 1988. 156 p. Bibl., index. ISBN 0292703961 pbk.

Venezuela

607. Freilich, Alicia. *Cláper.* Translated by Joan Friedman. Albuquerque, NM: University of New Mexico Press, 1998. 182 p. (Jewish Latin America.) ISBN 0826318541.

608. Gallegos, Rómulo. *Canaima.* Crit. ed. Translated by Will Kirkland. Pittsburgh, PA: University of Pittsburgh Press, 1996. 348 p. Bibl. (The Pittsburgh editions of Latin American Literature.) ISBN 0822938839.

609. Parra, Teresa de la. *Iphigenia: The Diary of a Young Lady Who Wrote Because She Was Bored.* 1st ed. Translated by Bertie Acker. Austin, TX: University of Texas Press, 1994. 354 p. (The Texas Pan American series.) ISBN 0292715706.

610. Torres, Ana Teresa. *Doña Inés vs. Oblivion: A Novel.* Translated by Gregory Rabassa. Baton Rouge, LA: Louisiana State University Press, 1999. 243 p. (Pegasus Prize for Literature.) ISBN 0807124761.

This work received the Mobil Pegasus Prize for Literature, 1998.

V

Social Sciences

GENERAL WORKS

This section includes works that cover more than one topic in the social sciences from multidisciplinary perspectives. The section is subdivided by geographic regions and countries.

Latin America

611. Bello, Andrés. *Selected Writings of Andrés Bello.* Edited by I. Jaksic, translated by F. M. López-Morillas. New York: Oxford University Press, 1997. 295 p. Bibl., index. (Library of Latin America.) ISBN 0195105451.

Available for the first time in English, this volume presents contributions by this influential nineteenth century statesman, educator, and journalist. The essays cover a wide range of topics from historiography to education and language studies.

612. Bethell, Leslie, ed. *Latin America: Economy and Society Since 1930.* New York: Cambridge University Press, 1998. 522 p. Bibl., ill., index. ISBN 052159393X.

This comparative and historical examination of the region's social and economic development also analyzes demographic and

economic trends, the transformation of urban and rural social structures, and the evolution of states and institutions.

613. Black, Jan Knippers, ed. *Latin America, Its Problems and Its Promise: A Multidisciplinary Introduction.* 3rd ed. Boulder, CO: Westview Press, 1998. 658 p. Bibl., ill., index. ISBN 0813327571.

This text surveys Latin America's enduring characteristics and contemporary changes. It includes the resolution of Central American conflicts; negative impacts of the drug trade and international debt; and the redemocratization trend in South America.

614. Blouet, Brian W., and Olwyn M. Blouet, eds. *Latin America and the Caribbean: A Systematic and Regional Survey.* 3rd ed. New York: Wiley, 1996. 512 p. Bibl., ill., index. ISBN 0471135704.

This thematic examination covers the region's physical environment and its socioeconomic setting.

615. Ewell, Judith, and William H. Beezley, eds. *The Human Tradition in Modern Latin America.* Wilmington, DE: SR Books, 1997. 277 p. (Latin American silhouettes.) ISBN 0842026126.

This includes brief biographies of ordinary men and women portraying different Latin American social, political, racial, and economic strata from the independence struggles through the twentieth century.

616. Fey, Ingrid, and Karen Racine, eds. *Strange Pilgrimages: Exile, Travel, and National Identity in Latin America, 1890–1990s.* Wilmington, DE: SR Books, 2000. 258 p. Bibl., ill. (Jaguar books on Latin America; 22.) ISBN 0842026932.

These essays examine the effect travel, foreign residency, and exile have had on the development of individual, national, and regional identities of Latin American intellectuals during the last one hundred years.

617. Grugel, Jean. *Politics and Development in the Caribbean Basin: Central America and the Caribbean in the New World Order.* Bloomington, IN: Indiana University Press, 1995. 270 p. Ill., index. ISBN 0253326834.

This comparative analysis of development dilemmas and challenges of Central American and Caribbean nations also examines would-be revolutionary regimes and those adopting neoliberalist policies.

618. Guillermoprieto, Alma. *The Heart That Bleeds: Latin America Now.* 1st ed. New York: Knopf, 1995. 345 p. ISBN 0679428844.

This is a collection of thirteen *New Yorker* articles, written between 1989 and 1993, which cover a variety of contemporary topics about the daily struggle for life in the region.

619. Hopkins, Jack W., ed. *Latin America: Perspectives on a Region.* 2nd ed. New York: Holmes & Meier, 1999. 320 p. Bibl., ill., index. ISBN 0841913622.

This introductory text presents the region's history, its peoples, and cultures, in a contemporary socioeconomic setting.

620. Keen, Benjamin, ed. *Latin American Civilization: History and Society, 1492 to the Present.* 7th ed. rev. and updated. Boulder, CO: Westview Press, 2000. 507 p. Bibl. ISBN 0813336236 pbk.

This survey covers a wide range of topics about Latin American civilization from the colonial period through the twentieth century.

621. Lehmann, David. *Democracy and Development in Latin America: Economics, Politics and Religion in the Post-War Period.* Philadelphia: Temple University Press, 1990. 235 p. Bibl., index. ISBN 0877227233.

This volume analyzes the political economy of development, the crisis of industrialization and related social thought, the role of the modern church, and contemporary social movements in the region.

622. MacDonald, Scott B., and Georges A. Fauriol. *Fast Forward: Latin America on the Edge of the 21st Century.* New Brunswick, NJ: Transaction Publishers, 1997. 318 p. Bibl., ill., index. ISBN 1560002077.

This introduction to contemporary Latin American politics and economics focuses on the seven largest countries and Cuba.

623. Meyer, Doris, ed. *Rereading the Spanish American Essay: Translations of 19th and 20th Century Women's Essays.* 1st ed. Austin, TX: University of Texas Press, 1995. 324 p. (The Texas Pan American series.) ISBN 0292751796.

These essays, by a diverse group of women writers, address the status of women in Latin American society and cover such topics as gender, religion, politics, economics, and other social issues.

624. Phillips, Lynne, ed. *The Third Wave of Modernization in Latin America: Cultural Perspectives on Neoliberalism.* Wilmington, DE: SR Books, 1998. 200 p. Bibl. (Jaguar books on Latin America; 16.) ISBN 0842026061.

This examines the impact of free market economics and politics on health, education, and the environment in rural and urban settings.

625. Rosenberg, Mark, and A. Douglas Kincaid. *Americas: An Anthology.* New York: Oxford University Press, 1992. 380 p. Ill. ISBN 019507792X.

This multidisciplinary reader for a PBS television course presents an introductory survey of Latin America and the Caribbean that captures its complexity.

626. Savedoff, William D., ed. *Organization Matters: Agency Problems in Health and*

Education in Latin America. Washington, D.C.: Inter-American Development Bank, 1998. 285 p. Bibl., ill. ISBN 1886938199.

This work argues that improvements in public service organization can result in better access to health and education programs. Case studies for Brazil, Chile, Dominican Republic, Uruguay, and Venezuela, serve as illustrations.

627. Stepan, Alfred, ed. *Americas: New Interpretive Essays.* New York: Oxford University Press, 1992. 327 p. Bibl., index. ISBN 0195077954.

This is the study-guide that accompanies a PBS telecourse. The essays by distinguished experts cover themes and issues of modern Latin America including changing women's role, migration, religion, politics, and popular culture.

628. Wiarda, Howard J., ed. *Politics and Social Change in Latin America: Still a Distinct Tradition?* 3rd ed. fully rev. and upd. Boulder, CO: Westview Press, 1992. 354 p. Bibl. ISBN 0813310571.

This examines Latin America's politics and social structure through a cultural heritage model. (OP)

629. Wiarda, Howard J., and Harvey F. Kline, eds. *Latin American Politics and Development.* 5th ed. fully rev. and upd. Boulder, CO: Westview Press, 2000. 592 p. Bibl., ill., index. ISBN 0813337690 pbk.

This standard volume about contemporary Latin American politics also discusses the impact of neoliberal economic policies on the democratization process during the post–cold war period.

Argentina

630. Erro, Davide G. *Resolving the Argentine Paradox: Politics and Development, 1966–1992.* Boulder, CO: L. Rienner Publishers, 1993. 254 p. Bibl., ill., index. ISBN 1555873693.

This presents a summary of Argentine political and economic policies from 1966–1992.

631. Tulchin, Joseph S., and Allison M. Garland, eds. *Argentina: The Challenges of Modernization.* Wilmington, DE: SR Books, 1998. 346 p. Bibl., ill., index. (Latin American silhouettes.) ISBN 0842027211.

This analysis of contemporary Argentina covers economic, social, and political conditions since the restoration of democracy in 1983.

Belize

632. Bolland, O. Nigel. *Belize, a New Nation in Central America.* Boulder, CO: Westview Press, 1986. 157 p. Bibl., ill., index. (Westview profiles. Nations of contemporary Latin America.) ISBN 0813300053.

This profile of Belize describes its Maya past and colonial legacy, socioeconomic and political characteristics, and educational system. (OP)

633. Sutherland, Anne. *The Making of Belize: Globalization in the Margins.* Westport, CT: Bergin & Garvey, 1998. 202 p. Bibl., ill., index. ISBN 0897895797.

This presents Belize as a small nation in transition in the globalized age that will likely create new opportunities and challenges for the local culture.

Bolivia

634. Zulawski, Ann. *They Eat from Their Labor: Work and Social Change in Colonial Bolivia.* Pittsburgh, PA: University of Pittsburgh Press, 1995. 283 p. (Pitt Latin American series.) ISBN 0822911833.

This explores the economic and social history of seventeenth–eighteenth century Bolivia when an indigenous labor force developed to support Spanish mercantilism. (OP)

Brazil

635. Eakin, Marshall C. *Brazil: The Once and Future Country.* 1st ed. New York: St. Martin's Press, 1997. 301 p. Ill. ISBN 0312162006.

This is a summary of basic events in Brazilian history, politics, economy, society, and culture from the colonial period through the early 1970s.

636. Kinzo, Maria D'Alva G., ed. *Brazil, the Challenges of the 1990s.* London, England: University of London, ILAS, 1993. 214 p. Bibl., index. ISBN 1850436134.

This overview of Brazil's recent difficulties discusses the fragmentation of a political system that has impeded governability and implementation of coherent socioeconomic policies.

637. Page, Joseph A. *The Brazilians.* Reading, MA: Addison-Wesley, 1995. 540 p. Bibl., ill., index. ISBN 0201409135.

This is an overview of the history, culture, civilization, and current socioeconomic and political development of contemporary Brazil.

638. Purcell, Susan Kaufman, and Riordan Roett, eds. *Brazil Under Cardoso.* Boulder, CO: Lynne Rienner, 1997. 119 p. ISBN 1555874525.

This is an examination of the Cardoso presidency and its agenda to change political, social, and economic policies to render Brazil more democratic and competitive.

639. Schneider, Ronald M. *Brazil: Culture and Politics in a New Industrial Powerhouse.* Boulder, CO: Westview Press, 1996. 255 p. Bibl., index. (Nations of the modern world. Latin America.) ISBN 081332436X.

This is an introduction to Brazil's diverse cultural reality examined through socioeconomic, political, and historical perspectives.

640. Summ, G. Harvey, ed. *Brazilian Mosaic: Portraits of a Diverse People and Culture.* Wilmington, DE: SR Books, 1995. 209 p. Bibl., ill. (Latin American silhouettes: studies in history and culture.) ISBN 0824025913.

This summary of Brazil's heritage from historical, political, and socioeconomic perspectives focuses on the legacy of slavery and its contemporary social and cultural ramifications.

Caribbean Area

641. Burton, Richard D. E. *Afro-Creole: Power, Opposition, and Play in the Caribbean.* Ithaca, NY: Cornell University Press, 1997. 297 p. Bibl., ill., index. ISBN 0801432499.

This volume examines the culture of the English-speaking Caribbean as exemplified by the complex relationship between politics, culture, history, religion, and social change.

642. Farmer, Paul. *The Uses of Haiti.* Monroe, ME: Common Courage Press, 1994. 432 p. ISBN 1567510353.

This traces Haiti's long-standing social injustice from the eighteenth century slave economy to post-revolution feudalism, from the U.S. Marine invasion of 1915 to the deposition of President Aristide. (OP)

Central America

643. Barry, Tom. *Central America Inside Out: The Essential Guide to Its Societies, Politics, and Economies.* 1st ed. New York: Grove Weidenfeld, 1991. 501 p. Bibl., index. ISBN 0802111351.

This source provides basic socioeconomic and political information about Belize, Costa Rica, El Salvador, Guatemala, Honduras, and Panama.

644. Brockett, Charles D. *Land, Power, and Poverty: Agrarian Transformation and Political Conflict in Central America.* 2nd ed. Boulder, CO: Westview Press, 1998. 270 p. Bibl., index. (Thematic studies in Latin America.) ISBN 0813386950 pbk.

This examines the connections between changes in agrarian structure, deteriorating living conditions for peasants, and political conflict in Central America.

645. Langley, Lester D., and Thomas Schoonover. *The Banana Men: American Mercenaries and Entrepreneurs in Central America, 1880–1930.* Lexington, KY: University Press of Kentucky, 1995. 219 p. Bibl., ill., index. ISBN 0813118913.

This is a description of the activities of U.S. and Central American rogue political, economic, and military players, whose legacies continue to impact contemporary Central American society.

646. Weaver, Frederick Stirton. *Inside the Volcano: The History and Political Economy of Central America.* Boulder, CO: Westview Press, 1994. 276 p. Bibl., ill., index. (Series in political economy and economic development in Latin America.) ISBN 0813309786.

This traces the history and political economy of the five Central American countries from colonial times to the present.

647. Weinberg, Bill. *War on the Land: Ecology and Politics in Central America.* Atlantic Highlands, NJ: Zed Books, 1991. 203 p. Bibl., ill., index. ISBN 0862329469.

This volume argues that Central American ecological and sociopolitical crises stem from oligarchic control of land supported by U.S. and international development agencies.

Costa Rica

648. Biesanz, Mavis Hiltunen et al. *The Ticos: Culture and Social Change in Costa Rica.* Boulder, CO: Lynne Rienner Publishers, 1999. 307 p. Bibl., ill., index. ISBN 1555877249.

This general introduction to Costa Rica presents its culture, history, politics, economy, and religion in the late twentieth century.

649. Wilson, Bruce M. *Costa Rica: Politics, Economics, and Democracy.* Boulder, CO: Lynne Rienner Publishers, 1998. 187 p. Bibl., ill., index. ISBN 1555874851.

This study of Costa Rica's political and economic development examines the country's policies throughout its history and finds that Costa Rica's approach to dealing with profound economic issues differs significantly from common patterns in the region.

Cuba

650. Centeno, Miguel Angel, and Mauricio Font. *Toward a New Cuba?: Legacies of a Revolution.* Boulder, CO: Lynne Rienner Publishers, 1997. 245 p. Bibl., index. ISBN 1555876323.

This systematic analysis of recent economic and political transformations suggests how these changes may affect Cuba's future transition.

651. Marshall, Peter H. *Cuba Libre: Breaking the Chains?.* Boston: Faber and Faber, 1988. 300 p. Bibl., index. ISBN 0571129854.

This is a balanced survey of achievements of revolutionary Cuba in education, health, welfare, and racial equality. It also includes the regime's failures such as totalitarianism, militarism, and machismo through the mid–1980s. (OP)

652. Mesa-Lago, Carmelo, ed. *Cuba After the Cold War.* Pittsburgh, PA: University of Pittsburgh Press, 1993. 383 p. Ill. (Pitt Latin American series.) ISBN 0822937492.

These essays examine the future of Fidel Castro and Cuba in the post-cold war setting. Among the topics discussed are foreign relations, the economic crisis, and political issues.

653. Roca, Sergio, ed. *Socialist Cuba: Past Interpretations and Future Challenges.* Boulder, CO: Westview Press, 1988. 253 p. Bibl., index. (Westview special studies on Latin America and the Caribbean.) ISBN 0813374618 pbk.

This is an analysis of Cuban political, economic, and social policies of the post–1959 period. (OP)

Ecuador

654. Clark, A. Kim. *The Redemptive Work: Railway and Nation in Ecuador, 1895–1930.* Wilmington, DE: SR Books, 1998. 244 p. Bibl., ill., index. (Latin American silhouettes.) ISBN 0842026746.

This is a survey of Ecuador's liberal era when the national economy, society, and politics were transformed during the first third of the twentieth century.

Guatemala

655. Barry, Tom. *Inside Guatemala.* 1st ed. Albuquerque, NM: Inter-Hemispheric Education Resource Center, 1992. 307 p. Bibl., ill. (Inside Central America.) ISBN 0911213406 pbk.

This is a summary of contemporary Guatemala's social, political, and economic forces including U.S. influence.

656. Grandin, Greg. *The Blood of Guatemala: A History of Race and Nation.* Durham, NC: Duke University Press, 2000. 343 p. Bibl., ill., index. (Latin America otherwise.) ISBN 082232458X.

This examines the violent historical and political relationship between Guatemala's Maya citizens and the non–Indian dominated government.

657. Menchú, Rigoberta. *Crossing Borders.* Translated by Ann Wright. New York: Verso, 1998. 242 p. Index. ISBN 1859848931.

This is a continuation of the 1992 Nobel Prize winner's 1984 autobiography. In this volume, Menchú provides a primer on Maya culture as she discusses Guatemala's human rights situation, relations between landowners and the military, and the plight of indigenous peoples.

658. Menchú, Rigoberta. *I, Rigoberta Menchú: An Indian Woman in Guatemala.* Edited by E. Burgos-Debray, translated by A. Wright. London, England: Verso, 1987. 251 p. Bibl. ISBN 0860917886 pbk.

This autobiography of the 1992 Nobel Prize winner presents her life as a peasant in rural Guatemala and the development of her own political consciousness within the context of Guatemalan politics and society.

659. Stoll, David. *Rigoberta Menchú and the Story of All Poor Guatemalans.* Boulder, CO: Westview Press, 1999. 336 p. Bibl., ill., index. ISBN 0813335744.

This critique characterizes Menchu's autobiography as a manipulated dramatization of her life to draw international attention to the atrocities committed by the Guatemalan army.

Mexico

660. Benjamin, Thomas. *A Rich Land, a Poor People: Politics and Society in Modern Chiapas.* Rev. ed. Albuquerque, NM: University of New Mexico Press, 1996. 376 p. Bibl., ill., index. ISBN 0826317138 pbk.

This is a description of Mexico's southernmost state in a context of political and economic changes. A basic theme of this work is the acute poverty of the people in Chiapas who live in rich agricultural areas that produce coffee, cattle, and other international agricultural commodities.

661. Byrd, Bobby, and Susannah M. Byrd, eds. *The Late Great Mexican Border: Reports from a Disappearing Line.* 1st ed. El Paso, TX: Cinco Puntos Press, 1996. 227 p. Bibl., ill. ISBN 0938317245.

This history of the U.S.-Mexico border examines its contemporary reality as a result of new international pressures such as NAFTA.

662. Harvey, Neil, ed. *Mexico: Dilemmas of Transition.* New York: Distributed in North America by St. Martin's Press, 1993. 381 p. Bibl., ill., index. ISBN 1850435146.

This is an overview of contemporary Mexican political and economic reforms and shifting patterns of state and society relations as the country evolves into a more democratic political system.

663. Raat, W. Dirk, and William H. Beezley, eds. *Twentieth-Century Mexico.* Lincoln, NE: University of Nebraska Press, 1986. 318 p. Bibl., ill., index. ISBN 0803238681.

This survey of twentieth century Mexico includes interviews with labor and political leaders who discuss the serious socioeconomic and political challenges facing the nation.

664. Ruiz, Ramón Eduardo. *On the Rim of Mexico: Encounters of the Rich and Poor.* Boulder, CO: Westview Press, 1998. 258 p. Bibl., ill., index. ISBN 0813334993.

This analysis of problems in the U.S.-Mexico border region includes a discussion of migration, the drug trade, poverty, and pollution on both sides of the border.

Nicaragua

665. Gould, Jeffrey L. *To Die in This Way: Nicaraguan Indians and the Myth of Mestizaje, 1880–1965.* Durham, NC: Duke University Press, 1998. 305 p. Bibl., ill., index. (Latin America otherwise.) ISBN 0822320843.

This volume examines the Nicaraguan myth of ethnic homogeneity and its relationship to political power as background for understanding the Sandinista revolution.

666. Ramírez, Sergio. *Hatful of Tigers: Reflections on Art, Culture, and Politics.* 1st English ed. Translated by D. J. Flakoll. Willimantic, CT: Curbstone Press, 1995. 135 p. ISBN 0915306980.

Ramírez, vice-president of the Sandinista government, presents a collection of reminiscences, travel notes, and observations about the Sandinista revolution that sought national, political, and economic independence from the U.S.

667. Walker, Thomas W. *Nicaragua, the Land of Sandino.* 3rd ed. rev. and updated. Boulder, CO: Westview Press, 1991. 202 p. Bibl., ill., index. (Westview profiles. Nations of contemporary Latin America.) ISBN 0813310903.

This is a historical study of Nicaragua's economic, political, and social systems including its role in the international sphere. (OP)

Panama

668. Zimbalist, Andrew S., and John Weeks. *Panama at the Crossroads: Economic Development and Political Change in the Twentieth Century.* Berkeley, CA: University of California Press, 1991. 219 p. Bibl., index. ISBN 0520073118.

This analysis of recent Panamanian events links political economy with history and international relations. (OP)

Paraguay

669. Miranda, Carlos R. *The Stroessner Era: Authoritarian Rule in Paraguay.* Boulder, CO: Westview Press, 1990. 177 p. Bibl., ill., index. ISBN 0813309956.

This is an overview of cultural, political, historical, and economic events of Stroessner's authoritarian regime from 1954 to 1989. (OP)

670. Roett, Riordan, and Richard Scott Sacks. *Paraguay: The Personalist Legacy.* Boulder, CO: Westview Press, 1991. 188 p. Bibl., ill., index. (Westview profiles. Nations of contemporary Latin America.) ISBN 0865312729.

This history of Paraguay from its colonial experience to the post–Stroessner era also discusses politics, economics, social issues, and the drug trade. (OP)

Peru

671. Kirk, Robin. *The Monkey's Paw: New Chronicles from Peru.* Amherst, MA: University of Massachusetts Press, 1997. 215 p. Ill. ISBN 1558491082.

Through interviews, memoirs and analysis, this work surveys Peru's socioeconomic and political difficulties during the last fifteen years.

672. Mariátegui, José Carlos. *Seven Interpretive Essays on Peruvian Reality.* Translated by Marjory Urquidi. Austin, TX: University of Texas Press, 1971 (reiss. 1988). 301 p. Bibl. (The Texas Pan American series.) ISBN 029277611X pbk.

This classic work, by one of Latin America's leading twentieth century social thinkers, examines social, economic, and religious issues of Peru that are as relevant today as when the essays were written in the 1930s. (OP)

673. Rudolph, James D. *Peru: The Evolution of a Crisis.* New York: Praeger, 1992. 166 p. Bibl., ill., index. (Politics in Latin America.) ISBN 0275941469.

This is an interpretation of contemporary Peru, its economic, political, and social problems since the restoration of democratic rule in 1980. It includes an in-depth study of Alan García's Aprista government, 1985–1990.

Surinam

674. Chin, Henk E. and Hans Buddingh'. *Surinam: Politics, Economics, and Society.* New York: F. Pinter, 1987. 192 p. Ill. (Marxist regimes series.) ISBN 0861875168.

This summarizes Surinam's history, social structure, political, and economic systems. (OP)

ANTHROPOLOGY

This section includes all types of cultural manifestations such as archaeology and ethnology of indigenous pre–Columbian peoples and their contemporary descendants. Mayas are listed under Central America; Aztecs under Mexico; and Incas under the Andean region. Smaller national groups are found under the corresponding country. The section is subdivided by geographic regions and countries.

Latin America

675. Adams, Richard E.W., and Murdo J. MacLeod, eds. *Mesoamerica.* New York: Cambridge University Press, 2000. 1064 p. Bibl., ill., index. (The Cambridge history of the native peoples of the Americas; 2 .) ISBN 0521652057.

This two-part set surveys Mesoamerica's native cultures beginning with Paleo-indian and classical societies through the present. The Aztec, Maya, Olmec, Tarascan, and Zapotec peoples are covered including contact, exchange, adaptation, and survival since the European arrival.

676. Brysk, Alison. *From Tribal Village to Global Village: Indian Rights and International Relations in Latin America.* Stanford, CA: Stanford University Press, 2000. 370 p. ISBN 0804734585.

This studies the rapidly changing national and international status of Latin American indigenous groups as a result of their own involvement and coordination with non-governmental organizations concerned with identity politics.

677. Coe, Sophie D. *America's First Cuisines.* 1st ed. Austin, TX: University of Texas Press, 1994. 276 p. Bibl., ill., index. ISBN 0292711557.

Although this work is a synthesis of the New World's contributions to world foods, it also presents how these foodstuffs contributed to the Maya, Aztec, and Inca cultures.

678. Díaz Polanco, Héctor. *Indigenous Peoples in Latin America: The Quest for Self-determination.* Translated by Lucía Rayas. Boulder, CO: Westview Press, 1997. 162 p. Bibl., index. (Latin American perspectives series; 18.) ISBN 0813386985.

This leading Mexican anthropologist examines the centuries-long tensions between Latin America's indigenous peoples and their respective governments from anthropology and political economy perspectives.

679. Dow, James W., ed. *The Encyclopedia of World Cultures, V. 8: Middle America and the Caribbean.* Boston: G.K. Hall, 1995. 329 p. Bibl., ill., index. ISBN 0816118167.

This reference work provides demographic, historical, socioeconomic, political, and religious information about Central America and Caribbean indigenous cultures.

680. Evans, Susan Toby, and David L. Webster. *Archaeology of Ancient Mexico and Central America: An Encyclopedia.* New York: Garland Pub., 2000. 700 p. Bibl., ill., index. ISBN 0815308876.

This one-volume encyclopedia covers pre–Columbian archaeology of Mesoamerica and includes findings from recent scholarship. A wide range of cultural practices of daily life are described for well- and lesser-known sites.

681. Fagan, Brian M. *Kingdoms of Gold, Kingdoms of Jade: The Americas Before Columbus.* New York: Thames and Hudson, 1991. 240 p. Bibl., ill., index. ISBN 0500050627.

This catalog accompanied the Smithsonian traveling exhibitions "Circa 1492" and "Seeds of Change" and presents an overview of the rise and fall of New World empires through archaeological, mythological, and ethnographic materials. (OP)

682. Ferguson, William M., and Arthur H. Rohn. *Mesoamerica's Ancient Cities: Aerial Views of Pre–Columbian Ruins in Mexico, Guatemala, Belize, and Honduras.* 1st ed. Niwot, CO: University Press of Colorado, 1990. 251 p. Bibl., ill., index. ISBN 0870811738.

Over three hundred aerial and ground photographs present fifty-one reconstructed archaeological sites in Mesoamerica.

683. Jara, René, and Nicholas Spadaccini, eds. *Amerindian Images and the Legacy of Columbus.* Minneapolis, MN: University of Minnesota Press, 1992. 758 p. Ill. (Hispanic issues; 9.) ISBN 0816621667 .

These essays reassess Columbus and the image of Native Americans as Europeans attempted to dominate them. It also presents Amerindian resistance to protect their way of life.

684. Kubler, George. *The Art and Architecture of Ancient America: The Mexican, Maya, and Andean Peoples.* 3rd ed. New Haven, CT: Yale University Press, 1993. 576 p. Bibl., ill., index. ISBN 0300053258.

This volume presents the development of the principal styles of ancient architecture, sculpture, and painting through the middle of the sixteenth century.

685. Marzal, Manuel M. et al. *The Indian Face of God in Latin America.* Translated by Penelope R. Hall. Maryknoll, NY: Orbis Books, 1996. 245 p. Bibl., index. (Faith and cultures series.) ISBN 1570750548.

This work examines the contemporary theological significance of indigenous religious traditions of Peru, Mexico, Bolivia, and Paraguay.

686. Miller, Mary Ellen, and Karl A. Taube. *An Illustrated Dictionary of the Gods and Symbols of Ancient Mexico and the Maya.* New York: Thames and Hudson, 1997. 216 p. Bibl., ill., index. ISBN 0500279284 pbk.

This reference work introduces the myths, symbols, and beliefs of the Olmec, Zapotec, Maya, Teotihuacan, Mixtec, Toltec, and Aztec peoples of pre–Columbian Mexico.

687. Pasztory, Esther. *Pre-Columbian Art.* New York: Cambridge University Press, 1998. 176 p. Bibl., ill., index. ISBN 0521645514 pbk.

This title focuses on recent research that enhances our understanding of Mesoamerican and Andean ideological systems that shaped political, historical, and social periods from 2500 BCE through the sixteenth century.

688. Salomon, Frank, and Stuart B. Schwartz, eds. *South America.* New York: Cambridge University Press, 2000. 1400 p. Bibl., ill., index. (The Cambridge history of the native peoples of the Americas; 3 .) ISBN 0521333938.

This is a survey of research about South

America's indigenous groups from pre–Columbian times through the twentieth century. While the volume focuses on South American groups, Caribbean and Central American peoples connected by language or culture also are included.

689. Schobinger, Juan. *The First Americans.* Grand Rapids, MI: Eerdmans, 1994. 193 p. Bibl., ill. ISBN 0802837662.

This summarizes contemporary knowledge about the origins of agriculture and cultural history of the Olmec, Maya, Teotihuacán, Chavín, and Tiahuanaco cultures during late pre-history. (OP)

690. Townsend, Richard F. *The Ancient Americas: Art from Sacred Landscapes.* Chicago: Art Institute of Chicago, 1992. 397 p. Bibl., ill. ISBN 3791311883.

This was the exhibit catalog of twelve pre–Columbian cultures from the national museums of Mexico, Guatemala, Colombia, Ecuador, Peru, Bolivia, and Chile.

691. Van Cott, Donna Lee, ed. *Indigenous Peoples and Democracy in Latin America.* New York: St. Martin's Press, 1994. 271 p. Bibl., ill., index. ISBN 0312122926.

These essays examine the relationship between indigenous groups and democratic development in Bolivia, Colombia, Peru, Ecuador, Guatemala, Mexico, Brazil, and Paraguay. The January 1994 Chiapas uprising is also discussed.

692. Wright, Ronald. *Stolen Continents: The Americas Through Indian Eyes Since 1492.* Boston: Houghton Mifflin, 1992. 424 p. Bibl., ill., index. ISBN 0395565006.

This is an alternative interpretation to the Eurocentric version of the conquest that focuses on Aztec, Maya, and Inca perspectives about cultural destruction and change as a result of European contact. (OP)

Amazon Region

693. Arhem, Kaj. *Makuna: Portrait of an Amazonian People.* Washington, DC: Smith-sonian Institution Press, 1998. 172 p. Bibl., ill., index. ISBN 1560988746.

This illustrated work presents contemporary Makuna culture and creation myths including challenges posed by the vanishing rainforest.

694. Balée, William L. *Footprints of the Forest: Ka'apor Ethnobotany; the Historical Ecology of Plant Utilization by an Amazonian People.* New York: Columbia University Press, 1994. 396 p. Bibl., ill., index. (Biology and resource management in the tropics series.) ISBN 0231074840.

This volume documents how the Ka'apor people use, name, manage, and classify plants in their habitat. Their approach is representative of Amazon culture and accounts for the delicate balance between its peoples, habitats, and resources.

695. Braun, Barbara, ed. *Arts of the Amazon.* New York: Thames and Hudson, 1995. 128 p. Bibl., ill., index. ISBN 0500278245.

This illustrated text highlights basketry, masks, ceramics, and featherwork of the Amazon region Indians.

696. Descola, Philippe. *In the Society of Nature: A Native Ecology in Amazonia.* Translated by Nora Scott. New York: Cambridge University Press, 1994. 372 p. Bibl., ill., index. (Cambridge studies in social and cultural anthropology; 93.) ISBN 0521411033.

This work presents the sophisticated approaches to resource management practiced by the Achuar Indians of the upper Amazon. Their technical expertise is well developed and it is interwoven with their cosmology and the role of nature in society.

697. Descola, Philippe. *The Spears of Twilight: Life and Death in the Amazon Jungle.* Translated by Janet Lloyd. New York: New Press, 1998. 458 p. Bibl., ill., index. ISBN 1565844386 pbk.

This is an ethnological account of the Achuar Jívaro in the Ecuadorian Amazon.

698. Hemming, John. *Amazon Frontier: The Defeat of the Brazilian Indians.* Cambridge,

MA: Harvard University Press, 1987. 647 p. Bibl., ill., index. ISBN 0674017250.

This work relates the tragic history of Brazilian Indians from 1755 to 1910. (OP)

699. Meunier, Jacques, and A. M. Savarin. *The Amazonian Chronicles.* Translated by Carol Christensen. San Francisco: Mercury House, 1994. 169 p. Ill. ISBN 1562790536.

This reviews the history of Amazonia from sixteenth century explorers and missionaries to contemporary traders, miners, and loggers.

700. Muscutt, Keith. *Warriors of the Clouds: A Lost Civilization of the Upper Amazon of Peru.* Albuquerque, NM: University of New Mexico Press, 1998. 128 p. Bibl., ill. ISBN 0826319793.

This is a historical and contemporary exploration of the Kuelap ruin where the Chachapoya peoples live in a remote region of the Peruvian upper Amazon.

701. Peters, John F. *Life Among the Yanomami: The Story of Change Among the Xilixana on the Mucajai River in Brazil.* Peterborough, Canada: Broadview Press, 1998. 292 p. Bibl., ill., index. ISBN 1551111934 pbk.

The author, a former missionary, presents a detailed ethnography of the Xilixana Yanomami.

702. Plotkin, Mark J. *Tales of a Shaman's Apprentice: An Ethnobotanist Searches for New Medicines in the Amazon Rain Forest.* New York: Viking, 1993. 318 p. Bibl., ill. ISBN 0670831379.

This is a chronicle of journeys to remote Amazonian communities in search of old remedies known only to disappearing elder tribal leaders.

703. Ricciardi, Mirella. *Vanishing Amazon.* New York: Harry N. Abrams, 1991. 240 p. Bibl., ill., index. ISBN 0810939150.

This photographic essay presents members of three Amazon tribes: Kampa, Maruba, and Yanomami peoples. (OP)

704. Tierney, Patrick. *Darkness in El Dorado: How Scientists and Journalists Devastated the Amazon.* New York: W.W. Norton, 2000. 417 p. Bibl., ill., index. ISBN 0393049221.

This examines the ground-breaking work of Napoleon Chagnon with the Yanomami Indians. It argues that social scientists and journalists used the Yanomami for their own selfish ends and contributed to the degradation of their way of life.

Andean Region

705. Arriaza, Bernardo T. *Beyond Death: The Chinchorro Mummies of Ancient Chile.* Washington, DC: Smithsonian Institution Press, 1995. 176 p. Bibl., ill., index. ISBN 1560985127.

This presents evidence of the oldest prepared mummies known and also explores the cultural context of mummification.

706. Bauer, Brian S. *The Development of the Inca State.* 1st ed. Austin, TX: University of Texas Press, 1992. 185 p. Bibl., ill., index. ISBN 0292715633.

This interdisciplinary analysis of Inca archaeology, ethnohistory, and mythology challenges traditional views of Inca society.

707. Bauer, Brian S., and David S. P. Dearborn. *Astronomy and Empire in the Ancient Andes: The Cultural Origins of Inca Sky Watching.* 1st ed. Austin, TX: University of Texas Press, 1995. 220 p. Bibl., ill., index. ISBN 0292708297.

This exploration of Inca sky watching proposes a new model of Inca cosmology and its role in social structure. (OP)

708. Betanzos, Juan de. *Narrative of the Incas.* 1st ed. Translated and edited by R. Hamilton and D. Buchanan. Austin, TX: University of Texas Press, 1996. 326 p. Bibl., ill., index. ISBN 0292755600.

This is an early chronicle about the Inca political system written in the 1550s. It presents the Inca world view from the personal experiences and oral traditions as told to the chronicler by his Inca wife, Doña Angelina, and other members of the Inca aristocracy.

709. Burger, Richard L. *Chavín and the Origins of Andean Civilization.* New York: Thames and Hudson, 1993. 248 p. Bibl., ill., index. ISBN 0500050694.

This is a synthesis of Peruvian prehistory focusing on the artistic production of its cultures.

710. Cameron, Ian. *Kingdom of the Sun God: A History of the Andes and Their People.* London, England: Century, 1990. 224 p. Bibl., ill., index. ISBN 0712625372.

This work summarizes the formation of the Andes range 200 million years ago and the arrival of its first settlers about 10,000 BC. (OP)

711. Cobo, Bernabé. *Inca Religion and Customs.* 1st ed. Edited and translated by Roland Hamilton. Austin, TX: University of Texas Press, 1990. 279 p. Bibl., ill., index. ISBN 0292738617 pbk.

This classic, written by the seventeenth century Spanish priest, describes Inca religion and myth. The work also reveals Cobo's mindset and that of his contemporaries and how their observations were the product of specific spatial and temporal contexts.

712. Hyslop, John. *Inka Settlement Planning.* 1st ed. Austin, TX: University of Texas Press, 1990. 377 p. Bibl., ill., index. ISBN 0292738528.

This encyclopedic inventory of known Inca architectural sites examines the composition of the Andean metropolis. (OP)

713. Kolata, Alan L. *Valley of the Spirits: A Journey into the Lost Realm of the Aymara.* New York: Wiley, 1996. 288 p. Ill., index. ISBN 0471575070.

This examines the ancient culture of the contemporary Aymara in Lake Titicaca who continue to live in spiritual harmony in this desolate environment.

714. Malpass, Michael Andrew. *Daily Life in the Inca Empire.* Westport, CT: Greenwood Press, 1996. 164 p. Bibl., ill., index. (The Greenwood Press "Daily life through history" series; 1080-4749.) ISBN 0313293902.

This work combines archaeological, ethnographic, and ethnohistorical sources to describe the lifestyle of the Inca ruling and other classes and the people they conquered.

715. Morris, Craig, and Adriana von Hagen. *The Inka Empire and Its Andean Origins.* 1st ed. New York: Abbeville Press, 1993. 251 p. Bibl., ill., index. ISBN 1558595562.

This survey of early Inca culture includes Moche, Chinchorro, and Nazca peoples.

716. Moseley, Michael Edward. *The Incas and Their Ancestors: The Archaeology of Peru.* New York: Thames and Hudson, 1992. 272 p. Bibl., ill., index. ISBN 0500050635.

This is a summary and interpretation of Peruvian archaeology from the arrival of the first humans through the Spanish conquest.

717. Paternosto, César. *The Stone and the Thread: Andean Roots of Abstract Art.* 1st ed. Austin, TX: University of Texas Press, 1996. 272 p. Bibl., ill., index. ISBN 0292765657.

This analysis of ancient Andean art (textile, pottery, sculpture, carved rock) explores the intimate connection between artistic development and social evolution.

718. Urton, Gary. *The History of a Myth: Pacariqtambo and the Origin of the Inkas.* 1st ed. Austin, TX: University of Texas Press, 1990. 172 p. Bibl., ill., index. ISBN 0292730578.

This work examines the Inca myth of origins including the social, geographic, and calendrical meanings of the different versions of the myth for clues about Cuzco, the capital of the Inca empire.

719. Vega, Garcilaso de la. *Royal Commentaries of the Incas, and General History of Peru.* Translated by Harold v. Livermore. Austin, TX: University of Texas Press, 1987. 740 p. (The Texas Pan American series.) ISBN 0292770383 pbk.

This classic deals with the origin, development, and destruction of the Inca empire. The author was the son of a Spanish conqueror and an Inca princess. (OP)

Caribbean Area

720. Dacal Moure, Ramón, and Manuel Rivero de la Calle. *Art and Archaeology of Pre-Columbian Cuba.* Edited by D. Sandweiss and D. Watters, translated by D. Sandweiss. Pittsburgh, PA: University of Pittsburgh Press, 1997. 134 p. (Pitt Latin American series.) ISBN 082293955X.

This discussion of the development of the Ciboney and Taino cultures focuses on their art and religion.

721. Hul, Peter, ed. *Wild Majesty: Encounters with Caribs from Columbus to the Present day; an Anthology.* New York: Oxford University Press, 1992. 369 p. Bibl., ill., index. ISBN 0198112262.

This anthology presents Carib history from their perspective and focuses on cultural survival despite centuries-long oppression by dominant groups. (OP)

722. Perrin, Michel. *The Way of the Dead Indians: Guajiro Myths and Symbols.* Translated by Michael Fineberg. Austin, TX: University of Texas Press, 1987. 195 p. Bibl., ill., index. ISBN 0292790325.

This volume provides socioeconomic and anthropological insights about the Guajiro Indians of Colombia and Venezuela.

723. Rouse, Irving. *The Tainos: Rise & Decline of the People Who Greeted Columbus.* New Haven, CT: Yale University Press, 1992. 211 p. Bibl., ill., index. ISBN 0300051816.

This is a description of the Taino people of the northern Caribbean beginning with their prehistory in 4,000 BCE through their contact with Columbus and his followers.

Central America

724. Bassie-Sweet, Karen. *From the Mouth of the Dark Cave: Commemorative Sculpture of the Late Classic Maya.* 1st ed. Norman, OK: University of Oklahoma Press, 1991. 287 p. Bibl, ill., index. ISBN 0806123230.

This is a study of late classic Maya textual and iconographic materials related to caves. This work also includes an introduction to Maya hieroglyphic writing and calendar system.

725. Canby, Peter. *The Heart of the Sky: Travels Among the Maya.* 1st ed. New York: Harper Collins, 1992. 368 p. Ill. ISBN 006016705X.

This examines the lifestyle of seven million contemporary Mayas who live in Mexico and Central America and their adaptation to life in the twentieth century.

726. Coe, Michael D. *The Maya.* 6th ed. rev. exp. New York: Thames and Hudson, 1999. 256 p. Ill., index. (Ancient peoples and places.) ISBN 0500280665.

This synthesis of Maya culture includes results of recent discoveries about their writing.

727. Drew, David. *The Lost Chronicles of the Maya Kings.* Berkeley, CA: University of California Press, 1999. 450 p. Bibl., ill., index. ISBN 0520226127.

This history of Maya art and architecture, political systems, and religion presents recent research findings that have revealed additional knowledge about their material and intellectual culture.

728. Everton, Macduff. *The Modern Maya: A Culture in Transition.* 1st ed. Edited by Ulrich Keller and Charles Demangate. Albuquerque, NM: University of New Mexico Press, 1991. 259 p. ill. ISBN 0826312403.

This photographic essay presents the contemporary Maya of the Yucatán peninsula.

729. Gillette, Douglas. *The Shaman's Secret: The Lost Resurrection Teachings of the Ancient Maya.* New York: Bantam Books, 1997. 278 p. Bibl., ill., index. ISBN 0553101544.

This work explores ancient Maya beliefs and practices to elucidate the Maya worldview.

730. Gonzalez, Nancie L. Solien. *Sojourners of the Caribbean: Ethnogenesis and Ethnohistory of the Garifuna.* Urbana, IL: University of Illinois Press, 1988. 253 p. Bibl., ill., index. ISBN 0252014537.

This is a study of the Garifuna or Black Caribs presently living in Central America. (OP)

731. Hoepker, Thomas. *Return of the Maya.* 1st Am. ed. New York: H. Holt, 1998. 144 p. Ill. ISBN 0805060073.

These color photographs of contemporary Mayas from Guatemala focus on their current efforts to reconnect with their ancient culture.

732. Longhena, Maria. *Maya Script: A Civilization and Its Writing.* 1st ed. New York: Abbeville Press, 2000. 180 p. Bibl., ill., index. ISBN 0789206536.

Approximately 200 symbolic characters of the Maya writing system are presented in this work.

733. Love, Bruce. *The Paris Codex: Handbook for a Maya Priest.* 1st ed. Austin, TX: University of Texas Press, 1994. 124 p. ill. ISBN 0292746741.

This reproduction and analysis of the Paris codex includes its hieroglyphs, painted figures, and calendrical calculations.

734. Marcus, Joyce. *Mesoamerican Writing Systems: Propaganda, Myth, and History in Four Ancient Civilizations.* Princeton, NJ: Princeton University Press, 1992. 495 p. Bibl., ill., index. ISBN 0691094748.

This examines the ancient writing systems of the Aztec, Zapotec, Mixtec, and Maya peoples.

735. Milbrath, Susan. *Star Gods of the Maya: Astronomy in Art, Folklore, and Calendars.* 1st ed. Austin, TX: University of Texas Press, 1999. 348 p. Bibl., ill., index. (The Linda Schele series in Maya and pre–Columbian studies.) ISBN 0292752253.

This is a pathfinder for ancient Maya astronomy and cosmology as presented in pre–Columbian art and as practiced by contemporary descendants of the ancient Maya.

736. Miller, Mary Ellen. *Maya Art and Architecture.* New York: Thames and Hudson, 1999. 240 p. Bibl., ill., index. (The world of art.) ISBN 050020327X pbk.

This volume addresses basic questions about Maya art and includes recent archaeological discoveries and decipherments.

737. Montejo, Víctor. *The Bird Who Cleans the World and Other Mayan Fables.* 1st ed. Translated by Wallace Kaufman. Willimantic, CT: Curbstone Press, 1991. 120 p. Ill. ISBN 091530693X.

This collection of approximately three dozen stories from the Jakaltek-Maya of Guatemala represent their cultural and moral values.

738. Morris, Walter F. *Living Maya.* New York: H.N. Abrams, 2000. 215 p. Bibl., ill. ISBN 0810927454 pbk.

The culture, art, and religion of the contemporary Maya living in Chiapas are the subject of this volume.

739. Proskouriakoff, Tatiana. *Maya History.* 1st ed. Edited by Rosemary A. Joyce. Austin, TX: University of Texas Press, 1993. 212 p. Bibl., ill., index. ISBN 0292750854.

The glyphic record from numerous sites is the basis for a reconstruction of the Maya classic period, AD 250–900. (OP)

740. Restall, Matthew. *Maya Conquistador.* Boston: Beacon Press, 1998. 254 p. Bibl., ill., index. ISBN 0807055069.

These documents, authored by Maya noblemen from the 1500s to the early 1800s, relate foretold events whose nature was one of adaptation and survival rather than wholesale destruction of the native cultures by foreign conquerors.

741. Restall, Matthew. *The Maya World: Yucatec Culture and Society, 1550–1850.* Stanford, CA: Stanford University Press, 1997. 441 p. Bibl., index. ISBN 0804727457.

This work covers Maya society beginning in the colonial period through the end of the Caste War in the nineteenth century.

742. Sabloff, Jeremy A. *The New Archaeology and the Ancient Maya.* New York: Scientific American Library, 1990. 193 p. Bibl., ill., index. (Scientific American Library series; 30.) ISBN 0716750546.

This is a chronology of evolving scholarly interpretations of the Maya and their world.

743. Sawyer-Laucanno, Christopher, trans. *The Destruction of the Jaguar: Poems from the Books of Chilam Balam.* San Francisco: City Lights Book, 1987. 59 p. Bibl., ill. ISBN 0872862100 pbk.

This collection of poems from the *Books of Chilam Balam* deal with Maya history, mythology, prophesy, and calendrical commentary.

744. Scarborough, Vernon L., and David R. Wilcox, eds. *The Mesoamerican Ballgame.* Tucson, AZ: University of Arizona Press, 1991. 404 p. Bibl., ill., index. ISBN 0816511802.

This collection of essays about the first American pastime discusses the sociopolitical context of the game among the various native cultures that practiced it.

745. Schele, Linda, and David Freidel. *A Forest of Kings: The Untold Story of the Ancient Maya.* 1st ed. New York: Morrow, 1990. 542 p. Bibl., ill., index. ISBN 0688074561.

This volume focuses on Maya royal history and the political activities of dynasties and states. It presents a vivid picture of the Maya world of cyclical time and multiple levels of reality.

746. Schele, Linda, and Peter Matthews. *The Code of Kings: The Language of Seven Sacred Maya Temples and Tombs.* New York: Scribner, 1998. 431 p. Bibl., ill., index. ISBN 068480106X.

This presents recently deciphered Maya scripts and includes visits to several ruins. A glossary of religious figures and key to pronunciation accompany the volume.

747. Schevill, Margot Blum et al., eds. *The Maya Textile Tradition.* New York: Abrams, 1997. 232 p. Bibl., ill., index. ISBN 0810942917.

This colorful work explores Maya embroidered and woven textiles including their cultural relevance in historical and contemporary contexts.

748. Sharer, Robert J. *Daily Life in Maya Civilization.* Westport, CT: Greenwood Press, 1996. 236 p. Bibl., ill., index. (The Greenwood Press "Daily life through history" series; 1080-4749.) ISBN 0313293422.

This work combines recent research findings from several disciplines to revise current interpretations of Maya civilization from its early development to the Spanish conquest in the sixteenth century.

749. Smith, Carol A., ed. *Guatemalan Indians and the State, 1540 to 1988.* Austin, TX: University of Texas Press, 1990. 316 p. Bibl., ill., index. (Symposia on Latin America series.) ISBN 0292727445.

This collection of essays presents the history of the Maya of Guatemala and their reactions to economic and political developments since the end of the eighteenth century. (OP)

750. Stone, Andrea Joyce. *Images from the Underworld: Naj Tunich and the Tradition of Maya Cave Painting.* 1st ed. Austin, TX: University of Texas Press, 1995. 284 p. Bibl., ill., index. ISBN 029275552X.

This overview of Mesoamerican cave art is followed by a catalog of the Naj Tunich cave paintings discovered in 1979 in Guatemala.

751. Tedlock, Dennis, trans. *Popol Vuh: The Mayan Book of the Dawn of Life .* Rev. ed. New York: Simon & Schuster, 1996. 388 p. Bibl., ill., index. ISBN 0684818450.

This sacred Maya-Quiché text describes the creation of life in Mesoamerica and describes daily life prior to the Spanish conquest.

752. Tsouras, Peter. *Warlords of the Ancient Americas: Central America.* London, England: Arms and Armour, 1996. 240 p. Bibl., ill., index. ISBN 1854092375.

This account of distinguished military leaders of pre–Columbian Central America reveals many aspects of Maya and Aztec military technology.

Chile

753. Bahn, Paul G., and John Flenley. *Easter Island, Earth Island.* New York: Thames and

Hudson, 1992. 240 p. Bibl., ill., index. ISBN 0500050651.

This work describes recent archaeological studies of the island that contribute to a better understanding of its origins, vegetation, as well as social and cultural issues. (OP)

754. Faron, Louis C. *The Mapuche Indians of Chile.* Prospects Heights, IL: Waveland Press, 1986. Bibl., ill. ISBN 088133247X.

This is the history of the Mapuche's human adaptation and their contemporary economic, political, and social adjustments.

Colombia

755. Labbé, Armand J. *Colombia Before Columbus: The People, Culture, and Ceramic Art of Prehispanic Colombia.* New York: Rizzoli, 1986. 207 p. Bibl., ill., index. ISBN 0847807703.

This work examines Colombian art from specific cultural regions and explains its milieu, use, and iconography. (OP)

Ecuador

756. Newson, Linda A. *Life and Death in Early Colonial Ecuador.* Norman, OK: University of Oklahoma Press, 1995. 505 p. Bibl., ill., index. ISBN 0806126973.

The demographic changes in pre–Columbian and colonial Ecuador due to the Inca and Spanish conquests are the subject of this work.

Mexico

757. Baldwin, Neil. *Legends of the Plumed Serpent: Biography of a Mexican God.* 1st ed. New York: PublicAffairs, 1998. 205 p. Bibl., ill., index. ISBN 1891620037.

The endurance and resilience of Mesoamerican culture in contemporary Mexico is examined through the myth of Queltzalcoatl, the plumed serpent and principal deity of the Aztec and Maya cultures.

758. Benson, Elizabeth P., and Beatriz de la Fuente, eds. *Olmec Art of Ancient Mexico.* Washington, DC: National Gallery of Art, 1996. 288 p. Bibl., ill., index. ISBN 0810963280.

This is the catalog of an Olmec art exhibit at the National Art Gallery, Washington, D.C., June 1996. Essays by experts in the field explore art and its place in the Olmec world.

759. Bonfil Batalla, Guillermo. *México Profundo: Reclaiming a Civilization.* 1st ed. Translated by Philip A. Dennis. Austin, TX: University of Texas Press, 1996. 198 p. Bibl., index. (Translations from Latin America series.) ISBN 0292708440.

The author, an important Mexican anthropologist, argues that Mexico's traditional cultures make continuous and important contributions to contemporary life while mainstream culture downplays their significance.

760. Boone, Elizabeth Hill. *Stories in Red and Black: Pictorial Histories of the Aztecs and Mixtecs.* Austin, TX: University of Texas Press, 2000. 296 p. Bibl., ill., index. ISBN 0292708769.

This is an analysis of stories depicted in picture books made by Aztecs and Mixtecs through the 1600s. Subjects covered are historical, religious, social, and dramatic events.

761. Broda, Johanna et al. *The Great Temple of Tenochtitlán: Center and Periphery in the Aztec World.* Berkeley, CA: University of California Press, 1988. 184 p. Bibl., ill., index. ISBN 0520056027.

The great temple was the most important site of Aztec culture. This work summarizes the results of recent excavations that support new perspectives about Aztec religion, empire, and history. (OP)

762. Carrasco, David. *Daily Life of the Aztecs.* Westport, CT: Greenwood Press, 1998. 164 p. Bibl., ill., index. (The Greenwood Press "Daily life through history" series; 1080-4749.) ISBN 0313295581.

This work combines archaeological, ethnographic, and ethnohistorical sources to describe lifestyle of the ruling and other classes and the peoples they conquered.

763. Carrasco, David, and Eduardo Matos Moctezuma. *Moctezuma's Mexico: Visions of the Aztec World.* Niwot, CO: University Press of Colorado, 1992. 188 p. Ill. ISBN 0870812637.

These color reproductions of Aztec art include essays about their lifestyle, history, and modes of thought.

764. Crosby, Harry. *The Cave Paintings of Baja California: Discovering the Great Murals of an Unknown People.* San Diego, CA: Sunbelt Publications, 1997. 246 p. Bibl., ill., index. (Sunbelt natural history books.) ISBN 0932653235.

This journal, illustrated with photographs, maps, and drawings, recounts an amateur archaeologist's search for the prehistoric murals of central Baja California.

765. Davies, Nigel. *The Aztec Empire: The Toltec Resurgence.* 1st ed. Norman, OK: University of Oklahoma Press, 1987. 341 p. Bibl., ill., index. (The Civilization of the American Indian series; 187.) ISBN 0806120983.

This volume focuses on the thought and society of the Nahuatl cultures of Central Mexico from the rise of the Toltecs to the fall of Mexica-Aztecs. (OP)

766. Durán, Diego. *The History of the Indies of New Spain.* Translated by Doris Heyden. Norman, OK: University of Oklahoma Press, 1994. 642 p. Ill. (The Civilization of the American Indian series; 210.) ISBN 0806126493.

Written originally in 1580, this is a rich source of information about Aztec history, customs, religion, political, and social organization.

767. Edmonson, Munro S. *Heaven Born Mérida and Its Destiny: The Book of Chilam Balam of Chumayel.* 1st ed. Austin, TX: University of Texas Press, 1986. 309 p. Bibl., ill., index. (The Texas Pan American series.) ISBN 0292730276.

This presents the Xiu (or Western) perspective on Yucatecan ethnohistory. (OP)

768. Florescano, Enrique. *The Myth of Quetzalcoatl.* Translated by Lysa Hochroth.

Baltimore, MD: Johns Hopkins University Press, 1999. 287 p. Bibl., ill., index. ISBN 0801859999.

Although this work examines the archaeological record of the history and cultural significance of Quetzalcoatl, the principal deity of Mesoamerican peoples, it also includes a comparison with vegetation gods of Mesopotamia and Mediterranean cultures.

769. Gruzinski, Serge. *Painting the Conquest: The Mexican Indians and the European Renaissance.* Translated by Deke Dusinberre. Paris, France: Unesco, Flammarion, 1992. 236 p. Bibl., ill., index. ISBN 208013521X.

This illustrated anthology of twenty-five codices includes lengthy explanatory captions and an essay that explains the importance of the documents.

770. Hassig, Ross. *Aztec Warfare: Imperial Expansion and Political Control.* 1st ed. Norman, OK: University of Oklahoma Press, 1988. 404 p. Bibl., ill., index. (The civilization of the American Indian series; 188.) ISBN 0806121211.

This work examines the role of war in Aztec culture and empire expansion.

771. León Portilla, Miguel, and J. Jorge Klor de Alva. *The Aztec Image of Self and Society: An Introduction to Nahua Culture.* Salt Lake City, UT: University of Utah Press, 1992. 248 p. Ill. ISBN 0874803608.

This narrative of the official view of the Aztec-Nahua story is written by the foremost Mexican scholar on the subject. The introduction includes a survey of the last two decades of research in Nahua studies.

772. Lockhart, James. *The Nahuas After the Conquest: A Social and Cultural History of the Indians of Central Mexico, Sixteenth Through Eighteenth Centuries.* Stanford, CA: Stanford University Press, 1992. 650 p. Bibl., ill., index. ISBN 0804719276.

This account of Nahua culture in the sixteenth–eighteenth centuries is from documents produced by Nahuas for their own use. This work helps to correct a distorted view of post-conquest lifestyle created by historians and anthropologists relying heavily on Spanish sources.

773. Lockhart, James, ed. and trans. *We People Here: Nahuatl Accounts of the Conquest of Mexico.* Berkeley, CA: University of California Press, 1993. 335 p. Bibl., ill., index. (Repertorium Columbianum; 1.) ISBN 0520078756.

This is the first Nahuatl, Spanish, and English translation of Fray Bernardino de Sahagún's accounts of the conquest of Mexico, Book Twelve of the *Florentine Codex.*

774. Ortiz de Montellano, Bernard R. *Aztec Medicine, Health, and Nutrition.* New Brunswick, NJ: Rutgers University Press, 1990. 308 p. Bibl., ill., index. ISBN 0813515629.

This is a description of the highly developed Aztec public health and food distribution system that existed when the Spanish arrived. This volume also illustrates the durability of Aztec culture as represented by many contemporary practices in Mexican society.

775. Pasztory, Esther. *Teotihuacan: An Experiment in Living.* Norman, OK: University of Oklahoma Press, 1997. 380 p. Bibl., ill., index. ISBN 080612847X.

This volume examines the arts (architecture, sculpture, ceramics, and mural painting) of Teotihuacan through eight centuries and compares them with the arts of the New and Old World civilizations.

776. Piña Chan, Román. *The Olmec: Mother Culture of Mesoamerica.* Edited by L. L. Minelli, translated by W. McManus. New York: Rizzoli, 1989. 240 p. Bibl., ill., index. ISBN 0847810445.

This classic provides a pictorial and narrative introduction to Olmec archaeology and history. (OP)

777. Pollard, Helen Perlstein. *Tariacuri's Legacy: The Prehispanic Tarascan State.* Norman, OK: University of Oklahoma Press, 1993. 266 p. Bibl., ill., index. (The Civilization of the American Indian series; 209.) ISBN 0806124970.

This is a comprehensive overview of the Tarascan state, one of the two great political powers encountered by the Spanish in the early sixteenth century. (OP)

778. Quiñones Keber, Eloise. *Codex Telleriano-Remensis: ritual, divination, and history in a pictorial Aztec manuscript.* 1st ed. Austin, TX: University of Texas Press, 1995. 365 p. Bibl., ill., index. ISBN 0292769016.

This is a color facsimile of a codex that was spared during the conquest. It includes a ritual calendar, an almanac for divination, and a 400-year, post-conquest history. An interpretation of the codex in its broader context is also provided.

779. Raat, W. Dirk, and George R. Janecek. *Mexico's Sierra Tarahumara: A Photohistory of the People of the Edge.* Norman, OK: University of Oklahoma Press, 1996. 212 p. Bibl., index. ISBN 0806128151.

The human geography, regional ecology, historical, and economic evolution of northern Mexico's Sierra Tarahumara is presented in this work.

780. Sabloff, Jeremy A. *The Cities of Ancient Mexico: Reconstructing a Lost World.* New York: Thames and Hudson. 1989. 224 p. Ill., index. ISBN 0500050538.

This is a study of eight Mesoamerican archaeological sites from the Olmec (1200 BCE) to Aztec (1521 CE) periods.

781. Sahagún, Bernardino de. *Conquest of New Spain: 1585 Revision.* Translated by Howard F. Cline. Salt Lake City, UT: University of Utah Press, 1989. 672 p. Bibl., ill. ISBN 087480311X.

Fray Bernardino de Sahagún's classic work describes Aztec life at the time of the conquest.

782. Sahagún, Bernardino de. *Primeros Memoriales.* Facsim. ed. Norman, OK: University of Oklahoma Press, 1993. 1 v. Ill. (The Civilization of the American Indian series; 200.) ISBN 0806116889.

This photographic facsimile of the colonial pictorial manuscript provides information about pre–Hispanic Aztec religion, calendrics, and iconography. The text is in Nahuatl.

783. Sandstrom, Alan R. *Corn Is Our Blood: Culture and Ethnic Identity in a Contemporary Aztec Indian Village.* 1st ed. Norman, OK: University of Oklahoma Press, 1992. 420 p. Bibl., ill., index. (The Civilization of the American Indian series; 206.) ISBN 0806123990.

This detailed portrait of contemporary Aztecs includes Nahua religion, economy, society, and conflict with non–Nahua Mexicans.

784. Schaefer, Stacy B., and Peter Furst, eds. *People of the Peyote: Huichol Indian History, Religion & Survival.* 1st ed. Albuquerque, NM: University of New Mexico Press, 1996. 560 p. Bibl., index. ISBN 0826316840.

The Huichol have been successful in maintaining almost intact their religious practices that focus on the peyote cactus. This work gathers contributions by several experts on Huichol culture of western Mexico.

785. Smith, Michael Ernest. *The Aztecs.* Cambridge, MA: Blackwell, 1996. 361 p. Bibl., index. (The peoples of America.) ISBN 1557864969.

This is a revisionist history of Aztec social, political, and cultural institutions based on archaeological findings from the last fifteen years.

786. Stephen, Lynn. *Zapotec Women.* 1st ed. Austin, TX: University of Texas Press, 1991. 316 p. Bibl., ill., index. (Texas Press sourcebooks in anthropology; 16.) ISBN 0292790643.

This is an analysis of gender role in indigenous peasant communities in Teotitlán, Oaxaca, Mexico.

787. Townsend, Richard F. *The Aztecs.* Rev. 2nd ed. New York: Thames and Hudson, 2000. 232 p. Bibl., ill., index. (Ancient peoples and places; 107.) ISBN 05000281327.

This describes the Aztec world in the twelfth through sixteenth centuries and includes a discussion of their social structure, economic system, religious beliefs and practices, and the Spanish conquest.

Panama

788. Howe, James. *A People Who Would Not Kneel: Panama, the United States, and the San Blas Kuna.* Washington, DC: Smithsonian Institution Press, 1998. 390 p. Bibl., ill., index. (Smithsonian series in ethnography inquiry.) ISBN 1560988908.

This account of Kuna resistance during the early years of the twentieth century describes their struggle against state domination and repression and success in achieving their goals.

789. Tice, Karin E. *Kuna Crafts, Gender, and the Global Economy.* 1st ed. Austin, TX: University of Texas Press, 1995. 232 p. Bibl., ill., index. ISBN 0292781334.

This work examines the commercialization of Kuna *mola* textiles, popular tourist souvenirs, and its impact on Kuna society.

790. Ventocilla, Jorge, Heraclio Herrera, and Valerio Nuñez. *Plants and Animals in the Life of the Kuna.* 1st ed. Translated by Elisabeth King. Austin, TX: University of Texas Press. 1995. 150 p. Bibl., ill., index. (Translations from Latin America series.) ISBN 0292787251.

This environmental and artistic portrait of Panama's Kuna people depicts the environmental degradation that threatens their culture.

Paraguay

791. Abou, Sélim. *The Jesuit "Republic" of the Guaranís (1609–1768) and Its Heritage.* Translated by Lawrence J. Johnson. New York: Crossroad, 1997. 160 p. Bibl., ill. ISBN 0824517067.

While this work examines events in the seventeenth and eighteenth centuries it also provides a survey of the early Jesuit presence in the New World and examines its contemporary legacy.

792. Clastres, Pierre. *Chronicle of the Guayaki Indians.* Translated by Paul Auster. New

York: Zone Books, 1998. 349 p. Ill. ISBN 0942299779.

This documents the life of the Guayaki people from eastern Paraguay who lived in harmony with nature until their extinction.

Peru

793. Aveni, Anthony F. *Between the Lines: The Mystery of the Giant Ground Drawings of Ancient Nasca, Peru.* 1st ed. Austin, TX: University of Texas Press, 2000. 257 p. Bibl., ill., index. (Texas film studies series.) ISBN 0292704968.

This work seeks to answer some of the nagging questions concerning the origin of these lines and images in the Peruvian desert.

794. Berrin, Kathleen, ed. *The Spirit of Ancient Peru: Treasures from the Museo Arqueológico Rafael Larco Herrera.* New York: Thames and Hudson, 1997. 216 p. Bibl., ill., index. ISBN 0500018022.

This is the catalog of middle Andean and pre–Columbian treasures exhibited in 1997 at the Fine Arts Museum of San Francisco. Accompanying essays present the historical, environmental, and ideological background for these cultural artifacts.

795. Hadingham, Evan. *Lines to the Mountain Gods: Nazca and the Mysteries of Peru.* 1st ed. New York: Random House, 1987. 307 p. Ill. ISBN 0394542355.

This volume presents and interprets the lines made by pre–Inca Nazca Indians in the Peruvian desert.

796. Kirkpatrick, Sidney. *Lords of Sipan: A Tale of Pre–Inca Tombs, Archaeology, and Crime.* 1st ed. New York: Morrow, 1992. 256 p. Bibl., ill., index. ISBN 0688103960.

This exposes the trail of stolen Sipan artifacts as they passed from the archaeological site in Peru to London and finally to California. (OP)

797. Sawyer, Alan Reed. *Early Nasca Needlework.* London, England: Lawrence King, 1997. 175 p. Bibl., ill., index. ISBN 1856690881.

This is an examination of pre–Columbian textiles from Peru's Ica and Nasca valleys.

798. Shimada, Izumi. *Pampa Grande and the Mochica Culture.* 1st ed. Austin, TX: University of Texas Press, 1994. 323 p. Bibl., ill., index. ISBN 0292776748.

This work presents recent information about Moche history, its culture and society concentrating on socioeconomic and political aspects of life in Pampa Grande, the most important city in the late Moche period.

South America

799. Key, Mary Ritchie. *Language Change in South American Indian Languages.* Philadelphia: University of Pennsylvania Press, 1991. 297 p. Bibl., ill., index. ISBN 0812230604.

These essays examine languages from various cultures and eras with a focus on their classification, grammar, and affinities.

800. Mcewan, Colin et al., eds. *Patagonia: Natural History, Prehistory, and Ethnography at the Uttermost End of the Earth.* Princeton, NJ: Princeton University Press, 1998. 200 p. Bibl., ill., index. (Princeton paperbacks.) ISBN 0691058490.

Although this work's primary focus is the Fuego-Patagonia region where three groups of native peoples lived, it also provides archaeological and anthropological information about the first inhabitants of this area.

801. Salzano, Francisco M., and Sidia M. Callegari-Jacques. *South American Indians: A Case Study in Evolution.* New York: Oxford University Press, 1988. 259 p. Bibl., ill., index. (Oxford science publications.) ISBN 0198576358.

This volume presents a synthesis of research in the field of South American Indian evolution. It examines population origins and history, physiological adaptation, and genetic variation, among other topics. (OP)

802. Wilbert, Johannes, ed. *The Encyclopedia of World Cultures, V. 7: South America.*

Boston: G.K. Hall, 1994. 425 p. Bibl., ill., index. ISBN 0816118132.

This reference work provides demographic, historical, socioeconomic, political, and religious information about South America's indigenous cultures and their evolution.

803. Wilson, David J. *Indigenous South Americans of the Past and Present.* Boulder, CO: Westview Press, 1999. 480 p. Bibl., ill., index. ISBN 0813336090.

This summary of archaeological research about South American indigenous groups from coastal Peru and the Amazon region covers findings from the last fifty years.

DRUG TRADE

This section includes all aspects of the illicit drug trade in the region in one alphabetical list.

804. Clawson, Patrick, and Lee Rensselaer, III. *The Andean Cocaine Industry.* 1st ed. New York: St. Martin's Press, 1996. 276 p. ISBN 0312124007.

This analyzes contemporary issues in the Andean region that focus on the Colombian drug cartels. The study presents evidence of failed U.S. efforts to eradicate and introduce alternative development projects.

805. Duzán, María Jimena. *Death Beat: A Colombian Journalist's Life Inside the Cocaine Wars.* 1st ed. Translated by Peter Eisner. New York: Harper Collins, 1994. 282 p. ISBN 0060170573.

This is an account of how the drug trade has left political, social, and economic scars on Colombia and its people. (OP)

806. Hargreaves, Clare. *Snowfields: The War on Cocaine in the Andes.* New York: Holmes & Meier, 1992. 202 p. Ill., index. ISBN 0841913277.

Producers, users, and enforcers are interviewed in this examination about the illicit drug business in Bolivia.

807. Joyce, Elizabeth, and Carlos Malamud, eds. *Latin America and the Multinational Drug Trade.* New York: St. Martin's Press, 1998. 243 p. Bibl., ill., index. (Institute of Latin American Studies series.) ISBN 0312176155.

This is a study of the socioeconomic and political impact of the drug trade on Bolivia, Colombia, Mexico, and Peru. U.S. policies to curtail supply, drug consumption in the U.S. and Europe are presented as background to the study.

808. MacDonald, Scott B. *Mountain High, White Avalanche: Cocaine and Power in the Andean States and Panama.* New York: Praeger. 1989. 153 p. Bibl., ill., index. (The Washington papers; 137.) ISBN 0275932346.

This volume assesses the structure of the cocaine industry and narcoterrorism in the Andean region and Panama.

809. MacGregor, Felipe E., ed. *Coca and Cocaine: An Andean Perspective.* Translated by Jonathan Cavanagh. Westport, CT: Greenwood Press, 1993. 155 p. Bibl., index. (Contributions in criminology and penology; 37.) ISBN 0313285306.

The focus of this volume is the historical and contemporary Andean perspectives on cocaine trade. Andean interpretation contradicts that of U.S. policy makers.

810. Morales, Edmundo. *Cocaine: White Gold Rush in Peru.* Tucson, AZ: University of Arizona Press, 1989. 228 p. Bibl., ill., index. ISBN 0816510660.

This work traces several aspects of the illicit cocaine traffic in contemporary Peru.

811. Painter, James. *Bolivia and Coca: A Study in Dependency.* Boulder, CO: Lynne Rienner Publishers, 1994. 194 p. Bibl., ill., index. (Studies on the impact of the illegal drug trade; 1.) ISBN 1555874908.

This volume examines the production of cocaine from coca leaves in the Chapare region of Bolivia. It also examines the interdiction efforts that have failed to decrease production.

812. Scott, Peter Dale, and Jonathan Marshall. *Cocaine Politics: Drugs, Armies, and the CIA in Central America.* Upd. ed. Berkeley, CA: University of California Press, 1998. 279 p. Bibl., index. ISBN 0520214498.

This is an in-depth exploration of the tangled connection between the Nicaraguan Contras, U.S. supporters, and the flow of cocaine from Central America to the North.

813. Simpson, John. *In the Forests of the Night: Encounters in Peru with Terrorism, Drug-Running and Military Oppression.* 1st U.S. ed. New York: Random House, 1994. 307 p. Bibl., ill., index. ISBN 0679432973.

This journalistic report describes all segments of Peruvian society affected by and involved in the drug trade.

814. Toro, María Celia. *Mexico's "War" on Drugs: Causes and Consequences.* Boulder, CO: L. Rienner Publishers, 1995. 105 p. Bibl., ill., index. (Studies on the impact of the illegal drug trade; 3.) ISBN 1555875483.

This is an analysis of the social, economic, and political impacts of the illegal drug trade on Mexico including the policy influences of the U.S. "war on drugs."

815. Walker, William O., ed. *Drugs in the Western Hemisphere: An Odyssey of Cultures in Conflict.* Wilmington, DE: Scholarly Resources, 1996. 262 p. Bibl. (Jaguar books on Latin America; 12.) ISBN 0842024220.

These essays trace the complex relationship between Latin American and U.S. drug cultures including history of drug use (1920s–1940s) in the latter, cultivation in Latin America, legalization and security, and current policies.

ECONOMICS

This section includes economic conditions and policies; business and industry; commerce and trade; economic theory and development; regional trade agreements; agriculture and *agrarian reform; and labor. The section is subdivided by geographic regions and countries.*

Latin America

816. Brown, Jonathan C., ed. *Workers' Control in Latin America, 1930–1979.* Chapel Hill, NC: University of North Carolina Press, 1997. 328 p. Bibl., ill., index. ISBN 0807823627.

The labor conditions of the sugar, oil, mining, textiles, and railroad industries of several Latin American countries are examined in this volume.

817. Bulmer-Thomas, Victor. *The Economic History of Latin America Since Independence.* New York: Cambridge University Press, 1995. 485 p. Bibl., ill., index. (Cambridge Latin American studies; 77.) ISBN 0521363292.

This survey and synthesis of Latin American economic history explores the political and social effects of economic policy in Brazil, Chile, Honduras, and Mexico. Recent redistribution of income policies also are examined.

818. Bulmer-Thomas, Victor, ed. *The New Economic Model in Latin America and Its Impact on Income Distribution and Poverty.* New York: St. Martin's Press, 1996. 370 p. Bibl., ill., index. (Institute of Latin American Studies series.) ISBN 0312160380.

This work examines the effects of neoliberal economic policies implemented by Latin American governments after the 1982 debt crisis.

819. Cruz-Saco, María Amparo, and Carmelo Mesa-Lago, eds. *Do Options Exist?: The Reform of Pension and Health Care Systems in Latin America.* Pittsburgh, PA: University of Pittsburgh Press, 1998. 444 p. Bibl., index. (Pitt Latin American series.) ISBN 0822940795.

This describes various policies regarding social security and health care reform including a current assessment of progress.

820. Dávila Carlos, and Rory Miller, eds. *Business History in Latin America: The Experience of Seven Countries.* Translated by G. Mills and R. Miller. Liverpool, England: Liverpool University Press, 1999. 241 p. Bibl., index. (Liverpool Latin American Studies; 1.) ISBN 853237239.

This volume provides a balanced introduction to Latin American business history focusing on its socioeconomic background. Also included is an objective assessment to counterbalance past studies that were often influenced by the rhetoric of the times.

821. Domínguez, Jorge I., ed. *Economic Strategies and Policies in Latin America.* New York: Garland, 1994. 388 p. Bibl., ill. (Essays on Mexico, Central and South America; 1.) ISBN 081531485X.

The first volume in this series presents a summary of scholarly debates by Latin American experts in the field of economic strategies. These range from import-substitution industrialization of the 1950s to more recent market-oriented economic growth policies.

822. Green, John Duncan. *Silent Revolution: The Rise of Market Economics in Latin America.* New York: Distributed in North America by Monthly Review Press, 1995. 266 p. Bibl., ill., index. (Global issues.) ISBN 0304334561.

This balanced overview and analysis of Latin American economies since the 1980s debt crisis includes a country-by-country guide to the region.

823. Greenfield, Gerald Michael, and Sheldon L. Maram, eds. *Latin American Labor Organizations.* New York: Greenwood Press, 1987. 929 p. Index. ISBN 0313228345.

This is a brief history with an annotated list of labor organizations in twenty-six countries.

824. Harrison, Lawrence E. *The Pan-American Dream: Do Latin America's Cultural Values Discourage True Partnership with the United States and Canada?* 1st ed. New York: BasicBooks, 1997. 310 p. ISBN 046508916X.

Attributing slow economic progress in Latin America to Ibero-American Catholic values, the author applies his theory to the region and four case studies.

825. Lustig, Nora, ed. *Coping with Austerity: Poverty and Inequality in Latin America.* Washington, DC: Brookings Institution, 1995. 460 p. Bibl., index. ISBN 0815753187.

This regional and countries survey examines the impact of the 1980s debt crisis resulting in economic adjustments that exacerbated poverty and inequality.

826. Marichal, Carlos. *A Century of Debt Crises in Latin America: From Independence to the Great Depression, 1820–1930.* Princeton, NJ: Princeton University Press, 1989. 283 p. Bibl., ill., index. ISBN 0691077924.

This is a synthesis of the economic and political forces that have led Latin American governments to borrow funds abroad and default on their obligations. (OP)

827. Mayer, Frederick W. *Interpreting NAFTA: The Science and Art of Political Analysis.* New York: Columbia University Press, 1998. 374 p. Bibl., index. ISBN 0231109806.

This is an in-depth examination of the conceptualization and start-up of NAFTA. It includes detailed information about negotiations with Mexico including the political dimensions of the treaty in both countries.

828. McCreery, David J. *The Sweat of Their Brow: A History of Work in Latin America.* Armonk, NY: M.E. Sharpe, 2000. 209 p. Bibl., index. (Latin American realities.) ISBN 0765602075.

This comparative social history examines the changing nature of work in Latin America during the last five hundred years.

829. Mesa-Lago, Carmelo. *Changing Social Security in Latin America: Toward Alleviating the Social Costs of Economic Reform.* Boulder, CO: L. Rienner Publishers, 1994. 213 p. Bibl., index. ISBN 155587486X.

This is an analysis of the negative impact of Latin American economic reforms focusing on the effects on the region's neediest groups. (OP)

830. O'Brien, Thomas F. *The Century of U.S. Capitalism in Latin America.* 1st ed. Albuquerque, NM: University of New Mexico Press, 1999. 199 p. Bibl., ill., index. (Diálogos.) ISBN 0826319955.

This examines the depth of involvement of U.S. business people in Latin American commerce since the beginning of the nineteenth century.

831. O'Brien, Thomas F. *The Revolutionary Mission: American Enterprise in Latin America, 1900–1945.* New York: Cambridge University Press, 1996. 356 p. Bibl., ill., index. (Cambridge Latin American studies; 81.) ISBN 0521550157.

This is an assessment of the role of U.S. corporate culture and its social impact on several Latin American countries focusing on the 1920–1930s.

832. Pastor, Robert A., ed. *Latin America's Debt Crisis: Adjusting to the Past or Planning for the Future?* Boulder, CO: L. Rienner Publishers, 1987. 176 p. Bibl., index. ISBN 1555870538.

This analyzes the debt crisis from two perspectives: 1) as a long-run development problem and not a short-term financial issue, and 2) as long-term solutions from the debtor and lender perspectives.

833. Petras, James F. et al. *Latin America: Bankers, Generals, and the Struggle for Social Justice.* Totowa, NJ: Rowman & Littlefield, 1986. 187 p. Bibl., ill., index. ISBN 084767505X.

This volume examines changes in power relations from modernization theory (that focused on growth of national economies) to the contemporary globalized economy model dominated by world-market forces.

834. Rakowski, Cathy A., ed. *Contrapunto: The Informal Sector Debate in Latin America.* Albany, NY: State University of New York Press, 1994. 336 p. Bibl., ill., index. (SUNY series in power and political economy.) ISBN 0791419053.

The growth of informal sector economies is a worldwide phenomenon. This work introduces the topic and examines economic policies adopted by Latin American governments in response to this development.

835. Roett, Riordan, ed. *Mercosur: Regional Integration, World Markets.* Boulder, CO: Lynne Rienner, 1999. 139 p. Bibl., index. ISBN 1555878377.

This work provides background information about the history and future role of Mercosur as a model for trade within the hemisphere.

836. Roseberry, William, L. Gudmundson, and M. S. Kutschbach, eds. *Coffee, Society, and Power in Latin America.* Baltimore, MD: Johns Hopkins University Press, 1995. 304 p. Bibl., ill., index. (Johns Hopkins studies in Atlantic history and culture.) ISBN 0801848849.

This work studies the coffee industry of Brazil, Costa Rica, Guatemala, Puerto Rico, Colombia, and El Salvador from cultural, economic, political, and social perspectives.

837. Scheman, L. Ronald, ed. *The Alliance for Progress: A Retrospective.* New York: Praeger, 1988. 272 p. Bibl., index. ISBN 0275927636.

This collection analyzes the Alliance's history, evaluates its successes and failures, and its relevance and limitations as a current policy guide.

838. Thiesenhusen, William C. *Broken Promises: Agrarian Reform and the Latin American Campesino.* Boulder, CO: Westview, 1995. 226 p. Bibl., index. ISBN 0813384583.

This historical examination of agrarian reform in Bolivia, Chile, El Salvador, Guatemala, Nicaragua, and Mexico summarizes the accomplishments and failures of the policies. (OP)

839. Thorp, Rosemary. *Progress, Poverty and Exclusion: An Economic History of Latin America in the 20th Century.* Washington, DC: Inter-American Development Bank, 1998. 369 p. Bibl., ill. ISBN 1886938350 pbk.

This is an analysis of the main themes of Latin American development (industrialization, the state, poverty, debt) including economic policy failures and successes. The conditions of the region are examined as a whole as are individual countries.

840. Topik, Steven C., and Allen Wells, eds. *The Second Conquest of Latin America: Coffee, Henequen, and Oil During the Export Boom, 1850–1930.* 1st ed. Austin, TX: University of Texas Press, 1998. 271 p. Bibl., ill., index. (ILAS critical reflections on Latin America.) ISBN 0292781571.

This overview of the Latin American economic boom of the late nineteenth century also includes a focused treatment of the three main commodities.

841. Tuller, Lawrence W. *Doing Business in Latin America and the Caribbean: Including Mexico, the U.S. Virgin Islands, and Puerto Rico, Central America, South America.* New York: AMACOM, 1993. 348 p. Index. ISBN 0814450350.

This introduction to business protocol provides tips for travelers, information about business assistance programs, and trade promotion organizations in the region. (OP)

842. Weaver, Frederick Stirton. *Latin America in the World Economy: Mercantile Colonialism to Global Capitalism.* Boulder, CO: Westview Press, 2000. 252 p. Bibl., index. ISBN 081333747X pbk.

This volume explores the interrelations of external and internal factors in the evolution of Latin American economic development from the colonial period to the present.

Argentina

843. Balze, Felipe A. M. de la. *Remaking the Argentine Economy.* New York: Council on Foreign Relations Press, 1995. 197 p. Bibl., ill., index. ISBN 0876091710 pbk.

This concise study provides insights into the process of economic and political change

in Argentina during the twentieth century. (OP)

844. Di Tella, Guido, and D. C. M. Platt, eds. *The Political Economy of Argentina, 1880–1946.* New York: St. Martin's Press, 1986. 217 p. Ill., index. ISBN 031262252X.

These ten essays present a synthesis of Argentina's economic history. (OP)

845. Lewis, Paul H. *The Crisis of Argentine Capitalism.* Chapel Hill, NC: University of North Carolina Press, 1990. 573 p. Ill., index. ISBN 0807818623.

This analysis focuses on pressure groups that shaped interaction between politics and economics that caused stagnation and instability in the 1910–1987 period.

846. Peralta-Ramos, Mónica. *The Political Economy of Argentina: Power and Class Since 1930.* Boulder, CO: Westview Press, 1992. 191 p. Bibl., index. (Westview special studies on Latin America and the Caribbean.) ISBN 0813375568.

This summarizes the instability and illegitimacy of the 1930s as government industrialization policies led to class conflict. (OP)

847. Ranis, Peter. *Argentine Workers: Peronism and Contemporary Class Consciousness.* Pittsburgh, PA: University of Pittsburgh Press, 1992. 313 p. Bibl., index. (Pitt Latin American series.) ISBN 0822937034.

This is a study of Argentine laborers as individuals who are concerned with their personal material well-being, upward mobility, and political freedoms while having a commitment to political and social democracy.

Bolivia

848. Ferry, Stephen. *I Am Rich Potosí: The Mountain That Eats Men.* New York: Monacelli Press, 1999. 155 p. ISBN 158093028X.

This chiefly illustrated work presents the history of the silver mountain that has enslaved the indigenous population since the conquest, has provided their livelihood, while often also taking their lives.

849. Tandeter, Enrique. *Coercion and Market: Silver Mining in Colonial Potosí, 1692–1826.* 1st ed. Albuquerque, NM: University of New Mexico Press, 1993. 332 p. Bibl., ill., index. ISBN 0826314309.

This work examines the social, economic, and technological history of the silver mining center in Upper Peru or modern Bolivia. (OP)

Brazil

850. Baer, Werner. *The Brazilian Economy: Growth and Development.* 4th ed. Westport, CT.: Praeger, 1995. 415 p. Bibl., ill., index. ISBN 027594509X.

The author surveys and analyzes Brazil's economic history from the colonial period through the early 1990s. (OP)

851. Gomes, Gustavo Maia. *The Roots of State Intervention in the Brazilian Economy.* New York: Praeger, 1986. 376 p. Bibl., ill., index. ISBN 0275921441.

This survey of Brazilian economic and political history focuses on the post 1930 period.

852. Pereira, Luiz Carlos Bresser. *Economic Crisis and State Reform in Brazil: Toward a New Interpretation of Latin America.* Boulder, CO: L. Rienner Publishers, 1996. 258 p. Bibl., index. ISBN 1555875327.

This work focuses on the Brazilian economic crisis of the 1980s and 1990s and challenges neoliberal views about the role of the state in economic recovery.

853. Randall, Laura. *The Political Economy of Brazilian Oil.* Westport, CT: Praeger, 1993. 315 p. Bibl., ill., index. ISBN 0275940918.

This is an analytical history of PETROBRAS, the state-owned Brazilian oil monopoly, including its organization, administration, operations, and efficiency.

854. Stanfield, Michael Edward. *Red Rubber, Bleeding Trees: Violence, Slavery, and Empire in Northwest Amazonia, 1850–1933.* 1st ed. Albuquerque, NM: University of New Mexico Press, 1998. 270 p. Bibl., ill., index. ISBN 0826319866.

This work studies the regional, national, and international factors that contributed to the rubber boom in northwestern Amazonia. It also includes a discussion of effects of this economic activity on the indigenous peoples of the region.

Caribbean Area

855. Bolles, Augusta Lynn. *We Paid Our Dues: Women Trade Union Leaders of the Caribbean.* Washington, DC: Howard University Press, 1996. 250 p. Bibl., index. ISBN 0882580868 pbk.

This summarizes contributions made by women to Anglophone Caribbean labor history.

856. Deere, Carmen Diana, and Peggy Antrobus. *In the Shadows of the Sun: Caribbean Development Alternatives and U.S. Policy.* Boulder, CO: Westview Press, 1990. 246 p. Ill., index. ISBN 0813310296.

This examines the 1980s economic crisis and its impact on the most disadvantaged sectors, particularly women. (OP)

857. Hope, Kempe R. *Economic Development in the Caribbean.* New York: Praeger, 1986. 215 p. ISBN 0275921816.

This is an analysis of economic development, security issues, and ethnic relations in Trinidad and Tobago, Barbados, Guyana, and Jamaica,

858. Pryor, Frederic L. *Revolutionary Grenada: A Study in Political Economy.* New York: Praeger, 1986. 395 p. Bibl., ill. ISBN 0275921557.

This is a study of the economic successes and failures of the People's Revolutionary Government of Grenada.

Central America

859. Barry, Tom, and Deb Preusch. *The Soft War: The Uses and Abuses of U.S. Economic Aid in Central America.* 1st ed. New York:

Grove Press, 1988. 304 p. Index. ISBN 0802100031.

This examination of the role of U.S. economic assistance in the area concludes that this aid supports local military policy instead of promoting the well-being of Central America's poor. (OP)

860. Bulmer-Thomas, Victor. *The Political Economy of Central America Since 1920.* New York: Cambridge University Press, 1987. 416 p. Bibl., ill., index. (Cambridge Latin American studies; 63.) ISBN 0521342848.

This sophisticated examination of the historic role of failed economic policies in the region seeks to develop more successful future strategies. (OP)

861. Torres-Rivas, Edelberto. *History and Society in Central America.* 1st ed. Translated by Douglass Sullivan-González. Austin, TX: University of Texas Press, 1993. 193 p. Bibl., ill., index. (Translations from Latin America series.) ISBN 0292781288.

This work traces 125 years of Central America's dependence on agricultural exports, foreign capital, and foreign markets.

Chile

862. Edwards, Sebastián, and Alejandra Cox Edwards. *Monetarism and Liberalization: The Chilean Experiment.* New York: Cambridge University Press, 1987. 233 p. Bibl., index. ISBN 0887301053.

This is a case study of neoliberal economic policies adopted by the Chilean government after the military coup in 1973 through the economic crisis of 1982.

863. Valdés, Juan Gabriel. *Pinochet's Economists: The Chicago School in Chile.* New York: Cambridge University Press, 1995. 334 p. Bibl., index. (Historical perspectives on modern economics.) ISBN 0521451469.

This reworked Ph.D. thesis examines how University of Chicago free market philosophy came to dominate Chile's military government economic policies. It also exposes

the clash between these policies and the emerging democratic process.

Colombia

864. Kofas, Jon V. *Dependence and Underdevelopment in Colombia.* Tempe, AZ: Arizona State University, Center for Latin American Studies, 1986. 201 p. Bibl. ISBN 0879180625.

This is an analysis of U.S. government influence on the evolution of Colombia's political economy from 1920 to 1960.

Costa Rica

865. Gudmundson, Lowell. *Costa Rica Before Coffee: Society and Economy on the Eve of the Export Boom.* Baton Rouge, LA: Louisiana State University Press, 1986. 204 p. Bibl., ill., index. ISBN 0807112747.

Changes in land holding patterns, demography, and class structure since the advent of the coffee cycle more than one hundred years ago, is the focus of this study.

Cuba

866. Kaplowitz, Donna Rich. *Anatomy of a Failed Embargo: U.S. Sanctions Against Cuba.* Boulder, CO: Lynne Rienner Publishers, 1998. 246 p. Bibl., ill., index. ISBN 1555876161.

This historical study of U.S. sanctions against Cuba from 1960 through 1997 focuses on the contradictory forces that created, weakened, amended, and again strengthened the sanctions that so deeply affect its citizens.

867. Pérez-López, Jorge F. *The Economics of Cuban Sugar.* Pittsburgh, PA: University of Pittsburgh Press, 1991. 313 p. Bibl., ill., index. (Pitt Latin American series.) ISBN 0822936631.

This is an overview of Cuban sugar industry research with a focus on its evolving economic influence since 1959. (OP)

868. Schwab, Peter. *Cuba: Confronting the U.S. Embargo.* 1st ed. New York: St. Martin's Press, 1999. 226 p. Bibl., index. ISBN 0312216203.

This examines the contemporary impact of the U.S. embargo on the lives of average Cubans. It also explores the political situation, human rights, and religion.

869. Zimbalist, Andrew S., ed. *Cuba's Socialist Economy Toward the 1990s.* Boulder, CO: Lynne Rienner Publishers, 1987. 188 p. Bibl., ill., index. ISBN 1555870805.

This volume presents different perspectives on the Cuban socialist economy between 1959 and 1986. (OP)

Ecuador

870. Andrien, Kenneth J. *The Kingdom of Quito, 1690–1830: The State and Regional Development.* New York: Cambridge University Press, 1995. 255 p. Bibl., ill., index. (Cambridge Latin American studies; 80.) ISBN 0521481252.

This work analyzes the effect of colonial public policy on the socioeconomic development of Ecuador. It argues that established colonial policies benefited Spain while long-term impact was mostly negative to the local and regional economies.

871. Martz, John D. *Politics and Petroleum in Ecuador.* New Brunswick, NJ: Transaction, 1987. 432 p. ISBN 0887381324.

This examines the Ecuadorian oil company and its relationship with the state since oil deposits were discovered in the 1960s.

872. Pineo, Ronn F. *Social and Economic Reform in Ecuador: Life and Work in Guayaquil.* Gainesville, FL: University Press of Florida, 1996. 227 p. Bibl., ill., index. ISBN 0813014379.

Ecuador's domination as the world supplier of cacao in the late nineteenth and early twentieth centuries is presented in this work

along with its contemporary economic and social underdevelopment.

El Salvador

873. Lindo-Fuentes, Héctor. *Weak Foundations: The Economy of El Salvador in the Nineteenth Century, 1821–1898.* Berkeley, CA: University of California Press, 1990. 239 p. ISBN 0520069277.

This detailed economic history of nineteenth century El Salvador concludes that weak foundations and legacy of disintegration from the colonial past still are apparent.

Mexico

874. Barrett, Elinore M. *The Mexican Colonial Copper Industry.* 1st ed. Albuquerque, NM: University of New Mexico Press, 1987. 143 p. Bibl., ill., index. ISBN 0826309291.

This is an overview of production, processing, and utilization of copper over a period of more than three hundred years. (OP)

875. Barry, Tom. *Zapata's Revenge: Free Trade and the Farm Crisis in Mexico.* Boston: South End Press, 1995. 317 p. Bibl., ill., index. ISBN 0896085007.

This work examines the role of subsistence agriculture in contemporary Mexico.

876. Brannon, Jeffery, and Eric N. Baklanoff. *Agrarian Reform & Public Enterprise in Mexico: The Political Economy of Yucatán's Henequen Industry.* Tuscaloosa, AL: University of Alabama Press, 1987. 237 p. Bibl., ill., index. ISBN 0817302824.

This analyzes agrarian reforms resulting from the Mexican revolution and the sector's subsequent dependence on international markets. It describes the wealthiest region in Mexico at the beginning of the twentieth century and how it became one of the poorest by the 1970s. (OP)

877. Brown, Jonathan C., and Alan Knight, eds. *The Mexican Petroleum Industry in the*

Twentieth Century. Austin, TX: University of Texas Press, 1992. 315 p. Bibl., ill., index. (Symposia on Latin America series.) ISBN 0292765339.

This work studies the role of the petroleum sector on Mexico's economic, social, and political development.

878. Bulmer-Thomas, Victor et al., eds. *Mexico and the North American Free Trade Agreement: Who Will Benefit?* New York: St. Martin's Press, 1994. 257 p. Bibl., ill., index. ISBN 0312121768.

This provides an overview of perspectives by scholars and public officials regarding the long-term effects of the treaty on Mexico.

879. Castañeda, Jorge G. *The Mexican Shock: Its Meaning for the United States.* New York: The New Press, 1995. 254 p. ISBN 1565843118.

This work analyzes the Chiapas crisis, the 1994 elections, and the factors contributing to the economic collapse of the 1990s.

880. Cross, John C. *Informal Politics: Street Vendors and the State in Mexico City.* Stanford, CA: Stanford University Press, 1998. 272 p. Bibl., index. ISBN 0804730601.

This study of street vendors in Mexico City includes background information about the vendors' political organizing activities.

881. Fatemi, Khosrow. *North American Free Trade Agreement: Opportunities and Challenges.* New York: St. Martin's Press, 1993. 301 p. Bibl., ill., index. ISBN 0312099762.

This balanced view of the treaty addresses macroeconomics, national perspectives and bilateral issues, cross-border and industry-specific issues, and environmental concerns.

882. González de la Rocha, Mercedes. *The Resources of Poverty: Women and Survival in a Mexican City.* Cambridge, MA: Blackwell, 1994. 311 p. Bibl., ill., index. (Studies in urban and social change.) ISBN 0631192239.

This is an interpretation of how the daily lives of poor women unfold in a context of urban poverty. (OP)

883. Gregory, Peter. *The Myth of Market Failure: Employment and the Labor Market*

in Mexico. Baltimore: Johns Hopkins University Press, 1986. 299 p. (A World Bank research publication.) ISBN 0810833434.

The premise of this provocative work is that underemployment and unemployment are minor problems in Mexico and that government policies have efficiently allocated labor among regions and sectors.

884. Hoberman, Louisa Schell. *Mexico's Merchant Elite, 1590–1660: Silver, State, and Society.* Durham, NC: Duke University Press, 1991. 352 p. Bibl., ill., index. ISBN 0822311348.

This work addresses the multifaceted roles of the Mexican merchant class in the seventeenth century.

885. La Botz, Dan. *The Crisis of Mexican Labor.* New York: Praeger, 1988. 206 p. Bibl., index. ISBN 0275926001.

This brief survey examines unionism in Mexico from a socialist perspective.

886. Lustig, Nora. *Mexico, the Remaking of an Economy.* 2nd ed. Washington, DC: The Brookings Institution, 1998. 287 p. Bibl., index. ISBN 0815775822.

This analyzes the transformation of Mexico's economic policy during the economic crisis of the 1980s.

887. Nolan, James et al. *Mexico Business: The Portable Encyclopedia for Doing Business with Mexico.* San Rafael, CA: World Trade Press, 1994. 488 p. (World Trade Press country business guides.) ISBN 096318640X pbk.

This guide includes preliminary investment research and tax information with cultural and travel details, bilingual glossaries, and other basic information for the business professional.

888. Roett, Riordan, ed. *The Mexican Peso Crisis: International Perspectives.* Boulder, CO: L. Rienner Publishers, 1996. 130 p. Bibl., ill., index. ISBN 1555876676 pbk.

This concise introduction to the Mexican financial crisis of the 1990s presents diverse perspectives concerning the causes and suggests possible solutions.

889. Roett, Riordan, ed. *Mexico's Private Sector: Recent History, Future Challenges.*

Boulder, CO: L. Rienner, 1998. 241 p. Bibl., index. ISBN 1555877133.

These essays examine the changing role of Mexico's private sector from the 1980s through the present.

890. Sanderson, Steven E. *The Transformation of Mexican Agriculture: International Structure and the Politics of Rural Change.* Princeton, NJ: Princeton University Press, 1986. 324 p. Bibl., ill., index. ISBN 0691076936.

This analysis of the Mexican agricultural system includes policy issues, U.S.-Mexican agricultural interests, and food imports. (OP)

891. Semo, Enrique. *The History of Capitalism in Mexico: Its Origins, 1521–1763.* 1st ed. Translated by Lidia Lozano. Austin, TX: University of Texas Press, 1993. 201 p. Bibl., index. (Translations from Latin America series.) ISBN 0292730691.

This classic presents an in-depth introduction to colonial Mexican economic history.

892. Sklair, Leslie. *Assembling for Development: The Maquila Industry in Mexico and the United States.* Upd. expd. ed. San Diego, CA: UCSD Center for U.S.-Mexican Studies, 1993. 287 p. (U.S.-Mexico contemporary perspectives series; 5.) ISBN 1878367129.

This is an overview study of the *maquila,* or assembly-for-export industry, in the border and interior.

893. Teichman, Judith A. *Privatization and Political Change in Mexico.* Pittsburgh, PA: University of Pittsburgh Press, 1996. 291 p. Bibl., index. (Pitt Latin American series.) ISBN 0822939282.

This examines economic privatization policies and questions the validity of this neoliberal economic reform within the context of a complex economic, political, and bureaucratic reality.

Nicaragua

894. Collins, Joseph. *Nicaragua: What Difference Could a Revolution Make?: Food*

and Farming in the New Nicaragua. 3rd updated and rev ed. New York: Grove Press, 1986. 311 p. Bibl., ill. (Food first.) ISBN 0394622952.

This is an analysis of Nicaragua's food policy within the context of changes in land holding patterns. (OP)

895. Luciak, Ilja A. *The Sandinista Legacy: Lessons from a Political Economy in Transition.* Gainesville, FL: University of Florida Press, 1995. 238 p. Bibl., index. ISBN 0813013690.

This describes Sandinista economic policy that was committed to long-term construction of socialism while also implementing a strategy that maintained the majority of the economy in private hands.

896. Martínez Cuenca, Alejandro. *Sandinista Economics in Practice: An Insider's Critical Reflections.* Translated by Nick Cooke. Boston: South End Press, 1992. 178 p. ISBN 0896084310 pbk.

In a question-answer format, this work examines the inner-workings of Sandinista economic policy and also includes a chronology of recent Nicaraguan history.

Paraguay

897. Kleinpenning, J. M. G. *Rural Paraguay, 1870–1932.* Amsterdam, The Netherlands: CEDLA, 1992. 525 p. Bibl., ill., index. (Latin America studies; 66.) ISBN 9070280647.

This study presents sixty years of Paraguayan economic history when this nation was a supplier of agricultural raw materials after the ruins of the Chaco War.

Peru

898. Gootenberg, Paul. *Between Silver and Guano: Commercial Policy and the State in Postindependence Peru.* Princeton, NJ: Princeton University Press, 1989. 234 p. Bibl., ill., index. ISBN 0691078106.

This studies Peruvian trade policy after

independence. The author argues that Peruvian leaders were nationalistic and conservative and that their selfish policies perpetuated a Peruvian economy highly dependent on external finance and commerce. (OP)

899. Scheetz, Thomas Edward. *Peru and the International Monetary Fund.* Pittsburgh, PA: University of Pittsburgh Press, 1986. 257 p. Bibl., ill., index. (Pitt Latin American series.) ISBN 0822938162.

This is an analysis of Peru's balance of payments problems including the conflict between growing expectations of new employment prospects and IMF stabilization policies that usually hurt the poor. (OP)

Puerto Rico

900. Baver, Sherrie L. *The Political Economy of Colonialism: The State and Industrialization in Puerto Rico.* Westport, CT: Praeger, 1993. 153 p. Bibl., index. ISBN 0275945030.

This examines the power structure of Puerto Rican industrial policy since World War II that made the economy more dependent on the mainland rather than increasing its autonomy.

901. Dietz, James L. *Economic History of Puerto Rico: Institutional Change and Capitalist Development.* Princeton, NJ: Princeton University Press, 1986. 337 p. Bibl, ill., index. ISBN 0691077169.

This general survey of Puerto Rico's economy from the early sixteenth century through the 1980s is based on secondary sources and includes an analysis of Operation Bootstrap.

Venezuela

902. Naím, Moisés. *Paper Tigers and Minotaurs: The Politics of Venezuela's Economic Reforms.* Washington, DC: Carnegie Endowment for International Peace, 1993. 180 p. Bibl., ill., index. ISBN 0870030256.

This volume examines economic deregulation and privatization policies adopted in 1989 in response to World Bank recommendations.

EDUCATION

This section includes all educational levels and pedagogy in one alphabetical list.

903. Albornoz, Orlando. *Education and Society in Latin America.* Pittsburgh, PA: University of Pittsburgh Press, 1993. 185 p. Bibl., index. (Pitt Latin American series.) ISBN 0822911752.

This work covers the major issues of education and society such as educational reform, the political role of the university, private and public institutions, among other topics.

904. Arnove, Robert F. *Education and Revolution in Nicaragua.* New York: Praeger, 1986. 160 p. Bibl., ill., index. (Praeger special studies series in comparative education.) ISBN 0275921387.

While this work focuses on the Sandinista educational system during the early period of the Nicaraguan revolution, it also examines education under the Somoza regime.

905. Britton, John A., ed. *Molding the Hearts and Minds: Education, Communications, and Social Change in Latin America.* Wilmington, DE: SR Books, 1994. 249 p. Bibl., ill. (Jaguar books on Latin America; 4.) ISBN 0842024891.

This collection of essays covers diverse topics including formal and non-formal education and social issues that span the nineteenth century through the present.

906. Freire, Paulo. *The Paulo Freire Reader.* Edited by A. M. Araújo Freire and D. Macedo. New York: Continuum, 1998. 291 p. ISBN 082641088X.

This anthology collects several of Freire's most influential writings about his educational philosophy.

907. Freire, Paulo. *Pedagogy of the Heart.* Translated by Donaldo Macedo and Alexandre Oliveira. New York: Continuum, 1997. 141 p. Bibl. ISBN 0826410391.

This work contains some of Freire's latest writing in which he contrasts pedagogical preparation and practice in terms of neoliberal and conservative perspectives.

908. Freire, Paulo. *Pedagogy of the Oppressed.* New rev. ed. New York: Continuum, 1993. 164 p. ISBN 0826406114.

Freire's classic work outlines the foundations for a democratic pedagogical theory.

909. Leonard, V. W. *Politicians, Pupils, and Priests: Argentine Education Since 1943.* New York: P. Lang, 1989. 456 p. Bibl., ill. (American university studies. Series XXII, Latin American studies; 2.) ISBN 0828407488.

This author describes Argentine education in the second half of the twentieth century from various social, political, and religious perspectives.

910. Stromquist, Nelly P., ed. *Women and Education in Latin America: Knowledge, Power, and Change.* Boulder, CO: L. Rienner Publishers, 1992. 310 p. Bibl., index. (Women and change in the developing world .) ISBN 1555872867.

This is an exploration of Latin American women's formal and informal education including its effect on women's role in society. (OP)

911. Torres, Carlos Alberto, and Adriana Puiggrós, eds. *Latin American Education: Comparative Perspectives.* Boulder, CO: Westview, 1997. 375 p. Bibl. ISBN 081338978X.

This collection of essays addresses several aspects of public education (primary, secondary, and higher) in the region.

GEOGRAPHY

This section includes physical geography, atlases, land use, and urban development in one alphabetical list.

912. Brawer, Moshe. *Atlas of South America.* New York: Simon & Schuster, 1991. 144 p. Bibl., ill., index. ISBN 0130506427.

This atlas covers climate, flora and fauna, resources, and population of South America and its individual countries. (OP)

913. Burnett, D. Graham. *Masters of All They Surveyed.* Chicago: University of Chicago Press, 2000. 298 p. Bibl., ill., index. ISBN 0226081206.

This work examines the early years of the former colony and the history of geography and mapmaking in Guyana as the British empire was forming in northern South America.

914. Greenfield, Gerald Michael. *Latin American Urbanization: Historical Profiles of Major Cities.* New York: Greenwood Press, 1994. 536 p. Bibl., ill. ISBN 0313259372.

This profiles twenty-one Latin American cities from the colonial period to the twentieth century describing their commonalities and differences.

915. Hoberman, Louisa Schell, and Susan M. Socolow, eds. *Cities & Society in Colonial Latin America.* 1st ed. Albuquerque, NM: University of New Mexico Press, 1986. 350 p. Bibl., ill., index. ISBN 0826308449 pbk.

These essays trace the historical evolution of key groups within the social hierarchy of colonial Latin American cities.

916. Kandell, Jonathan. *La Capital: The Biography of Mexico City.* 1st ed. New York: Random House, 1988. 640 p. Bibl., ill., index. ISBN 0394540697.

This is a historical portrait of Mexico City from the conquest to the present including social, political, artistic, and intellectual background. (OP)

917. Pick, James B., Edgard W. Butler, and Elizabeth L. Lanzer. *Atlas of Mexico.* Boulder, CO: Westview Press, 1989. 367 p. Bibl., ill., index. ISBN 0813376955.

This atlas of demographic data is based on Mexican census records, 1895–1980. (OP)

918. Pineo, Ronn F., and James A. Baer, eds. *Cities of Hope: People, Protests, and Progress* *in Urbanizing Latin America, 1870–1930.* Boulder, CO: Westview Press, 1998. 285 p. Bibl., ill., index. ISBN 0813314432.

This history of major Latin American urban centers focuses on the lifestyle of ordinary citizens as they organized to improve urban living conditions.

919. Tomaselli-Moschovitis, Valerie. *Latin America on File.* New York: Facts on File, 1995. 1 atlas. Bibl., ill., index. ISBN 0816032254.

Loose-leaf pages present current physical, political, administrative, population, and land use maps for the entire region.

HISTORY

This section includes long- and short-term historical accounts of people, events, and places from the conquest to the present; biographies, memoirs, chronicles, and historical dictionaries. The section is subdivided by geographic regions and countries. For pre–Columbian history see "Anthropology."

Latin America

920. Adams, Jerome R. *Liberators and Patriots of Latin America: Biographies of 23 Leaders from Doña Marina (1505–1530) to Bishop Romero (1917–1980).* Jefferson, NC: McFarland, 1991. 289 p. Bibl., ill., index. ISBN 089950602X.

This work provides biographical information in chronological order for Latin American leaders, revolutionaries, and visionaries from the sixteenth century to the present. It also includes their views of Latin American culture.

921. Archer, Christon, ed. *The Wars of Independence in Spanish America.* Wilmington, DE: SR Books, 2000. 325 p. Bibl. ISBN 0842024689.

This volume presents the parallels between Spain's loss of its American empire and similar twentieth-century "independence" strug-

gles throughout the world. It examines recent interpretations about the nature of insurgencies that give rise to new nations.

922. Bedini, Silvio A., ed. *The Christopher Columbus Encyclopedia.* New York: Simon & Schuster, 1992. 2 vols. Bibl., ill., index. ISBN 0131426621 set.

More than 350 signed articles with abundant cross-references and bibliographies examine Columbus, his era, and his legacy from all perspectives.

923. Bethell, Leslie, ed. *The Cambridge History of Latin America.* New York: Cambridge University Press, 1984–1995. 11 vols. Bibl., ill., index. ISBN 0521-

This source synthesizes Spanish and Portuguese American history since the European discovery. 1–2, Colonial L.A. (232236; 245168); 3, Independence to 1870 (232244); 4–5, 1870–1930 (232252; 245176); 6, L.A. since 1930: Economy, Society, and Politics (232260; 465567); 7, L.A. since 1930: Mexico, Central America, and the Caribbean (245184); 8, L.A. since 1930: Spanish South America (266521); 9–10, L.A. since 1930: Ideas, Culture, Society (495946); 11, Bibliographical essays (395259).

924. Brading, D. A. *The First America: The Spanish Monarchy, Creole Patriots, and the Liberal State, 1492–1867.* New York: Cambridge University Press, 1991. 761 p. Bibl., ill., index. ISBN 052139130X.

Based on contributions by Latin American intellectuals, this work examines the development of the American identity from the arrival of the Spaniards in 1492 through the restoration of the Mexican liberal state in 1867. (OP)

925. Burkholder, Mark A., and Lyman L. Johnson. *Colonial Latin America.* 3rd ed. New York: Oxford University Press, 1998. 376 p. Bibl., ill., index. ISBN 0195105354.

This overview of the Latin American colonial period includes not only traditional topics but also new ones, that are the result of late twentieth century research, such as racial adjustment, Indian immigration and life in the empire.

926. Burns, E. Bradford. *Latin America: A Concise Interpretive History.* 6th ed. Englewood Cliffs, NJ: Prentice Hall, 1994. 372 p. Bibl., ill., index. ISBN 0135013216.

This thematic text examines the region's history from the conquest to the contemporary period.

927. Bushnell, David, and Neill Macaulay. *The Emergence of Latin America in the Nineteenth Century.* 2nd ed. New York: Oxford University Press, 1994. 341 p. Bibl., ill., index. ISBN 0195084012.

Thirteen chapters compare socioeconomic and political experiences of the major Latin American countries during the period when national institutions were created and consolidated.

928. Casas, Bartolomé de las. *A Short Account of the Destruction of the Indies.* 1st ed. Translated and edited by Nigel Griffin. New York: Penguin Books, 1992. 143 p. Bibl., ill., index. ISBN 0140445625.

Father Las Casas, an ardent defender of the Indians, describes the mistreatment of the native population during the early years of the Spanish conquest.

929. Chasteen, John Charles, and Joseph S. Tulchin, eds. *Problems in Modern Latin American History: A Reader.* Wilmington, DE: SR Books, 1994. 339 p. Bibl. (Latin American silhouettes.) ISBN 0842023275.

This survey addresses topics of contemporary interest such as urban populism, revolutionary movements in Central America, cultural identity, and women's issues, in addition to standard themes.

930. Columbus, Christopher. *The Voyage of Christopher Columbus: Columbus' Own Journal of Discovery.* 1st U.S. ed. Restored and translated by John G. Cummins. New York: St. Martin's Press, 1992. 241 p. Bibl., ill., index. ISBN 0312078803.

This is a chronicle of Columbus' first voyage to the Americas. (OP)

931. Fuentes, Carlos. *The Buried Mirror: Reflections on Spain and the New World.* Boston: Houghton Mifflin, 1999. 399 p. Bibl., ill., index. ISBN 0395924995.

Fuentes reflects on the 500-year history of the Americas since the arrival of the Spanish conquerors, and in the process provides the reader with the story of Spain and Latin America from pre-conquest through the contemporary period.

932. Galeano, Eduardo H. *Memory of Fire.* Translated by Cedric Belfrage. New York: W.W. Norton, 1998. 3 vols. ISBN 039331-.

This well-known Uruguayan writer gathers perceptive vignettes that describe the Latin American way of life from pre–Columbian through the contemporary period. V. 1, Genesis; pre–Columbian era–1700 (-7730); V. 2, Faces and masks; Eighteenth-nineteenth centuries (-8060); V. 3 Century of the wind (-8079).

933. Galeano, Eduardo H. *Open Veins of Latin America: Five Centuries of the Pillage of a Continent.* Translated by Cedric Belfrage. New York: Monthly Review Press, 1998. 360 p. Bibl., index. ISBN 0853459916.

The twenty-fifth anniversary edition of Galeano's classic work examines Latin American history from a Marxist perspective.

934. Hanke, Lewis, and Jane M. Rausch, eds. *People and Issues in Latin American History: From Independence to the Present; Sources and Interpretations.* 2nd ed. upd. and enlg. New York: M. Wiener Pub., 1999. 367 p. Bibl., ill. ISBN 1558761950.

This is a survey of many key players of Latin American history since independence such as Simón Bolívar, Eva Perón, and Fidel Castro.

935. Hanke, Lewis, and Jane M. Rausch, eds. *People and Issues in Latin American History: The Colonial Experience; Sources and Interpretations.* New York: M. Wiener Pub., 1993. 356 p. Bibl., ill. ISBN 155876061X.

This volume presents key players of the Latin American colonial period and introduces perspectives about demographic, social, and economic issues.

936. Harvey, Robert. *Liberators: Latin America's Struggle for Independence.* New York:

Overlook, 2000. 561 p. Bibl., ill., index. ISBN 1585670723.

This work includes biographies of seven of the most influential leaders of the independence movement. They are Bolívar, Cochrane, Iturbide, Miranda, O'Higgins, Brazil's Pedro I, and San Martín.

937. Keen, Benjamin, and Mark Wasserman, eds. *A History of Latin America*. 5th ed. Boston: Houghton Mifflin Co., 1996. 622 p. Bibl., ill., index. ISBN 0395744555.

This one-volume historical survey covers the entire region since the conquest but its main focus is the colonial period through the wars of independence.

938. Kicza, John E. ed. *The Indian in Latin American History: Resistance, Resilience, and Acculturation*. Wilmington, DE: Scholarly Resources, 1999. 296 p. Bibl. (Jaguar books on Latin America; 1.) ISBN 0842028226.

The dynamics of Indian societies to adapt to new European systems is the subject of these essays. Indian societies are described as resilient in resisting European domination.

939. Kinsbruner, Jay. *Independence in Spanish America: Civil Wars, Revolutions, and Underdevelopment*. 2nd rev. ed. Albuquerque, NM: University of New Mexico Press, 1999. 187 p. Bibl., ill., index. (Diálogos.) ISBN 0826321771.

This is a thorough introduction to the upheaval of the early nineteenth century. It also includes a summary of recent scholarship that has changed the process and meaning of the Latin American independence movement.

940. Lane, Kris E. *Pillaging the Empire: Piracy in the Americas, 1500–1750*. Armonk, NY: M.E. Sharpe, 1998. 237 p. Bibl., index. (Latin American realities.) ISBN 0765602563.

This work examines the effects of French, English, and Dutch predators on Spanish shipping trade with its colonies in the Americas. Both well- and lesser-known pirates are presented as well as shipbuilding, navigation, sailor's diets, weaponry, and more.

941. Lynch, John. *Caudillos in Spanish America, 1800–1850*. New York: Oxford University Press, 1992. 468 p. Bibl., ill., index. ISBN 019821135X.

This volume presents a composite of the caudillo, a regional or national strongman, in several Latin American countries. It covers the period from the wars of independence through the 1850s.

942. Lynch, John, ed. *Latin American Revolutions, 1808–1826: Old and New World Origins*. Norman, OK: University of Oklahoma Press, 1994. 409 p. Bibl., ill., index. ISBN 0806126612.

This is a comprehensive introduction to the underlying reasons for the Latin American independence movement.

943. Mills, Kenneth, and William B. Taylor, eds. *Colonial Spanish America: A Documentary History*. Wilmington, DE: SR Books, 1998. 372 p. Bibl., ill., index. ISBN 0842025723.

This work presents cultural and social developments in colonial Latin America through primary and secondary non-literary sources, historical documents, and visual materials.

944. Moseley, Edward H. *Historical Dictionary of the United States–Mexican War*. Lanham, MD: Scarecrow Press, 1997. 345 p. Bibl., ill. (Historical dictionaries of wars, revolution, and civil unrest; 2.) ISBN 0810833344.

This volume covers a variety of subjects related to the war's background including its causes, development, and outcomes.

945. Muldoon, James. *The Americas in the Spanish World Order: The Justification for Conquest in the 17th Century*. Philadelphia: University of Pennsylvania Press, 1994. 239 p. Bibl., index. ISBN 0812232453.

This examines a legal document by Juan de Solórzano Pereira that justifies the Spanish conquest and settlement of Latin America. (OP)

946. Navarro, Marysa, and Virginia Sánchez Korrol. *Women in Latin America and the Caribbean: Restoring Women to History.*

Bloomington, IN: Indiana University Press, 1999. 128 p. Bibl., ill., index. (Restoring women to history.) ISBN 0253334799.

The role of Latin American women in pre–Columbian and colonial societies is explored in this volume.

947. Patch, Robert. *Maya and Spaniard in Yucatán, 1648–1812.* Stanford, CA: Stanford University Press, 1993. 329 p. Bibl., ill., index. ISBN 0804720622.

This work studies the evolution of Spanish and Maya societies over nearly three centuries.

948. Robinson, David J., ed. *Migration in Colonial Spanish America.* New York: Cambridge University Press, 1990. 399 p. Bibl., ill., index. (Cambridge studies in historical geography.) ISBN 0521362814.

Fourteen essays examine the movement of peoples of all classes and races in the viceroyalties of New Spain and South America from historical and socioeconomic perspectives.

949. Rodríguez O., Jaime E. *The Independence of Spanish America.* New York: Cambridge University Press, 1998. 274 p. Bibl., ill., index. (Cambridge Latin American studies; 84.) ISBN 0521622980.

This political history of Spanish American independence argues that the independence movements were not the result of anticolonial struggles but instead the unforeseen outcome of political upheaval in Spain.

950. Sale, Kirkpatrick. *The Conquest of Paradise: Christopher Columbus and the Columbian Legacy.* 1st ed. New York: Knopf, 1990. 453 p. Bibl., ill., index. ISBN 039457429X.

This work separates Columbus, the man, from his legend and legacy, from the fifteenth century through the present, and examines him as a historical and heroic figure. (OP)

951. Skidmore, Thomas E., and Peter H. Smith. *Modern Latin America.* 4th ed. New York: Oxford University Press, 1997. 465 p. Bibl., ill., index. ISBN 0195100166.

This one-volume history of the region focuses on the years after independence with particular emphasis on the twentieth century.

952. Weber, David J., and Jane M. Rausch. *Where Cultures Meet: Frontiers in Latin American History.* Wilmington, DE: SR Books, 1994. 233 p. Bibl. (Jaguar books on Latin America; 6.) ISBN 0842024778.

This collection of essays examines the theme of frontiers throughout Latin American history "as geographic zones of interaction between two or more distinctive cultures," countries or regions in the nineteenth and twentieth centuries.

953. Williamson, Edwin. *The Penguin History of Latin America.* New York: Penguin Books, 1992. 631 p. Bibl., ill., index. ISBN 0713990767.

This historical survey is organized topically with selected regional examples.

954. Winn, Peter. *Americas: The Changing Face of Latin America and the Caribbean.* Upd. ed. Berkeley, CA: University of California Press, 1999. 646 p. Bibl., ill., index. ISBN 0679411690.

This is the accompanying text to a television series and college telecourse. This work provides historical background including twentieth century history of the region in a thematic arrangement.

955. Yeager, Gertrude, ed. *Confronting Change, Challenging Tradition: Women in Latin American History.* Wilmington, DE: SR Books, 1994. 242 p. Bibl. (Jaguar books on Latin America; 7.) ISBN 0842024794.

This work presents Latin American women as defined by culture from the sixteenth century to the present.

956. Zea, Leopoldo. *The Role of the Americas in History.* Translated by Amy Oliver. Savage, MD: Rowman & Littlefield, 1992. 250 p. Bibl., index. (Social Philosophy Research Institute book series.) ISBN 0847677206.

This translation of Zea's important 1957 work presents a comprehensive overview of historical development in Latin America since the Reformation.

Argentina

957. Crassweller, Robert D. *Perón and the Enigmas of Argentina.* 1st ed. New York: Norton, 1987. 432 p. Bibl., ill., index. ISBN 0393023818.

This biography of J.D. Perón is based on primary and secondary sources including a concise history of Argentina.

958. Goodrich, Diana Sorensen. *Facundo and the Construction of Argentine Culture.* 1st ed. Austin, TX: University of Texas Press, 1996. 218 p. Bibl., index. (The Texas Pan American series.) ISBN 0292727895.

This work examines the construction of Argentine national identity through one of the nineteenth century's seminal works.

959. Rock, David. *Authoritarian Argentina: The Nationalist Movement, Its History, and Its Impact.* Berkeley, CA: University of California Press, 1993. 320 p. Bibl., index. ISBN 0520079205.

This volume covers the rise and transformation of the nationalist movement from the turn of the century through today by intertwining intellectual history with political, social, and economic history.

960. Shumway, Nicolás. *The Invention of Argentina.* Berkeley, CA: University of California Press, 1991. 325 p. Bibl., ill., index. ISBN 0520069064.

This analysis of Argentine intellectual history focuses on works of nineteenth century figures who explore ideas and cultural myths.

Bolivia

961. Klein, Herbert S. *Bolivia: The Evolution of a Multi-Ethnic Society.* 2nd ed. New York: Oxford University Press, 1992. 343 p. Bibl., ill., index. (Latin American histories.) ISBN 0195057341.

This is an account of Bolivian history as a nation that strives to develop a multi-racial and multi-ethnic society. The ongoing implications of the Pacific and Chaco wars, the 1952 revolution, and 1980s transition to democracy are highlighted.

962. Larson, Brooke. *Cochabamba, 1550–1900: Colonialism and Agrarian Transformation in Bolivia.* Exp. ed. Durham, NC: Duke University Press, 1998. 422 p. Bibl., ill., index. ISBN 0822320886.

This volume examines the transformation of the Bolivian countryside during the colonial period.

963. Morales, Waltraud Q. *Bolivia: Land of Struggle.* Boulder, CO: Westview Press, 1992. 234 p. Bibl., ill., index. (Westview profiles. Nations of contemporary Latin America.) ISBN 0813301971.

This is a historical, introductory outline of Bolivia from its integral role in the Inca empire to the present period. (OP)

Brazil

964. Abreu, João Capistrano de. *Chapters of Brazil's Colonial History, 1500–1800.* Translated by Arthur Brakel. New York: Oxford University Press, 1997. 236 p. Bibl., index. (Library of Latin America.) ISBN 0195103017.

This is the first English language translation of Abreu's classic work that presents a balanced analysis of Brazil's history prior to the Portuguese arrival through its independence struggles.

965. Conniff, Michael L., and Frank D. McCann, eds. *Modern Brazil: Elites and Masses in Historical Perspective.* Lincoln, NE: University of Nebraska Press, 1989. 305 p. Bibl., ill. (Latin American studies series.) ISBN 0803231318.

These original essays are drawn from several academic disciplines and present a comprehensive analysis of modern Brazilian life.

966. Levine, Robert M. *Brazilian Legacies.* Armonk, NY: M.E. Sharpe, 1997. 209 p. Bibl., ill., index. (Perspectives on Latin America & the Caribbean.) ISBN 0765600099.

This work studies the complex Brazilian reality by exploring several historical legacies such as colonial rule, religious beliefs, political culture, race and class, among others.

967. Levine, Robert M. *The History of Brazil.* Westport, CT: Greenwood Press, 1999. 208 p. Bibl., index. (The Greenwood histories of the modern nations.) ISBN 0313303908.

This general introduction focuses on the late nineteenth century through the present. Brazil's contemporary free market economy, its painful transition to democracy, and social issues are also examined.

968. Levine, Robert M., and John J. Crocitti, eds. *The Brazil Reader: History, Culture, Politics.* Durham, NC: Duke University Press, 1999. 527 p. Bibl., ill., index. (The Latin America readers.) ISBN 822322587.

This reader outlines Brazilian history from its early origins through its return to democracy via simultaneous, diverse voices (lower and upper classes, women, race relations), in an effort to paint an accurate portrait of its complex reality.

969. Macaulay, Neill. *Dom Pedro: The Struggle for Liberty in Brazil and Portugal, 1798–1834.* Durham, NC: Duke University Press, 1986. 361 p. Ill., index. ISBN 0822306816.

This is a detailed biography of Dom Pedro, Brazil's first emperor, 1821–1831.

970. Skidmore, Thomas E. *Brazil: Five Centuries of Change.* New York: Oxford University Press, 1999. 254 p. Bibl., index. (Latin American histories.) ISBN 0195058097.

This brief history of Latin America's largest nation outlines the birth and growth of the Portuguese colony, its independence, and the economic and political development of modern Brazil including social and racial issues.

Caribbean Area

971. Craton, Michael, and Gail Saunders. *Islanders in the Stream: A History of the Bahamian People.* Athens, GA: University of

Georgia Press, 1992–1998. 2 vols. Bibl., ill., index. ISBN 082031-.

This set presents a social history of ordinary Bahamians as they struggle for self-determination. Vol. 1, covers pre–Columbian times to the end of slavery (3823); Vol. 2, covers the end of slavery to the twentieth century (9260).

972. Price, Richard *The Convict and the Colonel.* Boston: Beacon Press, 1998. 284 p. ISBN 0807046507.

This work explores Martinique's twentieth century history through ethnography, oral history, and autobiography.

973. Rogozinski, Jan. *A Brief History of the Caribbean: From the Arawak and the Carib to the Present.* Rev. ed. New York: Facts on File, 1999. 415 p. Bibl., ill., index. ISBN 0816038112.

This volume traces the social, economic and political factors that shaped Caribbean history, including a discussion of its climate and vegetation.

974. Wucker, Michele. *Why the Cocks Fight: Dominicans, Haitians, and the Struggle for Hispaniola.* 1st ed. New York: Hill and Wang, 1999. 281 p. Bibl., index. ISBN 080903719X.

This work analyzes the historical roots for the often violent relationship between Haiti and the Dominican Republic, the two nations of the island of Hispaniola.

Central America

975. Booth, John A., and Thomas W. Walker. *Understanding Central America.* 3rd ed. Boulder, CO: Westview Press, 1999. 267 p. Bibl., ill., index. ISBN 081333070X.

This volume examines the historical roots, including U.S. policy, of the late twentieth century conflicts in the region.

976. Pérez Brignoli, Héctor. *A Brief History of Central America.* Translated by Ricardo and Susan Sawrey. Berkeley, CA: University of California Press, 1989. 223 p. Bibl., ill., index. ISBN 0520060490.

This is a comparative historical overview of the Central American republics from the sixteenth century to the present.

Chile

977. Bethell, Leslie, ed. *Chile Since Independence.* New York: Cambridge University Press, 1993. 240 p. Bibl., ill., index. ISBN 0521433754.

This introductory work surveys major periods of Chilean history with an emphasis on political and economic aspects.

978. Bizzarro, Salvatore. *Historical Dictionary of Chile.* 2nd ed. rev. enl. and upd. Metuchen, NJ: Scarecrow Press, 1987. 583 p. Bibl., ill. (Latin American historical dictionaries; 7.) ISBN 0810819643.

This revised and updated edition focuses on sociopolitical and historical transformations during the Allende and Pinochet regimes.

979. Collier, Simon, and William F. Sater. *A History of Chile, 1808–1994.* New York: Cambridge University Press, 1996. 427 p. Bibl., ill., index. (Cambridge Latin American studies; 82.) ISBN 0521560756.

This comprehensive survey of Chilean historiography focuses on four critical transition periods in modern times and takes the traditional position that history is intimately connected with politics.

Colombia

980. Bushnell, David. *The Making of Modern Colombia: A Nation in Spite of Itself.* Berkeley, CA: University of California Press, 1993. 334 p. Bibl., ill., index. ISBN 052078020.

This succinct work, organized chronologically, outlines the main events in Colombian history since independence as Colombians struggle with issues of political order while seeking to define national identity.

981. Davis, Robert H. *Historical Dictionary of Colombia.* 2nd ed. Metuchen, NJ: Scarecrow Press, 1993. 600 p. Bibl., ill., index. (Latin American historical dictionaries; 23.) ISBN 0810826364.

This dictionary provides background information about peoples, events, and places relevant to Colombian history.

982. McFarlane, Anthony. *Colombia Before Independence: Economy, Society, and Politics under Bourbon Rule.* New York: Cambridge University Press, 1993. 399 p. Ill. (Cambridge Latin American studies; 75.) ISBN 0521416418.

This work examines Bourbon reforms from 1700–1810 as they affected Nueva Granada in terms of its political, social, and economic history.

983. Rausch, Jane M. *The Llanos Frontier in Colombian History, 1830–1930.* 1st ed. Albuquerque, NM: University of New Mexico Press, 1993. 401 p. Ill. ISBN 0826313965.

This is an analysis of Colombia's historical development through the expansion of its frontier. (OP)

Costa Rica

984. Creedman, Theodore S. *Historical Dictionary of Costa Rica.* 2nd ed. Metuchen, NJ: Scarecrow Press, 1991. 338 p. Bibl., ill. (Latin American historical dictionaries; 16.) ISBN 0810822156.

This reference volume provides background information about significant historical events, people, and places with an emphasis on economic and social history of Costa Rica.

Cuba

985. Pérez, Louis A. *The War of 1898: The United States and Cuba in History and Historiography.* Chapel Hill, NC: University of Carolina Press, 1998. 171 p. Bibl., index. ISBN 0807824372.

This comprehensive overview of the

conflict explores the significance of the 1898 events including their place in world and regional history that resulted in Cuba's independence from Spain.

986. Schwartz, Rosalie. *Lawless Liberators: Political Banditry and Cuban Independence.* Durham, NC: Duke University Press, 1989. 297 p. Bibl., ill., index. ISBN 0822308827.

This work examines the Cuban situation at the end of the nineteenth century when it was waging its struggle for independence.

987. Simons, Geoff. *Cuba: From Conquistador to Castro.* New York: St. Martin's Press, 1996. 416 p. Bibl., index. ISBN 0312128223.

Although the author's perspective is partial to the accomplishments of the Cuban revolution (healthcare, education, distribution of wealth) and highly critical of U.S. policy, he provides thorough historical background about Cuba from pre–Columbian times to the present including U.S. Cuban relations.

Ecuador

988. Van Aken, Mark J. *King of the Night: Juan José Flores and Ecuador, 1824–1864.* Berkeley, CA: University of California Press, 1989. 382 p. Bibl., ill., index. ISBN 0520062779.

This political biography of Flores, a Venezuelan, who became president of Ecuador examines his regime within the wider context of Andean history. (OP)

Guatemala

989. McCreery, David. *Rural Guatemala, 1760–1940.* Stanford, CA: Stanford University Press, 1994. 450 p. Bibl., ill., index. ISBN 0804723184.

This is a study of the conditions in rural Guatemala in the nineteenth century with particular emphasis on the coffee revolution and its impact on Indian communities.

990. Woodward, Ralph Lee. *Rafael Carrera and the Emergence of the Republic of Guate-* *mala, 1821–1871.* Athens, GA: University of Georgia Press, 1993. 630 p. Bibl., ill., index. ISBN 082031448X.

This volume examines the caudillo's life, political career, and influence in Central America.

Haiti

991. Arthur, Charles, and Michael Dash, eds. *A Haiti Anthology: Libète.* Princeton, NJ: M. Wiener Pubs. 1999. 352 p. Bibl., ill., index. ISBN 1558762124.

This work covers Haitian history from its Arawak past through Aristide. All facets are covered from its insurmountable social problems to its rich, diverse culture.

992. Fick, Carolyn E. *The Making of Haiti: The Saint Domingue Revolution from Below.* 1st ed. Knoxville, TN: University of Tennessee Press, 1990. 355 p. ISBN 0870496581.

This political history of the Haitian Revolution of 1789–1803 focuses on the black struggle for emancipation and independence and the colony's south coast.

Honduras

993. Meyer, Harvey K., and Jessie H. Meyer. *Historical Dictionary of Honduras.* 2nd ed. rev. enl. and updated. Metuchen, NJ: Scarecrow Press, 1994. 708 p. Bibl., ill., index. (Latin American historical dictionaries; 25.) ISBN 0810828456.

This historical dictionary provides historical information about peoples, events, and places relevant to Honduras.

Jamaica

994. Campbell, Mavis Christine. *The Maroons of Jamaica, 1655–1796: A History of Resistance, Collaboration & Betrayal.* Westport, CT: Bergin & Garvey, 1988. 296 p. Ill. ISBN 0897891481.

This is a study of Jamaican maroons from the British conquest to the late eighteenth century.

995. Sherlock, Philip, and Hazel Bennett. *Story of the Jamaican People.* Princeton, NJ: M. Wiener Pub., 1998. 434 p. Bibl., index. ISBN 1558761454.

This one volume history of Jamaica presents events from the last four hundred years from an Afro-Jamaican perspective.

Mexico

996. Aguilar Camín, Héctor. *In the Shadow of the Mexican Revolution: Contemporary Mexican History, 1910–1989.* 1st ed. Translated by Lorenzo Meyer and Luis A. Fierro. Austin, TX: University of Texas Press, 1993. 287 p. Bibl., index. (Translations from Latin America series.) ISBN 0292704461.

This is a descriptive history that covers political changes in Mexico from the revolution of 1910 to the 1988 election.

997. Albro, Ward S. *Always a Rebel: Ricardo Flores Magón and the Mexican Revolution.* Fort Worth, TX: Texas Christian University Press, 1992. 219 p. Bibl., ill., index. ISBN 0875651089.

The thought of Flores Magón and its transformation during exile in the U.S. is examined in this work. He was a liberal journalist turned radical anarchist whose writings were influential during the Mexican revolution.

998. Benjamin, Thomas. *La Revolución: Mexico's Great Revolution as Memory, Myth, and History.* 1st ed. Austin, TX: University of Texas Press, 2000. 237 p. Bibl., ill., index. ISBN 0292708807.

The contemporary relevance of the Mexican revolution is analyzed in this work through present day fiestas, monuments, and official history.

999. Berler, Beatrice. *The Conquest of Mexico: A Modern Rendering of William H. Prescott's History.* San Antonio, TX: Corona Pub.

Co., 1988. 143 p. Bibl., ill., index. ISBN 0931722691.

This classic account of the conquest of Mexico was first published in 1843. This abridged version is rich in examples of the first encounter between Mexicans and Spaniards.

1000. Díaz del Castillo, Bernal. *The Discovery and Conquest of Mexico, 1517–1521.* 1st Da Capo Press ed. Edited by Genaro García. New York: Da Capo, 1996. 478 p. Ill. ISBN 0306806975.

Díaz del Castillo, eyewitness of the Spanish conquest, describes the pre–Columbian civilization and its destruction.

1001. Eisenhower, John S. D. *So Far from God: The U.S. War with Mexico, 1846–1848.* 1st ed. New York: Random House, 1989. 436 p. Bibl., ill., index. ISBN 0394560515.

This is a study of the conflict that preceded and shaped the war including an account of U.S.-Mexican relations.

1002. Fehrenbach, T. R. *Fire and Blood: A History of Mexico.* 1st Da Capo Press ed. New York: Da Capo, 1995. 683 p. Bibl., ill., index. ISBN 0306806282 pbk.

This one-volume history of Mexico summarizes its main events from pre–Columbian times to the present.

1003. Florescano, Enrique. *Memory, Myth, and Time in Mexico: From the Aztecs to Independence.* 1st ed. Translated by Albert and Kathryn Bork. Austin, TX: University of Texas Press, 1994. 282 p. Bibl., ill., index. (Translations from Latin America series.) ISBN 0292724853.

This classic work examines the changing discourses about history and time from the Spanish conquest through Mexican independence as represented in the writing of the Spanish chroniclers and creole writers.

1004. Fuentes, Patricia de. *The Conquistadors: First-Person Accounts of the Conquest of Mexico.* Norman, OK: University of Oklahoma Press, 1993. 264 p. Ill. ISBN 0806125624.

This work presents original Spanish

chronicles of the exploration and settlement of Mexico by the conquistadors.

1005. Gerhard, Peter. *A Guide to the Historical Geography of New Spain.* Rev. ed. Norman, OK: University of Oklahoma Press, 1993. 484 p. Bibl., ill., index. ISBN 0806125535.

This is an in-depth analysis of Mexico's colonial history and its administrative government in what is today southern and central Mexico.

1006. Gerhard, Peter. *The North Frontier of New Spain.* Rev. ed. Norman, OK: University of Oklahoma Press, 1993. 456 p. Bibl., ill., index. ISBN 0806125446.

This is a study of the Spanish advance up the coasts of Mesoamerica and crossing of northern Mexico's central plateau. (OP)

1007. Gerhard, Peter. *The Southeast Frontier of New Spain.* Rev. ed. Norman, OK: University of Oklahoma Press, 1993. 219 p. Bibl., ill., index. ISBN 0806125438.

This is an examination of eastern Mexico's colonial government and its administrative divisions.

1008. Green, Stanley C. *The Mexican Republic: the First Decade, 1823–1832.* Pittsburgh, PA: University of Pittsburgh Press, 1987. 314 p. Bibl., ill., index. (Pitt Latin American series.) ISBN 0822938170.

This is a synthesis of the beginning of the Mexican republic. (OP)

1009. Griswold del Castillo, Richard. *The Treaty of Guadalupe Hidalgo: A Legacy of Conflict.* 1st ed. Norman, OK: University of Oklahoma Press, 1990. 251 p. Bibl., ill., index. ISBN 0806122404.

This is an in-depth analysis of the treaty that ended the war between the U.S. and Mexico in 1848. In particular, it examines and interprets the implementation of the treaty by the U.S. legal system.

1010. Hale, Charles A. *The Transformation of Liberalism in Late Nineteenth-Century Mexico.* Princeton, NJ: Princeton University Press, 1989. 291 p. Bibl., index. ISBN 0691078149.

This volume analyzes the changing political ideas of Mexican intellectuals during the Benito Juárez presidency through the 1890s. During this period, liberalism was transformed by its encounter with the philosophy of positivism. (OP)

1011. Hamnett, Brian R. *Juárez.* New York: Longman, 1994. 301 p. Bibl., ill., index. (Profiles in power.) ISBN 0582050545.

This work attempts to demystify one of Mexico's most important nineteenth century political figures. It examines Juárez's role as president from 1858–1872 and restorer of the liberal republic.

1012. Hamnett, Brian R. *Roots of Insurgency: Mexican Regions, 1750–1824.* New York: Cambridge University Press, 1986. 276 p. Bibl., ill., index. (Cambridge Latin American studies; 59.) ISBN 0521321484.

This study of the Mexican independence period examines regional insurgencies in Morelia, Guadalajara, and Puebla and establishes a connection between the social tensions of the late colonial era and the independence movements. (OP)

1013. Hart, John M. *Revolutionary Mexico: The Coming and Process of the Mexican Revolution.* 10th anniversary ed. Berkeley, CA: University of California Press, 1997. 478 p. Bibl., index. ISBN 0520215311 pbk.

This work evaluates the historical roles of the Mexican peasantry, urban and industrial workers, petty bourgeoisie, and provincial elites since the Spanish colonial period.

1014. Himmerich y Valencia, Robert. *The Encomenderos of New Spain, 1521–1555.* 1st ed. Austin, TX: University of Texas Press, 1991. 348 p. Bibl., ill., index. ISBN 0292720688.

This is an analysis of individuals who held *encomiendas* (land grants) between 1521–1555 and the relationship of this institution to the Spanish conquest and settlement of Mexico.

1015. Katz, Friedrich. *The Life and Times of Pancho Villa.* Stanford, CA: Stanford University Press, 1998. 985 p. ISBN 0804730458.

This biography of the Mexican legendary revolutionary leader explores his pivotal role in the revolution, its ultimate failure and his legacy.

1016. Knight, Alan. *The Mexican Revolution*. Lincoln, NE: University of Nebraska Press, 1990. 2 vols. Bibl., ill., index. ISBN 0803277725.

This is a narrative, comprehensive history of the tumultuous 1910–20 decade. Vol. 1, covers Porfirians, Liberals and Peasants; Vol. 2, covers the Counter-revolution and Reconstruction. (OP)

1017. Krauze, Enrique. *Mexico: Biography of Power; a History of Modern Mexico, 1810–1996*. 1st ed. Translated by Hank Heifetz. New York: HarperCollins, 1997. 872 p. Ill., index. ISBN 0060163259.

Recurring themes and biographies of political leaders are the thread the authors use to weave Mexico's troubled history since independence through the mid–1990s.

1018. Le Clézio, Jean-Marie G. *The Mexican Dream, or, The Interrupted thought of Amerindian Civilizations*. Chicago: University of Chicago Press, 1993. 221 p. Bibl., ill. ISBN 0226110028.

This volume provides a historical account of pre–Columbian and post-conquest Mexican civilization including the devastation of the Amerindian cultures through their contact with the Spanish conquerors.

1019. Meyer, Michael, and William Beezley, eds. *The Oxford History of Mexico*. New York: Oxford University Press, 2000. 709 p. Bibl., ill., index. ISBN 0195112288.

These twenty essays reinterpret and re-evaluate Mexican history from pre-colonial times to the present. Several of the authors are Mexican historians whose work is not well known to English-reading audiences.

1020. Mier Noriega y Guerra, José Servando Teresa de. *The memoirs of Fray Servando Teresa de Mier*. Translated by Helen Lane. New York: Oxford University Press, 1998. 242 p. Bibl., index. ISBN 0195106733.

This work relates the experiences of the late eighteenth century Dominican friar who questioned the political and religious order of colonial Mexico for which he was imprisoned.

1021. Prescott, William Hickling. *History of the Conquest of Mexico*. New York: Modern Library, 1998. 1005 p. Index. (Modern library giant.) ISBN 0679602992.

This classic work was originally published in 1843 and even though it is a product of its time it remains a noteworthy interpretation of the arrival of the Spanish in Mexico and the downfall of the Aztec empire.

1022. Ridley, Jasper Godwin. *Maximilian and Juárez*. New York: Ticknor & Fields, 1992. 353 p. Bibl., ill., index. ISBN 0899199895.

This is a detailed account of Napoleon III's effort to install the Austrian Archduke, Ferdinand Maximilian, as emperor of Mexico.

1023. Robinson, Cecil. *The View from Chapultepec: Mexican Writers on the Mexican-American War*. Tucson, AZ: University of Arizona Press, 1989. 223 p. Bibl., index. ISBN 0816510830.

These essays represent the diverse views of twelve Mexican intellectuals, diplomats, and writers about the Mexican-American War in the latter part of the 1840s. (OP)

1024. Ruiz, Ramón Eduardo. *Triumphs and Tragedy: A History of the Mexican People*. New York: W.W. Norton, 1992. 512 p. Bibl., index. ISBN 0393030237.

This narrative covers Mexican history from pre–Columbian times to the present.

1025. Salas, Elizabeth. *Soldaderas in the Mexican Military: Myth and History*. 1st ed. Austin, TX: University of Texas Press, 1990. 163 p. Bibl., ill., index. ISBN 0292776306.

This inter-disciplinary study relates the participation of Mexican women in warfare, from pre–Columbian times to the present.

1026. Suchlicki, Jaime. *Mexico: From Montezuma to NAFTA, Chiapas, and Beyond*. Washington: Brassey's, 1996. 227 p. Bibl., ill., index. ISBN 1574880314.

This is a thematic examination of issues throughout Mexican history from the time of the conquest to the present such as regionalism, ethnic conflict, and church-state affairs.

1027. Thomas, Hugh. *Conquest: Montezuma, Cortés, and the Fall of Old Mexico.* New York: Simon & Schuster, 1993. 812 p. Bibl., ill., index. ISBN 0671705180.

This is an account of personalities, events, and the social setting leading to the destruction of Montezuma's Aztec empire by Cortés and his followers.

1028. Wasserman, Mark. *Everyday Life and Politics in Nineteenth Century Mexico: Men, Women, and War.* 1st ed. Albuquerque, NM: University of New Mexico Press, 2000. 248 p. Bibl., ill., index. (Diálogos.) ISBN 0826321704.

This work describes the influence of politicians in everyday life of nineteenth century common Mexican citizens. The three key figures are López de Santa Ana, Benito Juárez, and Porfirio Díaz.

1029. Womack, John, Jr., comp. and trans. *Rebellion in Chiapas: An Historical Reader.* New York: New Press, 1999. 372 p. Bibl., ill. ISBN 1565844521 pbk.

This collection of readings documents the current struggle of indigenous groups in the Mexican state of Chiapas. Historical as well as contemporary sources illuminate this complex struggle.

Nicaragua

1030. Burns, E. Bradford. *Patriarch and Folk: The Emergence of Nicaragua, 1798–1858.* Cambridge, MA: Harvard University Press, 1991. 307 p. Bibl., ill., index. ISBN 0674657969.

This is an analysis of the socioeconomic and political development of Nicaragua as it evolved from a colony to an independent state including foreign influences.

1031. Sandino, Augusto César. *Sandino Without Frontiers.* Edited by Karl Bermann. Hampton, VA: Compita Pub., 1988. 138 p. Bibl., ill. ISBN 0944824013.

This introduction to Sandino's thought during the struggle against U.S. occupation of Nicaragua, 1927–1933, also contains a short biography and overview of Nicaraguan history.

Panama

1032. La Feber, Walter. *The Panama Canal: The Crisis in Historical Perspective.* Updated ed. New York: Oxford University Press, 1989. 270 p. Bibl., ill. ISBN 0195061926.

This work examines the turbulent and often uneasy relationship between the U.S. and Panama through the 1980s, including the canal's creation, its administration, and treaty negotiations.

1033. McCullough, David G. *The Path Between the Seas: The Creation of the Panama Canal, 1870–1914.* New York: Simon & Schuster, 1999. 704 p. Bibl., ill., index. ISBN 0671225634.

This chronicles the creation of the Panama Canal.

Paraguay

1034. Nickson, R. Andrew. *Historical Dictionary of Paraguay.* 2nd ed. rev. enl. and updated. Metuchen, NJ: Scarecrow Press, 1993. 685 p. Bibl., ill., index. (Latin American historical dictionaries; 24.) ISBN 0810826437.

As one of the few comprehensive historical sources about Paraguay, this dictionary covers significant events, people, institutions, and places.

Peru

1035. Adorno, Rolena. *Guamán Poma: Writing and Resistance in Colonial Peru.* 2nd ed. Austin, TX: University of Texas Press, 2000. 194 p. Bibl., ill., index. (ILAS special publication.) ISBN 0292705034 pbk.

This work examines the contributions of

Guamán Poma de Ayala, an important chronicler of colonial Peru, who denounced the abuses committed by the Spanish colonial powers against the native population.

1036. Lockhart, James. *Spanish Peru, 1532–1560: A Social History.* 2nd ed. Madison, WI: University of Wisconsin Press, 1994. 320 p. Bibl., ill., index. ISBN 0299141608.

This analysis of the role of Spanish society in early colonial Peru concludes that the conquest and settlement represented similar peninsular social institutions.

Puerto Rico

1037. Santiago-Valles, Kelvin A. *"Subject People" and Colonial Discourses: Economic Transformation and Social Disorder 1898–1947.* Albany, NY: State University of New York Press, 1994. 304 p. Bibl., index. (SUNY series in society and culture in Latin America.) ISBN 0791415899.

This is an interdisciplinary study of Puerto Rican history between 1898–1947 including United States policy to turn the island into a wage-earning, consumption-addicted population amenable to capitalist development.

1038. Wagenheim, Kal, and Olga J. de Wagenheim, eds. *The Puerto Ricans: A Documentary History.* Princeton, NJ: M. Wiener Pub., 1994. 338 p. Bibl., ill., index. ISBN 1558760776.

This one-volume history begins with the arrival of the Spanish in the fifteenth century and ends with the institution of the commonwealth status after World War II.

South America

1039. Early, Edwin et al. *The History Atlas of South America.* New York: Macmillan, 1998. 160 p. Bibl., ill., index. (Macmillan continental history atlases.) ISBN 0028625838.

This atlas covers in images and text the pre–Columbian era, colonial period, independence revolt, post colonial years, and contemporary South America.

1040. Farcau, Bruce W. *The Chaco War: Bolivia and Paraguay, 1932–1935.* Westport, CT: Praeger, 1996. 254 p. Bibl., ill., index. ISBN 0275952185.

This is an analysis of the role of the military in both countries, their governments, and the weakness of the League of Nations in resolving the disputes between Bolivia and Paraguay in the 1930s.

1041. Sater, William F. *Chile and the War of the Pacific.* Lincoln, NE: University of Nebraska Press, 1986. 343 p. Bibl., index. ISBN 0803241550.

This is a general description of the expansionist War of the Pacific, 1879–84, involving Bolivia, Chile, and Peru. (OP)

Venezuela

1042. Oviedo y Baños, José de. *The Conquest and Settlement of Venezuela.* Translated by Jeannette J. Varner. Berkeley, CA: University of California Press, 1988. 305 p. Bibl., index. ISBN 05200058518.

This classic work details Venezuela's history from Columbus' arrival through 1600. (OP)

1043. Rudolph, Donna Keyse, and G. A. Rudolph. *Historical Dictionary of Venezuela.* 2nd ed. rev. enl. and updated. Lanham, MD: Scarecrow Press, 1996. 954 p. Bibl., ill. (Latin American historical dictionaries; 3.) ISBN 0810830299.

This dictionary provides background information about peoples, places, organizations, events and general subjects relevant to Venezuelan history.

POLITICS AND GOVERNMENT

This section contains all types of government systems; leaders and officials; political parties, movements, elections, theory, policy, and history; foreign and U.S.–Latin American relations; human rights and refugees; armed forces; and church-state relations. Due to the extensive coverage of politics, the section begins with general works for the region then is subdivided by these subtopics: "Armed Forces," "Foreign Relations," "Political Participation," "Revolutions," and "U.S. Relations." The section is subdivided by geographic regions and countries.

Latin America

1044. Agosín, Marjorie, and Monica Bruno, eds. *Surviving Beyond Fear: Women, Children and Human Rights in Latin America.* 1st ed. Fredonia, NY: White Pine Press, 1993. 217 p. (Human rights series; 2.) ISBN 1877727253 pbk.

These essays by U.S. Latin American scholars and human rights activists focus on women and children political prisoners and their families' relentless efforts to secure their freedom and/or discover their fate. (OP)

1045. Alexander, Robert Jackson, ed. *Biographical Dictionary of Latin American and Caribbean Political Leaders.* New York: Greenwood Press, 1988. 509 p. ISBN 0313243530.

This introductory biographical source covers 450 significant political figures from the nineteenth and twentieth centuries.

1046. Castañeda, Jorge G. *Utopia Unarmed: The Latin American Left After the Cold War.* 1st ed. New York: Knopf, 1993. 498 p. ISBN 0394582594.

This history of the Latin American left since World War II includes its personalities, ideals, conflicts, triumphs, failures, and future role.

1047. Child, Jack. *Antarctica and South American Geopolitics: Frozen Lebensraum.* New York: Praeger, 1988. 232 p. Ill. ISBN 0275928861.

This is a review of the legal validity of claims over Antarctica made by Chile, Argentina, and Brazil.

1048. Cleary, Edward L. *The Struggle for Human Rights in Latin America.* Westport, CT: Praeger, 1997. 181 p. ISBN 0275959805.

This work examines the history, development, and effects of the human rights movement in Latin America.

1049. Di Tella, Torcuato S. *Latin American Politics: A Theoretical Framework.* 1st ed. Austin, TX: University of Texas Press, 1990. 236 p. Bibl. (Translations from Latin America series.) ISBN 0292746644.

This basic source addresses requirements for democracy and the role of popular movements in Latin American social change.

1050. Gill, Anthony James. *Rendering Unto Caesar: The Catholic Church and the State in Latin America.* Chicago: University of Chicago Press, 1998. 269 p. Bibl., ill., index. ISBN 0226293831.

This work analyzes the evolution of the Latin American Catholic Church's relationship with the state since 1960. Included is a discussion of human rights and authoritarian governments, social issues (divorce, abortion, contraception, and homosexuality), and the growth of Protestant fundamentalism.

1051. Gunson, Phil, and Greg Chamberlain. *The Dictionary of Contemporary Politics of Central America and the Caribbean.* New York: Simon & Schuster, 1991. 397 p. Ill. ISBN 0132133725.

This compact political dictionary in a country-by-country arrangement provides general background information focusing on the latter half of the twentieth century. (OP)

1052. Klaiber, Jeffrey L. *The Church, Dictatorships, and Democracy in Latin America.* Maryknoll, NY: Orbis Books, 1998. 326 p. Bibl., index. ISBN 1570751994 pbk.

This is an overview of church-state relations of eleven countries under authoritarian regimes.

1053. Löwy, Michael, ed. *Marxism in Latin America from 1909 to the Present: An Anthology.* Translated by Michael Pearlman.

Atlantic Highlands, NJ: Humanities Press, 1992. 296 p. Bibl., index. (Revolutionary studies.) ISBN 0391037552.

This work identifies three periods in the history of Latin American Marxism: the 1920s–1935, when socialism and anti-imperialism were the focus; 1930s–1959, when Stalinism was the model; 1959–present, when the Cuban revolution has been the primary example in the region. Other related movements are also examined. (OP)

1054. Morris, Michael A., ed. *Great Power Relations in Argentina, Chile, and Antarctica.* New York: St. Martin's Press, 1990. 210 p. Bibl., ill., index. ISBN 0312036108.

This volume deals with issues related to the law of the sea, territorial rights, and power relations (United States, Great Britain, and the former Soviet Union) in the Southern Cone and Antarctica.

1055. Rossi, Ernest E., and Jack C. Plano. *Latin America: A Political Dictionary.* Santa Barbara, CA: ABC-CLIO, 1992. 242 p. Index. (Clio dictionaries in political science.) ISBN 0874366089.

Broad subject-oriented chapters cover the political changes in Latin America during the last decades of the twentieth century. (OP)

1056. Stoetzer, O. Carlos. *The Organization of American States.* 2nd ed. Westport, CT: Praeger, 1993. 443 p. Bibl., index. ISBN.

This is a concise account of the development, activities, and structure of the OAS, including the Pan-American movement.

1057. Vellinga, Menno, ed. *The Changing Role of the State in Latin America.* Boulder, CO: Westview Press, 1998. 312 p. Bibl., index. ISBN 0813321379.

This is an introduction to state reform, its relation to civil society and the economy, and the reasons for the evolution of the state throughout the region.

1058. Yundt, Keith W. *Latin American States and Political Refugees.* New York: Praeger, 1988. 236 p. Bibl., index. ISBN 0275929426.

This is an overview of treatment of political refugees in the region within the context of international, regional, national asylum, and refugee laws.

Latin America

Armed Forces

1059. Loveman, Brian. *For la Patria: Politics and the Armed Forces in Latin America.* Wilmington, DE: SR Books, 1999. 331 p. Bibl., ill., index. (Latin American silhouettes.) ISBN 842027726.

This analyzes the historical role of the military in Latin America's public life as the protector of the constitution.

1060. Loveman, Brian, and Thomas M. Davies, Jr. *The Politics of Antipolitics: The Military in Latin America.* Rev. and upd. Wilmington, DE: SR Books, 1997. 426 p. (Latin American silhouettes.) ISBN 0842026096.

Overview chapters by U.S. scholars focus on military power and democracy in the region. Primary resources (speeches by Latin American generals and U.S. military documents) enhance the usefulness of this volume that also covers contemporary redemocratization developments.

1061. Nunn, Frederick M. *The Time of the Generals: Latin American Professional Militarism in World Perspective.* Lincoln, NE: University of Nebraska Press, 1992. 349 p. Bibl., index. ISBN 0803233345.

This analyzes the emergence of professional militarism during the period from 1964 to 1989 in Argentina, Brazil, Chile, and Peru.

1062. Remmer, Karen L. *Military Rule in Latin America.* Boulder, CO: Westview Press, 1991. 213 p. Bibl., ill., index. ISBN 0813384508.

This study of the Latin American military institution includes the origins of authoritarianism and significance of military rule in the twentieth century. (OP)

1063. Rouquié, Alain. *The Military and the State in Latin America.* Translated by Paul E. Sigmund. Berkeley, CA: University of California Press, 1987. 469 p. Bibl., index. ISBN 0520055594.

This in-depth examination of the relationship between the armed forces and Latin American society includes linkages between political culture and the military.

1064. Wesson, Robert G., ed. *The Latin American Military Institution.* New York: Praeger, 1986. 234 p. Bibl., index. ISBN 0030070295.

This collection of essays focuses on the organization of the armed forces in Brazil, Chile, Argentina, Mexico, Colombia, Guatemala, Venezuela, Peru, and Panama.

Foreign Relations

1065. Adams, Jan S. *A Foreign Policy in Transition: Moscow's Retreat from Central America and the Caribbean, 1985–1992.* Durham, NC: Duke University Press, 1992. 248 p. Index. ISBN 0822312565.

This evaluates the impact of the end of the cold war on Soviet relations with the Caribbean and Central America, especially Cuba and Nicaragua.

1066. Armony, Ariel C. *Argentina, the United States, and the Anti-Communist Crusade in Central America, 1977–1984.* Athens: Ohio University Center for International Studies, 1997. 301 p. Bibl., ill., index. (MIS; Latin America series; 26.) ISBN 0896801969.

This work establishes a connection between Argentina's "dirty war," Central American death squads, U.S. intelligence, and human rights in Central America.

1067. Atkins, G. Pope. *Latin America in the International Political System.* 4th ed. Boulder, CO: Westview Press. 1998. 472 p. Bibl., ill., index. ISBN 0813333822.

This well-established source on Latin American international affairs also examines influential subregional organizations and the major theoretical thrusts for studying the region.

1068. Caballero, Manuel. *Latin America and the Comintern, 1919–1943.* New York: Cambridge University Press, 1986. 213 p. (Cambridge Latin American studies; 60.) ISBN 0521325811.

This work presents a synthesis of the history, theory and practice of the Third Communist International in Latin America from its founding in 1919 to 1943. It cites Brazilian, Chilean, Cuban, and Venezuelan examples. (OP)

1069. Domínguez, Jorge I., ed. *Latin America's International Relations and Their Domestic Consequences: War and Peace, Dependency and Autonomy, Integration.* New York: Garland, 1994. 451 p. Bibl. (Essays on Mexico, Central and South America; 6.) ISBN 0815314906.

This is a summary of scholarly debates by Latin American experts in foreign relations and regional integration, the 1980s debt crisis, the relationship between governments and multinational corporations, and U.S. interventions in the region.

1070. Miller, Nicola. *Soviet Relations with Latin America, 1959–1987.* New York: Cambridge University Press, 1989. 252 p. Bibl., index. (Cambridge Soviet paperbacks; 1.) ISBN 0521351936.

This volume examines Soviet-Latin American relations from economic, political, and military perspectives.

Political Participation

1071. Agüero, Felipe, and Jeffrey Stark, eds. *Fault Lines of Democracy in Post-Transition Latin America.* Coral Gables, FL: NS Center, University of Miami, 1998. 407 p. Bibl., index. ISBN 1574540467 pbk.

This is an analysis of the democratization trend in the era of globalization.

1072. Boeker, Paul H. *Lost Illusions: Latin America's Struggle for Democracy as Recounted by Its Leaders.* La Jolla, CA: Institute of the Americas, 1990. 333 p. ISBN 1558760237.

Twenty-six political leaders were interviewed as the democratization revival was developing in 1988. The interviews explore the strength of these democratization efforts.

1073. Camp, Roderic Ai, ed. *Democracy in Latin America: Patterns and Cycles.* Wilmington, DE: SR Books, 1995. 294 p. (Jaguar books on Latin America; 10.) ISBN 084202512X.

This collection of essays examines Latin America's efforts to strengthen participatory government within a context of historic economic instability.

1074. Collier, Ruth Berins, and David Collier. *Shaping the Political Arena: Critical Junctures, the Labor Movement, and Regime Dynamics in Latin America.* Princeton, NJ: Princeton University Press, 1991. 877 p. Bibl., index. ISBN 0691023131 pbk.

This comparative-historical analysis of eight countries examines trajectories of change resulting from different strategies of working class politics. These activities influenced regime changes that range from authoritarian to democratic paths. (OP)

1075. Conniff, Michael L., ed. *Populism in Latin America.* Tuscaloosa, AL: University of Alabama Press, 1999. 243 p. Bibl., index. ISBN 0817309594.

Latin American and U.S. social scientists propose a definition of the populist phenomenon in eight Latin American countries and explore the charismatic traits and electoral successes of populism in the region.

1076. Diamond, Larry et al., eds. *Democracy in Developing Countries, V. 4: Latin America.* 2nd ed. Boulder, CO: L. Rienner Publishers, 1999. 594 p. Ill., index. ISBN 1555877982.

This work analyzes the persistence and failure of democracy in the region and surveys its current state.

1077. Dietz, Henry A., and Gil Shidlo, eds. *Urban Elections in Democratic Latin America.* Wilmington, DE: SR Books, 1998. 298 p. Bibl., ill., index. (Latin American silhouettes.) ISBN 0842026274.

This analyzes local electoral politics after constitutional governments returned to power in the region.

1078. Domínguez, Jorge I., ed. *Authoritarian and Democratic Regimes in Latin America.* New York: Garland, 1994. 395 p. Bibl., ill. (Essays on Mexico, Central and South America; 2.) ISBN 0815314868.

The second volume of this series provides a summary of scholarly debates by Latin American experts in the rise and fall of democratic and authoritarian regimes.

1079. Domínguez, Jorge I., ed. *Parties, Elections, and Political Participation in Latin America.* New York: Garland, 1994. 411 p. Bibl., ill. (Essays on Mexico, Central and South America; 5.) ISBN 0815314892.

The fifth volume in the series provides a summary of scholarly debates by Latin American experts in political behavior. Parties, elections, and political participation are examined in the context of authoritarianism and the return to democratic regimes.

1080. Harris, Richard L. *Marxism, Socialism, and Democracy in Latin America.* Boulder, CO: Westview Press, 1992. 234 p. Bibl., index. (Latin American perspectives series; 8.) ISBN 0813313228.

This work focuses on the successes and failures of attempts to construct socialist societies in Cuba, Chile, Grenada, and Nicaragua. (OP)

1081. Jelin, Elizabeth, and Eric Hershberg, eds. *Constructing Democracy: Human Rights, Citizenship, and Society in Latin America.* Boulder, CO: Westview Press, 1996. 238 p. Bibl., index. ISBN 0813324386.

This is an examination of the relationship between grassroots organizations, human rights issues, and democratic regimes in the 1980s.

1082. Jonas, Susanne, and Nancy Stein, eds. *Democracy in Latin America: Visions and Realities.* Westport, CT: Bergin & Garvey, 1990. 224 p. ISBN 0897891651.

This volume evaluates different models of democracy in the region and exposes the differences between the myths and realities in practice.

1083. Lynch, Edward A. *Latin America's Christian Democratic Parties: A Political Economy.* Westport, CT: Praeger, 1992. 197 p. Bibl., index. ISBN 0275944646.

This work examines the Christian democratic movement in Latin America from its nineteenth century origins to the events of the 1990s.

1084. McManus, Philip, and Gerald Schlabach, eds. *Relentless Persistence: Nonviolent Action in Latin America.* Philadelphia: New Society Publishers, 1991. 312 p. Bibl., ill., index. ISBN 086571181X .

This proposes a new interpretive framework for Latin American non-violent political action that draws its inspiration from liberation theology. (OP)

1085. Nickson, R. Andrew. *Local Government in Latin America.* Boulder, CO: L. Rienner Publishers, 1995. 316 p. Bibl., ill., index. ISBN 1555873669.

This detailed country-by-country historical analysis of local governments in the region examines the relationship between democracy and development.

1086. Stotzky, Irwin P. *Transition to Democracy in Latin America: The Role of the Judiciary.* Boulder, CO: Westview Press, 1993. 401 p. Bibl. ISBN 0813384567.

This evaluation of the role of the judiciary in Latin America's democratic governments focuses on Argentina, Chile, Guatemala, and Haiti while also comparing U.S. and Latin American judicial systems and traditions. (OP)

Revolutions

1087. Castro, Daniel, ed. *Revolution and Revolutionaries: Guerrilla Movements in Latin America.* Wilmington, DE: SR Books, 1999. 236 p. (Jaguar books on Latin America; 17.) ISBN 0842026258.

This work presents the experience of guerrilla warfare as practiced by Zapatistas from the Mexican revolution, Nicaraguan Sandinistas, and Cuban revolutionaries.

1088. Hodges, Donald Clark. *Sandino's Communism: Spiritual Politics for the Twenty-First Century.* 1st ed. Austin, TX: University of Texas Press, 1992. 246 p. Bibl., index. ISBN 0292776578.

This examines the role of Sandino in the history of Latin American revolutions. Sandino is described as a "libertarian communist" who often distanced himself from avowed communists while trying to define his own philosophical position.

1089. Huggins, Martha Knisely. *Vigilantism and the State in Modern Latin America: Essays on Extralegal Violence.* New York: Praeger, 1991. 266 p. Bibl., index. ISBN 0275934764.

This volume deals with lynchings and popular justice, vigilantism and death squads, torture and extralegal police activities.

1090. Selbin, Eric. *Modern Latin American Revolutions.* 2nd ed. Boulder, CO: Westview Press, 1999. 236 p. Bibl., index. ISBN 0813335639 pbk.

This analysis of social revolutions in Bolivia, Cuba, Nicaragua, and Grenada after the 1950s examines the role of the individual in the revolutionary process, leadership, ideology, and strategy.

1091. Wickham-Crowley, Timothy P. *Guerrillas and Revolution in Latin America: A Comparative Study of Insurgents and Regimes Since 1956.* Princeton, NJ: Princeton University Press, 1992. 424 p. Bibl., ill., index. ISBN 0691078858.

This is an assessment of guerrilla insurgencies during the second half of the twentieth century.

1092. Wright, Thomas C. *Latin America in the Era of the Cuban Revolution.* New York: Praeger, 1991. 236 p. Bibl., ill., index. ISBN 0275935833.

This work surveys political reaction in Latin America to Castro's successful bid for power in Cuba.

U.S. Relations

1093. Black, George. *The Good Neighbor: How the United States Wrote the History of*

Central America and the Caribbean. 1st ed. New York: Pantheon Books, 1989. 200 p. Ill., index. ISBN.

This short, descriptive history of U.S. interventions in Central America and the Caribbean presents documentation of several U.S. actions. (OP)

1094. Black, Jan Knippers. *Sentinels of Empire: The United States and Latin American Militarism.* New York: Greenwood Press, 1986. 240 p. Bibl., index. (Contributions in political science; 144.) ISBN 031325155X.

This is a survey and indictment of U.S. policies and actions that have supported Latin American military governments in order to protect U.S. business interests.

1095. Carothers, Thomas. *In the Name of Democracy: U.S. Policy Toward Latin America in the Reagan Years.* Berkeley, CA: University of California Press, 1991. 309 p. ISBN 0520073193.

This is an assessment of U.S. policy toward the region in the 1980s.

1096. Dent, David W. *The Legacy of the Monroe Doctrine: A Reference Guide to U.S. Involvement in Latin America and the Caribbean.* Westport, CT: Greenwood Press, 1999. 418 p. Bibl., index. ISBN 0313301093.

This reference work presents a country-by-country introduction, with time line, to U.S.–Latin American relations.

1097. Gilderhus, Mark T. *The Second Century: U.S.–Latin American Relations Since 1889.* Wilmington, DE: SR Books, 2000. 282 p. Bibl., index. (Latin American silhouettes.) ISBN 0842024131.

This succinct summary of the issues and events that shaped U.S.–Latin American relations since the late 1880s also presents scholarly debates about the nature of the often conflictive relationship.

1098. Hartlyn, Jonathan et al., eds. *The United States and Latin America in the 1990s: Beyond the Cold War.* Chapel Hill, NC: University of North Carolina Press, 1992. 328 p. Bibl., ill., index. ISBN 0807820709.

This work examines post–cold war rela-

tions between the U.S. and its neighbors. Among the topics discussed are new actors and power configurations at the global, hemispheric and national levels, human rights, drug traffic, environmental politics, and migration.

1099. Johnson, John J. *A Hemisphere Apart: The Foundations of United States Policy Toward Latin America.* Baltimore, MD: Johns Hopkins University Press, 1990. 271 p. Bibl., index. (The Johns Hopkins symposia in comparative history.) ISBN 050183953X.

This analysis of the foundation of U.S. policy and attitudes toward Latin America examines the development of the relationship during the period 1815–1830. The basic question addressed is why the U.S. position changed from one that supported the independence insurgency to one of little interest in the affairs of the new republics.

1100. Johnson, John J. *Latin America in Caricature.* 1st pbk. ed. Austin, TX: University of Texas Press, 1993. 330 p. Bibl., ill., index. (The Texas Pan American series.) ISBN 029274031X.

This classic work explores U.S.–Latin American relations in the 1860s–1980s through political cartoons from U.S. media.

1101. Kryzanek, Michael J. *U.S.–Latin American Relations.* 3rd ed. Westport, CT: Praeger, 1996. 282 p. Bibl., ill., index. ISBN 0275950832.

This work examines the evolution of inter–American relations and emphasizes the players involved in the development and implementation of U.S. policy toward the region.

1102. Langley, Lester D. *America and the Americas: The United States in the Western Hemisphere.* Athens, GA: University of Georgia Press, 1989. 307 p. Bibl., index. (The United States and the Americas.) ISBN 0820311049.

This general history surveys inter–American relations from the colonial period through the Reagan presidency and includes a discussion of the cultural differences that separate the U.S. and Latin America.

1103. Musicant, Ivan. *The Banana Wars: A History of the United States Military Intervention in Latin America from the Spanish-American War to the Invasion of Panama.* New York: Macmillan Pub. Co. 1990. 470 p. Bibl., ill., index. ISBN 0025882104.

This volume explores the differences between dollar diplomacy and U.S. interventions in Central America and the Caribbean. (OP)

1104. Pike, Fredrick B. *FDR's Good Neighbor Policy: Sixty Years of Generally Gentle Chaos.* 1st ed. Austin, TX: University of Texas Press, 1995. 394 p. Bibl., ill., index. ISBN 0292765576.

This examines the origins and motives of the Good Neighbor policy toward Latin America during the last sixty years. According to the author, this successful policy bears responsibility for maintaining peace, order, and capitalist development in the hemisphere.

1105. Schoultz, Lars. *Beneath the United States: A History of U.S. Policy Toward Latin America.* Cambridge, MA: Harvard University Press, 1998. 476 p. Bibl., ill., index. ISBN 0674922751.

This comprehensive history of U.S. policy towards its southern neighbors argues that relations have always been affected by the U.S. perception that Latin America is culturally inferior and that this misperception continues to influence contemporary relations.

1106. Wesson, Robert G., and Heraldo Muñoz, eds. *Latin American Views of U.S. Policy.* New York: Praeger, 1986. 153 p. (Politics in Latin America.) ISBN 0030067146.

This representative sample of essays by Latin American scholars whose concern is furthering economic development is in stark contrast with their U.S. counterparts who focus on political issues and security matters.

Argentina

1107. Arditti, Rita. *Searching for Life: The Grandmothers of the Plaza de Mayo and the Disappeared Children of Argentina.* Berkeley,

CA: University of California Press, 1999. 235 p. Bibl., ill., index. ISBN 0520211138.

This is the history of the grandmothers of the Plaza de Mayo who demanded that the government provide answers to the disappearances of loved ones during the "dirty war," between 1976–1983.

1108. Di Tella, Guido, and Donald Cameron Watt, eds. *Argentina Between the Great Powers, 1939–46.* Pittsburgh, PA: University of Pittsburgh Press, 1990. 212 p. Bibl., ill., index. (Pitt Latin American series.) ISBN 0822911590.

Argentina's international relations during World War II are the focus of these essays. (OP)

1109. Dujovne Ortiz, Alicia. *Eva Perón.* 1st ed. Translated by Shawn Fields. New York: St. Martin's Press, 1996. 325 p. Ill., index. ISBN 0312145993.

This balanced view of this important Argentine figure places her in a national and international setting.

1110. Guest, Iain. *Behind the Disappearances: Argentina's Dirty War Against Human Rights and the United Nations.* Philadelphia: University of Pennsylvania Press, 1990. 605 p. Bibl., index. (Pennsylvania studies in human rights.) ISBN 0812282043.

This analyzes Argentina's international activities in the realm of military government sponsored human rights abuses in 1976–1983. (OP)

1111. Gustafson, Lowell S. *The Sovereignty Dispute over the Falkland (Malvinas) Islands.* New York: Oxford University Press, 1988. 268 p. Bibl., index. ISBN 0195041844.

This volume presents the historical background for Great Britain and Argentina's claims of sovereignty and self-determination of the Falkland (Malvinas) Islands.

1112. Hodges, Donald Clark. *Argentina's "Dirty War": An Intellectual Biography.* 1st ed. Austin, TX: University of Texas Press, 1991. 387 p. ISBN 0292704232.

This work traces the origin of the "dirty war" by examining the foundations of the major political parties and military movements. (OP)

1113. Ivereigh, Austen. *Catholicism and Politics in Argentina, 1810–1960.* New York: Macmillan Pub. Co. 1995. 275 p. Bibl., index. ISBN 0312124546.

This is a study of Argentine church-state debates, actions, and policy from the early nineteenth century to the end of the 1950s.

1114. Munck, Ronaldo, Ricardo Falcón, and Bernardo Galitelli. *Argentina, from Anarchism to Peronism: Workers, Unions, and Politics, 1855–1985.* Atlantic Highlands, NJ: Zed Books, 1987. 261 p. Bibl. ISBN 0862325706.

This is a history of the Argentine labor movements from the founding of the First International in Argentina in 1872 to their transformation under Perón and his heirs.

1115. Newton, Ronald C. *The "Nazi menace" in Argentina, 1931–1947.* Stanford, CA: Stanford University Press, 1992. 520 p. Bibl., ill., index. ISBN 0804719292.

This overview of the German community of Buenos Aires in 1900–1933 examines the changes within the community as Hitler rises to power including Nazi intentions in Argentina and U.S.–Western European overreaction to a perceived Nazi threat.

1116. Norden, Deborah L. *Military Rebellion in Argentina: Between Coups and Consolidation.* Lincoln, NE: University of Nebraska Press, 1996. 242 p. Bibl., index. ISBN 0803233396.

This volume examines the civil-military relationship in Argentina as the civilian governments of R. Alfonsín and C. Menem attempt to build democratic institutions during the 1980s.

1117. Smith, William C. *Authoritarianism and the Crisis of the Argentine Political Economy.* Stanford, CA: Stanford University Press, 1989. 395 p. Bibl., index. ISBN 0804716722.

This analysis of Argentina's failure to achieve economic and political stability covers the Onganía government of the 1960s to the Alfonsín presidency of the 1980s.

1118. Snow, Peter G., and Luigi Manzetti. *Political Forces in Argentina.* 3rd ed. Westport, CT: Praeger, 1993. 201 p. Bibl., ill., index. ISBN 0275933849.

This revised and updated edition describes and analyses the role played by the political parties, armed forces, labor unions, Catholic Church, and students in Argentine politics since 1979.

1119. Tulchin, Joseph S. *Argentina and the United States: A Conflicted Relationship.* New York: Twayne, 1990. 193 p. Bibl., ill., index. (Twayne's international history series; 5.) ISBN 0805779000.

While this work is primarily a historical account of the benign neglect of U.S. policy towards Argentina over time, it focuses on the Reagan years and includes Argentina's confrontational posture and unrealistic understanding of world affairs. (OP)

1120. Wynia, Gary W. *Argentina: Illusions and Realities.* 2nd ed. New York: Holmes & Meier, 1992. 240 p. Bibl., index. ISBN 0841912963 pbk.

This is an analysis of major Argentine political issues from 1973, when Perón returned to power, through the Falklands conflict and Raúl Alfonsín's election in 1983.

Bolivia

1121. Guevara, Ernesto. *The Bolivian Diary of Ernesto Che Guevara.* 1st ed. Edited by Mary-Alice Waters. New York: Pathfinder, 1994. 467 p. Bibl., ill., index. ISBN 0873487672.

This volume details Che Guevara's participation in the guerrilla war of the Bolivian altiplano in 1966.

1122. Malloy, James M., and Eduardo Gamarra. *Revolution and Reaction: Bolivia, 1964–1985.* New Brunswick, NJ: Transaction Books, 1988. 244 p. Bibl., index. ISBN 0887381596.

This survey analyzes Bolivian political personalities and public policy events. (OP)

1123. Prado Salmón, Gary. *The Defeat of Che Guevara: Military Response to Guerrilla Challenge in Bolivia.* Translated by John Deredita. New York: Praeger, 1990. 288 p. Bibl., ill. ISBN 0275932117.

This is an account of the capture and demise of Guevara in Bolivia in 1967. The author is the captain of the unit that captured him.

Brazil

1124. Alexander, Robert Jackson. *Juscelino Kubitschek and the Development of Brazil.* Athens, OH: Ohio University, Center for International Studies, 1991. 429 p. Bibl., ill. (Monographs in international studies. Latin America series; 16.) ISBN 0896801632 pbk.

This is a biography of Brazil's first developmentalist president whose objective was to industrialize the economy with the state as a prominent player. (OP)

1125. Barman, Roderick J. *Brazil: The Forging of a Nation, 1798–1852.* Stanford, CA: Stanford University Press, 1988. 334 p. Bibl., ill., index. ISBN 0804714371.

This interpretive study of the formation of modern Brazil covers the colony to imperial nation-state; development of an autonomous identity; process of state formation; and politics at the national level after independence in 1822.

1126. Catholic Church. Archdiocese of São Paulo, Brazil. *Torture in Brazil: A Shocking Report on the Pervasive Use of Torture by Brazilian Military Governments, 1964–1979.* Austin, TX: University of Texas Press, 1998. 238 p. (ILAS special publication.) ISBN 0292704844 pbk.

This document relies upon official proceedings of the military courts that reveal the systematic abduction, torture, and murder of Brazilians suspected of subversive activities.

1127. Dulles, John W. F. *Carlos Lacerda, Brazilian Crusader.* 1st ed. Austin, TX: University of Texas Press, 1991–1996. 2 vols. Bibl., ill., index. ISBN 029271-

Lacerda is among Brazil's most influential twentieth century politicians. This work recounts his radical family background and communist youth. Vol. 1 covers 1914–1960 (-1255); vol. 2 covers 1960–1977 (-5811).

1128. Hilton, Stanley E. *Brazil and the Soviet Challenge, 1917–1947.* Austin, TX: University of Texas Press, 1991. 287 p. Bibl., ill., index. ISBN 0292707819.

This volume argues that the modern Brazilian state was shaped by fear of Soviet communism.

1129. Levine, Robert M. *Father of the Poor?: Vargas and His Era.* New York: Cambridge University Press, 1998. 193 p. Bibl., ill., index. (New approaches to the Americas.) ISBN 0521585155.

This work examines the life, legacy, and times of Getûlio Vargas, Brazilian dictator and president from 1930–1954.

1130. Mainwaring, Scott. *The Catholic Church and Politics in Brazil, 1916–1985.* Stanford, CA: Stanford University Press, 1986. 328 p. Bibl., index. ISBN 0804713200.

This study of the political role of the Catholic church in Brazil argues that it is the most progressive in the world. (OP)

1131. Schneider, Ronald M. *Order and Progress: A Political History of Brazil.* Boulder, CO: Westview Press, 1991. 486 p. Bibl., ill., index. ISBN 0813310776.

This political history of Brazil covers the nineteenth century to the present. (OP)

1132. Selcher, Wayne A., ed. *Political Liberalization in Brazil: Dynamics, Dilemmas, and Future Prospects.* Boulder, CO: Westview Press, 1986. 272 p. Index. (Westview special studies on Latin America and the Caribbean.) ISBN 0813302633: pbk.

This collection of essays analyzes the process of political opening and restoration of democracy in Brazil since 1985. (OP)

1133. Skidmore, Thomas E. *The Politics of Military Rule in Brazil, 1964–85.* New York:

Oxford University Press, 1988. 420 p. Bibl., ill., index. ISBN 0195038983.

This volume examines the political and economic policies of Brazil's military regime.

Caribbean Area

1134. Black, Jan Knippers. *The Dominican Republic: Politics and Development in an Unsovereign State.* Boston: Allen & Unwin, 1986. 164 p. Bibl., ill., index. ISBN 0044970005.

This describes the political life of the Dominican Republic by examining its historical background and socioeconomic structures. (OP)

1135. Collin, Richard H. *Theodore Roosevelt's Caribbean: The Panama Canal, the Monroe Doctrine, and the Latin American Context.* Baton Rouge, LA: Louisiana State University Press, 1990. 598 p. Bibl., index. ISBN 080711507X.

This work focuses on Roosevelt's policies toward the Caribbean before World War I as the U.S. was extending its influence as a world rather than a regional power.

1136. Domínguez, Jorge I., Robert A. Pastor, and R. D. Worrell, eds. *Democracy in the Caribbean: Political, Economic, and Social Perspectives.* Baltimore, MD: Johns Hopkins University Press, 1993. 312 p. Bibl., ill., index. (A World Peace Foundation study.) ISBN 0801844509.

This collection of essays describes the democratic tradition in the Caribbean and discusses current destabilizing forces.

1137. Heine, Jorge, and Leslie Manigat, eds. *The Caribbean and World Politics: Cross Currents and Cleavages.* New York: Holmes & Meier, 1988. 385 p. Bibl., index. ISBN 0841910006.

These essays, written by Caribbeanists, focus on the international relations of the area in 1960–1980s.

1138. Hillman, Richard S., and Thomas J. D'Agostino. *Distant Neighbors in the Caribbean: The Dominican Republic and Jamaica in Comparative Perspective.* New York: Praeger, 1992. 197 p. Bibl., ill., index. ISBN 0275939278.

This summarizes the political history and traditions of the Dominican Republic and Jamaica.

1139. Lewis, Gordon K. *Grenada: The Jewel Despoiled.* Baltimore, MD: Johns Hopkins University Press, 1987. 239 p. Index. ISBN 0801834228.

This is an analysis of the Grenadian revolution, including its achievements and mistakes, and U.S. intervention. (OP)

1140. MacDonald, Scott B. *Trinidad and Tobago: Democracy and Development in the Caribbean.* New York: Praeger, 1986. 231 p. Bibl., index. ISBN 0275920046.

This reviews the evolution of Trinidadian politics from the post-colonial nineteenth century through the 1980s.

1141. Maingot, Anthony P. *The United States and the Caribbean: Challenges of an Asymmetrical Relationship.* Boulder, CO: Westview Press, 1994. 260 p. Bibl., index. ISBN 0813322421.

This survey of modern U.S.-Caribbean relations focuses on the period since the end of the cold war.

1142. Palmer, Ransford W., ed. *The Repositioning of U.S.-Caribbean Relations in the New World Order.* Westport, CT: Praeger, 1997. 222 p. Bibl., index. ISBN 0275958582.

This historical overview of the Caribbean includes a discussion of U.S.-Caribbean relations. The focus is on the contemporary period as these nations adjust to globalization.

Central America

1143. Anderson, Thomas P. *Politics in Central America: Guatemala, El Salvador, Honduras, and Nicaragua.* Rev. ed. New York: Praeger, 1988. 256 p. Bibl., index. ISBN 0275928055.

This historical chronology also includes a social and political overview of the four countries in the region during the second half of the twentieth century.

1144. Berryman, Phillip. *Stubborn Hope: Religion, Politics, and Revolution in Central America.* Maryknoll, NY: Orbis Books, 1994. 276 p. Bibl., index. ISBN 0883449625.

This examines Christian participation (leftist church workers, liberation theologists, and rightists evangelicals) in the revolutions of El Salvador, Guatemala, and Nicaragua. (OP)

1145. Booth, John A., and Mitchell A. Seligson, eds. *Elections and Democracy in Central America, Revisited.* New & enl. ed. Chapel Hill, NC: University of North Carolina Press, 1995. 299 p. Bibl., ill., index. ISBN 0807822329.

This work analyzes the level of democratic participation achieved in all five Central American countries after recent successful popular elections.

1146. Ferris, Elizabeth G. *The Central American Refugees.* New York: Praeger, 1987. 159 p. Index. ISBN 0275922219.

This volume presents the foreign and refugee policies of Mexico, Costa Rica, Honduras, Nicaragua, and the U.S.

1147. Goodman, Louis W. et al., eds. *Political Parties and Democracy in Central America.* Boulder, CO: Westview Press, 1992. 407 p. Bibl., index. ISBN 0813382424.

Twenty essays by U.S. Central American, Mexican, and European scholars examine the regional crisis (including Belize and Panama) within its international context beginning with the fall of Somoza in 1979. (OP)

1148. La Feber, Walter. *Inevitable Revolutions: The United States in Central America.* 2nd ed. New York: W.W. Norton, 1993. 452 p. Bibl., ill., index. ISBN 0393034348.

This work analyzes Washington's diplomatic track record in Central America and its profound involvement in shaping Central American history.

1149. LeoGrande, William M. *Our Own Backyard: The United States in Central America, 1977–1992.* Chapel Hill, NC: University of Carolina Press, 1998. 773 p. Bibl., ill., index. ISBN 0807823953.

This is a detailed analysis of the execution of U.S. policy in Central America during the Reagan administration.

1150. Leonard, Thomas M. *Central America and the United States: The Search for Stability.* Athens, GA: University of Georgia Press, 1991. 245 p. Bibl., ill., index. (The United States and the Americas.) ISBN 0820313203.

This overview of the history of U.S.–Central American relations argues that the 1980s crisis has historical roots. Since the 1820s, U.S. policy has sought to maintain the status quo by aligning itself with the ruling elite.

1151. Liss, Sheldon B. *Radical Thought in Central America.* Boulder, CO: Westview Press, 1991. 290 p. Ill., index. (Latin American perspectives series; 7.) ISBN 0813382084.

This work presents brief biographies of twenty-one Central American intellectuals whose thought and praxis illustrate the diversity of leftist philosophy. Among them are Rubén Darío, Augusto César Sandino, Graciela García, Farabundo Martí, Roque Dalton, Ernesto Cardenal, and Jaime Wheelock. (OP)

1152. Moreno, Darío. *The Struggle for Peace in Central America.* Gainesville, FL: University of Florida Press, 1994. 251 p. Bibl., index. ISBN 0813012740.

This political history combines research with personal interviews that describe the influence of the U.S. on its Central American neighbors.

1153. Schoonover, Thomas David. *The United States in Central America, 1860–1911: Episodes of Social Imperialism and Imperial Rivalry in the World System.* Durham, NC: Duke University Press, 1991. 253 p. Bibl., index. ISBN 0822311607.

This volume includes eight interpretive essays on U.S.–Central American relations.

The analysis relies primarily on non–U.S. documents to draw its conclusions.

1154. Walker, Thomas W., and Ariel C. Armony, eds. *Repression, Resistance, and Democratic Transition in Central America.* Wilmington, DE: SR Books, 2000. 301 p. Bibl., ill., index. ISBN 0842027661.

This is an analysis of the major forces shaping recent Central American political history. Its focus is the process of revolt and revolution as motors of political change in the region.

1155. Williams, Philip J. *The Catholic Church and Politics in Nicaragua and Costa Rica.* Pittsburgh, PA: University of Pittsburgh Press, 1989. 228 p. Bibl., ill., index. (Pitt Latin American series.) ISBN 0822911558.

This work details the activities in the realm of politics by the Catholic Church of Nicaragua and Costa Rica.

Chile

1156. Bitar, Sergio. *Chile: Experiment in Democracy.* Translated by Sam Sherman. Philadelphia: Institute for the Study of Human Issues, 1986. 243 p. Bibl., index. (Inter-American politics series; 6.) ISBN 0897270622.

This in-depth reassessment of the Allende regime's road to socialism includes its economic characteristics, objectives and strategies, and the rapidly changing political environment. (OP)

1157. Cockcroft, James D., ed. *Salvador Allende Reader: Chile's Voice of Democracy.* Translated by M. Espinoza and N. Nuñez. New York: Ocean, 2000. 287 p. Bibl., ill. ISBN 1876175249.

This is a collection of Salvador Allende's speeches and interviews from 1970 to 1973 during his turbulent presidency.

1158. Constable, Pamela, and Arturo Valenzuela. *A Nation of Enemies: Chile Under Pinochet.* 1st ed. New York: W.W. Norton, 1991. 367 p. Ill., index. ISBN 0393030013.

This rigorous examination of the Pinochet regime is based on interviews with Chileans of all backgrounds and political views.

1159. Drake, Paul, and Iván Jaksiac, eds. *The struggle for Democracy in Chile.* Rev. ed. Lincoln, NE: University of Nebraska Press, 1995. 358 p. ISBN 0803266006.

This work deals with Chilean politics, 1970–1992, and presents views of proponents and opponents of the Pinochet regime. It also examines the breakdown of the military regime through the restoration of democracy.

1160. Faúndez, Julio. *Marxism and Democracy in Chile: From 1932 to the Fall of Allende.* New Haven, CT: Yale University Press, 1988. 305 p. Bibl., index. ISBN 0300040245.

This is an overview of the participation by the Socialist and Communist parties in twentieth century Chilean politics.

1161. Garretón Merino, Manuel A. *The Chilean Political Process.* Translated by Sharon Kellum and Gilbert Merkx. Boston: Unwin Hyman, 1989. 220 p. Bibl., index. (Thematic studies in Latin America.) ISBN 0044970684.

This work summarizes the Chilean political process through 1973, the military regimes of the Southern Cone since the 1960s, and the evolution of the Chilean military government. (OP)

1162. Kaufman, Edy. *Crisis in Allende's Chile: New Perspectives.* New York: Praeger, 1988. 376 p. Bibl., ill., index. ISBN 0275928225.

The author examines international and domestic influences at work during the last weeks of the Popular Unity regime including the effect of long-term structural processes upon events in Chile at the time.

1163. Lowden, Pamela. *Moral Opposition to Authoritarian Rule in Chile, 1973–90.* New York: St. Martin's Press, 1996. 216 p. Bibl., index. (St. Antony's series.) ISBN 031215870X.

This volume focuses on the organized activities of the Catholic Church's Vicariate of Solidarity against the abuses of the Pinochet dictatorship.

1164. Oppenheim, Lois Hecht. *Politics in Chile: Democracy, Authoritarianism, and the Search for Development.* 2nd ed. Boulder, CO: Westview Press, 1998. 304 p. Bibl., index. ISBN 0813335655.

This volume traces political changes in Chile beginning with the Allende period in the early 1970s through the military regime. It concludes with the consolidation of democracy in the 1980–1990s.

1165. Pollack, Benny, and Hernán Rosenkranz-Schikler. *Revolutionary Social Democracy: The Chilean Socialist Party.* New York: St. Martin's Press, 1986. 234 p. Bibl., index. ISBN 0312680317.

This is a study of Chile's Socialist Party including its history, composition, leadership, and organization before and under military rule. (OP)

1166. Sater, William F. *Chile and the United States: Empires in Conflict.* Athens, GA: University of Georgia Press, 1990. 249 p. Bibl., index. (The United States and the Americas.) ISBN 0820312495.

This is the history of U.S.-Chilean relations from the nineteenth century through the 1980s.

1167. Scully, Timothy. *Rethinking the Center: Party Politics in Nineteenth- and Twentieth-Century Chile.* Stanford, CA: Stanford University Press, 1992. 287 p. Bibl., index. ISBN 0804719136.

This work highlights the historical continuities and discontinuities of Chilean politics focusing on centrist parties during the 1870–1950s.

Colombia

1168. Bergquist, Charles W. et al., eds. *Violence in Colombia: The Contemporary Crisis in Historical Perspective.* Wilmington, DE: SR Books, 1992. 337 p. Bibl., ill., index. (Latin American silhouettes.) ISBN 0842023690.

These essays examine Colombia's political and social history and emphasize the violence that has characterized its society for the past 150 years. Traditional explanations are questioned and the result is a proposal for rewriting Colombian history since independence.

1169. Dix, Robert H. *The Politics of Colombia.* New York: Praeger, 1987. 247 p. Bibl., ill., index. (Politics in Latin America.) ISBN 0275923150.

This work is an assessment of major political changes in Colombia since 1967.

1170. García Márquez, Gabriel. *News of a Kidnapping.* 1st American ed. Translated by Edith Grossman. New York: Knopf, 1997. 291 p. ISBN 0375400516.

This journalistic chronology of the events of 1993–94, when several prominent Colombian figures were kidnapped by members of the Colombian drug cartel, also presents an overview of contemporary Colombian society.

1171. Giraldo, Javier. *Colombia: The Genocidal Democracy.* Monroe, ME: Common Courage Press, 1996. 125 p. ISBN 1567510876.

This work exposes the relationship between human rights abuses and the Colombian drug trade.

1172. Kline, Harvey F. *State Building and Conflict Resolution in Colombia, 1986–1994.* Tuscaloosa, AL: University of Alabama Press, 1999. 240 p. Bibl., index. ISBN 0817309438.

This volume examines recent efforts by Colombian governments to overcome numerous and complex obstacles to create a stable and democratic state.

1173. Randall, Stephen J. *Colombia and the United States: Hegemony and Interdependence.* Athens, GA: University of Georgia Press, 1992. 325 p. Bibl., index. (The United States and the Americas.) ISBN 0820314013.

This describes the two-way relationship between Colombia and the U.S. since the beginning of the twentieth century. While the U.S. may have focused on common strategic interests, economic ties and ideological solidarity, Colombia successfully has resisted dependency.

1174. Zamosc, León. *The Agrarian Question and the Peasant Movement in Colombia, 1967–1981.* New York: Cambridge University Press, 1986. 289 p. Bibl., ill., index. (Cambridge Latin American studies; 58.) ISBN 0521320100.

This is a study of the evolution of a nascent national peasant movement in Colombia. The movement was initially reformist, became radical-revolutionary, and eventually reached a clientelist phase.

Costa Rica

1175. Booth, John A. *Costa Rica: Quest for Democracy.* Boulder, CO: Westview Press, 1998. 230 p. Bibl., ill., index. (Nations of the modern world. Latin America.) ISBN 0813376319.

This examines the breadth and depth of Costa Rica's democracy and focuses on the evolution of political participation and attitudes during the last twenty years.

1176. Honey, Martha. *Hostile Acts: U.S. Policy in Costa Rica in the 1980s.* Gainesville, FL: University of Florida Press, 1994. 640 p. Ill. ISBN 081301249X.

This chronicles regional events during the 1980s including the Reagan administration's Central American policy.

1177. Rolbein, Seth. *Nobel Costa Rica: A Timely Report on Our Peaceful Pro–Yankee, Central American Neighbor.* 1st ed. New York: St. Martin's Press, 1989. 253 p. Bibl. ISBN 031202262X.

This brief political history of Costa Rica includes contributions by Oscar Arias and José Figueres to their country's peaceful coexistence with neighbors in a turmoil-filled region. (OP)

Cuba

1178. Abel, Christopher, and Nissa Torrents, eds. *José Martí, Revolutionary Democrat.*

Durham, NC: Duke University Press, 1986. 238 p. Bibl., index. ISBN 0822306794.

This examines the contemporary significance of Martí's literary works and those expressing his political ideas. Martí's writings address issues of Cuban independence and its relationship with Spain and the U.S. (OP)

1179. Blight, James G. et al. *Cuba on the Brink: Castro, the Missile Crisis, and the Soviet Collapse.* New York: Pantheon Books, 1993. 509 p. Bibl., index. ISBN 0679421491.

This is an analysis of Cuban-U.S. relations from colonial times to the present. It contains extensive transcripts and observations regarding the Cuban missile crisis. (OP)

1180. Cabrera Infante, Guillermo. *Mea Cuba.* Translated by Kenneth Hall. New York: Farrar, Straus, Giroux, 1994. 503 p. ISBN 0374204977.

This collection of essays by one of Cuba's most renowned, self-exiled authors, critiques Castro's authoritarian policies.

1181. Castañeda, Jorge G. *Compañero: The Life and Death of Che Guevara.* Translated by Marina Castañeda. New York: Knopf, 1997. 457 p. Ill., index. ISBN 0679440348.

This work contains extensive details about Che's life as it sheds light on his contributions to Cuban and international affairs.

1182. Córdova, Efrén. *Castro and the Cuban Labor Movement: Statecraft and Society in a Revolutionary Period (1959–1961).* Lanham, MD: University Press of America, 1987. 341 p. Bibl., index. ISBN 0819159522.

This volume examines the labor movement and Castro's policies during the regime's early years. (OP)

1183. Domínguez, Jorge I. *To Make a World Safe for Revolution: Cuba's Foreign Policy.* New York: Harvard University Press, 1989. 365 p. Bibl., index. ISBN 0674893255.

This is a thematic survey of Cuba's foreign policy between 1979 and 1988.

1184. Domínguez, Jorge I., and Rafael Hernández, eds. *U.S.-Cuban Relations in the*

1990s. Boulder, CO: Westview Press, 1989. 324 p. Bibl., index. ISBN 0813308836.

This work examines prospects for improved relations between the U.S. and Cuba from binational perspectives. Issues such as national security and foreign policy, economic relations, and international law provide the backdrop for the studies. (OP)

1185. Fernández Revuelta, Alina. *Castro's Daughter: An Exile's Memoir of Cuba.* 1st US ed. Translated by Dolores M. Koch. New York: St. Martin's Press, 1998. 259 p. ISBN 0312193084.

Fidel Castro's daughter, one of his harshest critics, provides insights about everyday life in contemporary Cuba.

1186. Foss, Clive. *Fidel Castro.* Stroud, Gloucestershire: Sutton, 2000. 128 p. Ill. (Sutton brief biographies.) ISBN 0750923849.

This work presents a balanced account of one of the most enduring political figures of the hemisphere.

1187. Guevara, Ernesto. *Che Guevara Reader: Writings by Ernesto Che Guevara on Guerrilla Strategy, Politics & Revolution.* Edited by David Deutschmann. New York: Ocean Press, 1997. 400 p. Bibl., ill., index. ISBN 1875284931.

This representative compilation of Guevara's writings, mostly about his political economic philosophy, includes accounts of the Cuban insurrection, important speeches of his years in Cuba, and personal letters.

1188. Jordan, David C. *Revolutionary Cuba and the End of the Cold War.* Lanham, MD: University Press of America, 1993. 276 p. Bibl., ill., index. ISBN 0819189987.

This presents an overview of Cuban affairs since the end of the cold war.

1189. Kirk, John M. *Between God and the Party: Religion and Politics in Revolutionary Cuba.* Tampa, FL: University of South Florida Press, 1989. 231 p. Bibl., ill., index. ISBN 081300909X pbk.

This is a comprehensive survey of relations between the Catholic Church and the state in Castro's Cuba. (OP)

1190. Liss, Sheldon B. *Fidel!: Castro's Political and Social Thought.* Boulder, CO: Westview Press, 1994. 246 p. Bibl., index. (Latin American perspectives series; 13.) ISBN 0813386780.

This work analyzes Castro's political and social philosophy, based on studies of his writings and speeches.

1191. Oppenheimer, Andrés. *Castro's Final Hour: The Secret Story Behind the Coming Downfall of Communist Cuba.* New York: Simon & Schuster, 1996. 461 p. Bibl., ill., index. ISBN 0671728733.

This is a behind-the-scenes account of Castro's Cuba since the Soviet Union's withdrawal of economic subsidies. It is based on more than 500 interviews of individuals close to the government and those who oppose it.

1192. Paterson, Thomas G. *Contesting Castro: The United States and the Triumph of the Cuban Revolution.* New York: Oxford University Press, 1994. 352 p. Bibl., ill., index. ISBN 0195086309.

This is a reexamination of Cuban-U.S. relations during the insurrection against Batista and the role of the U.S. in Castro's rise to power.

1193. Pérez, Louis A. *Cuba and the United States: Ties of Singular Intimacy.* 2nd ed. Athens, GA: University of Georgia Press, 1997. 322 p. Bibl., ill., index. (The United States and the Americas.) ISBN 0820319368.

This analyzes the uneasy reciprocity between Cuba and the U.S. for more than two hundred years.

1194. Pérez-Stable, Marifeli. *The Cuban Revolution: Origins, Course, and Legacy.* 2nd ed. New York: Oxford University Press, 1998. 288 p. Bibl., index. ISBN 0195127498.

This work presents a comprehensive analysis of the failures and successes of the Cuban revolution through several fundamental characteristics: U.S. influence; the labor movement; monoculture sugar economy; political leadership crisis; and unbalanced modernization.

1195. Quirk, Robert E. *Fidel Castro.* 1st ed. New York: Norton, 1993. 898 p. Ill., index. ISBN 0393034852.

This lengthy volume presents a historical interpretation of Castro's complex life and times including his personal rise to power, the failures of the Cuban revolution, and the regime's recent difficulties.

1196. Rodríguez, Ana, and Glenn Garvin. *Diary of a Survivor: Nineteen Years in a Cuban Women's Prison.* 1st ed. New York: St. Martin's Press, 1995. 325 p. Index. ISBN 0312130503.

This is a documentary story-memoir of a Cuban political prisoner's life behind bars.

Ecuador

1197. Spindler, Frank MacDonald. *Nineteenth Century Ecuador: A Historical Introduction.* Fairfax, VA: George Mason University Press, 1987. 285 p. Bibl., ill., index. ISBN 0802600158.

This volume describes the nineteenth century political evolution of Ecuador emphasizing the conflict between liberals and conservatives regarding ecclesiastic and economic development issues.

El Salvador

1198. Byrne, Hugh. *El Salvador's Civil War: A Study of Revolution.* Boulder, CO: Lynne Rienner Publishers, 1996. 242 p. Bibl., ill., index. ISBN 1555876064.

This work explores the reasons for El Salvador's revolution and the profound role of the U.S. in strategies adopted by the Salvadoran government and insurgency. Declassified U.S. and FSLN documents and interviews support this analysis.

1199. Doggett, Martha. *Death Foretold: The Jesuit Murders in El Salvador.* Washington, DC: Georgetown University Press, 1993. 358 p. Ill., index. ISBN 0878405453.

This report summarizes the crime and evaluates its handling by the Salvadoran legal system including the role of the U.S. in the case.

1200. Duarte, José Napoleón, and Diana Page. *Duarte: My Story.* New York: Putnam, 1986. 284 p. Ill. ISBN 0399132023.

This surveys Duarte's personal views about Salvadoran politics including relations with the U.S. (OP)

1201. Hutchinson, Bill. *When the Dogs Ate Candles: A Time in El Salvador.* Niwot, CO: University Press of Colorado, 1998. 229 p. Bibl., ill., index. ISBN 0870814753.

This personalized account of human rights abuses of the civilian population by the Salvadoran military and death squads in the 1970–1980s also condemns U.S. government policy towards El Salvador.

1202. Montgomery, Tommie Sue. *Revolution in El Salvador: From Civil Strife to Civil Peace.* 2nd ed. Boulder, CO: Westview Press, 1995. 344 p. Bibl., ill., index. ISBN 0813300703.

This work examines the history of the war in El Salvador through the peace accords of 1992, considering factors such as the roles of the U.S., the Salvadoran Catholic Church and the political-military strategy of the FMLN.

Guatemala

1203. Dosal, Paul J. *Doing Business with the Dictators: A Political History of United Fruit in Guatemala, 1899–1944.* Wilmington, DE: SR Books, 1993. 256 p. Bibl., ill., index. (Latin American silhouettes.) ISBN 0842024751.

This is the history of the United Fruit Co. in Guatemala from 1899 to 1944, its involvement in Guatemalan politics, and U.S.-Guatemalan relations.

1204. Gleijeses, Piero. *Shattered Hope: The Guatemalan Revolution and the United States, 1944–1954.* Princeton, NJ: Princeton University Press, 1991. 430 p. Bibl., ill., index. ISBN 0691078173.

The region's first revolution was eventually subjected to U.S. intervention that contributed to its eventual downfall.

1205. Manz, Beatriz. *Refugees of a Hidden War: The Aftermath of Counterinsurgency in Guatemala.* Albany, NY: State University of New York Press, 1988. 283 p. Bibl., ill. (SUNY series in anthropological studies of contemporary issues.) ISBN 0887066755.

This is a chronicle of the tragic human effects of militarism and war in Guatemala.

1206. Painter, James. *Guatemala: False Hope, False Freedom: The Rich, the Poor, and the Christian Democrats.* Upd. ed. New York: Distribution by Monthly Review Press, 1989. 167 p. Bibl., ill., index. ISBN 0906156416.

This is a Catholic left polemic against the government of Guatemala. It argues that Christian Democrats will not be able to introduce necessary radical reforms while the military remains undisciplined.

1207. Schwantes, V. David. *Guatemala: A Cry from the Heart.* Minneapolis, MN: Health Initiatives Press, 1990. 218 p. Bibl., ill. ISBN 096250663X.

This analyzes U.S. involvement in Guatemala from political, ideological, economic, and moral perspectives. (OP)

1208. Trudeau, Robert H. *Guatemalan Politics: The Popular Struggle for Democracy.* Boulder, CO: L. Rienner Publishers, 1993. 220 p. Bibl., index. ISBN 1555874150.

This work examines Guatemala's formal transition to democracy in 1986 within the context of the region's movement toward constitutional regimes.

Haiti

1209. Abbott, Elizabeth. *Haiti: The Duvaliers and Their Legacy.* Rev. upd. 1st Touchstone ed. New York: Simon & Schuster, 1991. 402 p. Bibl., ill., index. ISBN 0671686208.

This is a detailed examination of the Duvalier dictatorships from 1957–1986. (OP)

1210. Aristide, Jean-Bertrand. *Dignity.* Translated by Carrol F. Coates. Charlottesville, VA: University Press of Virginia, 1996. 210 p. Bibl. ISBN 0813916747.

This work presents Aristide's political and humanitarian philosophy.

1211. Dupuy, Alex. *Haiti in the New World Order: The Limits of the Democratic Revolution.* Boulder, CO: Westview Press, 1997. 220 p. Bibl., index. ISBN 0813321131.

This analysis of Haiti's contemporary situation exposes the inability of the Haitian left to organize and present alternative policies while the Aristide regime is unable to implement its government program.

1212. Shacochis, Bob. *The Immaculate Invasion.* New York: Viking, 1999. 408 p. Index. ISBN 0670863041.

This chronicles the vagaries of "Operation Other than War" in Haiti as U.S. forces sought to support Haitian efforts to establish a new government.

1213. Shannon, Magdaline W. *Jean Price-Mars, the Haitian Elite and the American Occupation, 1915–1935.* New York: St. Martin's Press, 1996. 186 p. Bibl., index. ISBN 0312160372.

This historical background to the U.S. occupation of Haiti during the early part of the twentieth century also explores the reaction of Haitian intellectuals to the intervention.

1214. Stotzky, Irwin P. *Silencing the Guns in Haiti: The Promise of Deliberative Democracy.* Chicago: University of Chicago Press, 1997. 294 p. Bibl., ill., index. ISBN 0226776263.

This volume examines Haiti's difficult transition to representative government including the historical background of its numerous dictatorships.

1215. Trouillot, Michel-Rolph. *Haiti, State Against Nation: The Origins and Legacy of Duvalierism.* New York: Monthly Review Press, 1990. 282 p. Bibl., ill. ISBN 0853457557.

This work discusses the historical evolution of Haiti as background for understanding the rise of Duvalierism. (OP)

Honduras

1216. Euraque, Darío A. *Reinterpreting the Banana Republic: Region and State in Honduras, 1870–1972.* Chapel Hill, NC: University of North Carolina Press, 1996. 242 p. Bibl., ill., index. ISBN 080784604X.

This is an examination of the role of elites in Honduran politics including the evolution and role of the new bourgeoisie.

1217. Rosenberg, Mark, and Philip L. Shepherd, eds. *Honduras Confronts Its Future: Contending Perspectives on Critical Issues.* Boulder, CO: L. Rienner Publishers, 1986. 268 p. Bibl., index. ISBN 093147745X.

This collection of essays covers the contemporary Honduran political situation in its socioeconomic context. (OP)

1218. Schulz, Donald E., and Deborah Sundloff Schulz. *The United States, Honduras, and the Crisis in Central America.* Boulder, CO: Westview Press, 1994. 367 p. Bibl., ill., index. (Thematic studies in Latin America.) ISBN 0813313244.

The authors analyze U.S. and Honduras's role in the Central American crisis of the 1980s. Also presented are the features that distinguish Honduran politics from that of its neighbors.

Jamaica

1219. Campbell, Horace. *Rasta and Resistance: From Marcus Garvey to Walter Rodney.* 1st American ed. Trenton, NJ: Africa World Press, 1987. 234 p. Ill. ISBN 0865430349.

This is a study of the Rastafari movement and the effect of reggae music in its development and expansion.

1220. Keith, Nelson W., and Novella Z. Keith. *The Social Origins of Democratic Socialism in Jamaica.* Philadelphia: Temple University Press, 1992. 320 p. Bibl., index. ISBN 0877229066.

This volume examines Michael Manley's socialist government of the 1970s.

1221. Stone, Carl. *Class, State, and Democracy in Jamaica.* New York: Praeger, 1986. 198 p. (Politics in Latin America.) ISBN 0275920135.

This is an analysis of Jamaica's stable liberal democratic order.

Mexico

1222. Avalos, Francisco. *The Mexican Legal System.* 2nd ed. Littleton, CO: Fred Rothman, 2000. 254 p. Bibl., index. ISBN 0837702267.

This is an overview of the Mexican federal legal system.

1223. Brunk, Samuel. *Emiliano Zapata: Revolution & Betrayal in Mexico.* 1st ed. Albuquerque, NM: University of New Mexico Press, 1995. 360 p. Bibl., ill., index. ISBN 0826316190.

This work examines Zapata's personal leadership of the revolutionary movement he led to secure social justice for peasants in the state of Morelos.

1224. Camp, Roderic Ai. *Generals in the Palacio: The Military in Modern Mexico.* New York: Oxford University Press, 1992. 278 p. Bibl., index. ISBN 0195073002.

This surveys the Mexican military institution as it examines its similarities and also striking differences when compared with its Latin American neighbors. (OP)

1225. Camp, Roderic Ai. *Mexican Political Biographies, 1884–1935.* 1st ed. Austin, TX: University of Texas Press, 1991. 458 p. ISBN 0292751192.

This volume provides biographical information about Mexican political figures.

1226. Camp, Roderic Ai. *Mexican Political Biographies, 1935–1993.* 3rd ed. Austin, TX: University of Texas Press, 1995. 985 p. ISBN 0292711743.

See above listing.

1227. Camp, Roderic Ai. *Politics in Mexico: The Decline of Authoritarianism.* 3rd ed. New York: Oxford University Press, 1999. 279 p. Bibl., index. ISBN 019512412X pbk.

This work examines Mexican contemporary political culture focusing on the one-party system. An introduction to Mexican history, relations with the U.S. political values, recruitment and decision-making, are provided as background.

1228. Centeno, Miguel Angel. *Democracy Within Reason: Technocratic Revolution in Mexico.* University Park, PA: Pennsylvania State University Press, 1994. 272 p. Ill. ISBN 0271010207.

This is an analysis of late twentieth century Mexican economic and political developments.

1229. Domínguez, Jorge I., and James A. McCann. *Democratizing Mexico: Public Opinion and Electoral Choices.* Baltimore: Johns Hopkins University Press, 1996. 269 p. Bibl., ill. ISBN 0801851467.

This presents a thorough study of Mexican public opinion concerning the country's political life. It argues that Mexico is becoming increasingly democratic and that there is widespread public support for this development.

1230. Eisenhower, John S. D. *Intervention!: the United States and the Mexican Revolution, 1913–1917.* 1st ed. New York: W.W. Norton, 1993. 544 p. Bibl., ill., index. ISBN 0393035735.

This account of U.S.-Mexican relations from 1913 to 1917 includes details of the U.S. intervention in the Mexican revolution.

1231. Fuentes, Carlos. *A New Time for Mexico.* Translated by Marina G. Castañeda. New York: Farrar, Straus and Giroux, 1996. 216 p. ISBN 0374221707.

The renowned Mexican writer and critic analyzes the historical roots behind Mexico's current breaks with its ruling party, the Chiapas revolt, political assassinations, among other contemporary issues.

1232. La Botz, Dan. *Democracy in Mexico: Peasant Rebellion and Political Reform.* Boston: South End Press, 1995. 274 p. Bibl., ill., index. ISBN 0896085074.

This is a detailed history of Mexican political life focusing on its monolithic one-party system.

1233. O'Malley, Ilene V. *The Myth of the Revolution: Hero Cults and the Institutionalization of the Mexican State, 1920–1940.* New York: Greenwood Press, 1986. 199 p. Bibl., index. (Contributions to the study of world history; 1.) ISBN 0313251843.

This work analyzes the institutionalization and mythification of the Mexican revolution in order to perpetuate the bourgeois character of the regime.

1234. Oppenheimer, Andrés. *Bordering on Chaos: Guerrillas, Stockbrokers, Politicians, and Mexico's Road to Prosperity.* 1st ed. Boston: Little, Brown and Co. 1996. 367 p. ISBN 0316650951.

This is an in-depth examination of Mexico's political situation in the early 1990s.

1235. Paz, Octavio. *Itinerary: An Intellectual Journey.* Translated by Jason Wilson. New York: Harcourt, 1999. 129 p. Bibl. ISBN 0151005621.

This collection of essays presents the Nobel laureate's meditations on Mexican politics and history.

1236. Poniatowska, Elena. *Massacre in Mexico.* Columbia, MO: University of Missouri Press, 1991. 333 p. Ill. ISBN 0826208177.

This classic relates the bloody student massacre in Mexico City in 1968.

1237. Purcell, Susan Kaufman, and Luis Rubio, eds. *Mexico Under Zedillo.* Boulder, CO: L. Rienner Pub., 1998. 151 p. Bibl., ill., index. ISBN 1555873154 pbk.

This is an assessment of the Zedillo administration within the context of the political changes in Mexico since 1982 whose main characteristic has been demand for a more democratic and pluralist system.

1238. Rodríguez, Victoria E., ed. *Women's Participation in Mexican Political Life.* Boulder, CO: Westview Press, 1998. 260 p. Bibl., ill., index. ISBN 0813335299.

This anthology examines formal and informal participation of Mexican women in political affairs from historical and contemporary perspectives.

1239. Rodríguez O., Jaime E. *The Evolution of the Mexican Political System*. Wilmington, DE: SR Books, 1993. 322 p. Bibl., ill., index. (Latin American silhouettes.) ISBN 0842024484.

These essays evaluate the nature of Mexican politics in the nineteenth and twentieth centuries from local, regional, and national perspectives. (OP)

1240. Roett, Riordan, ed. *Mexico's External Relations in the 1990s*. Boulder, CO: L. Rienner Publishers, 1991. 279 p. Bibl., ill., index. ISBN 1555872387.

This work evaluates Mexico's external relations from political and economic perspectives within a global framework. (OP)

1241. Ross, John. *Rebellion from the Roots: Indian Uprising in Chiapas*. Monroe, ME: Common Courage Press, 1994. 424 p. Ill., index. ISBN 1567510434.

This volume recounts the story of the Zapatista guerrilla uprising in Chiapas on New Year's Day, 1994.

1242. Russell, Philip L. *Mexico Under Salinas*. Austin, TX: Mexico Resource Center, 1994. 485 p. Bibl., ill., index. ISBN 0963922300 pbk.

This is a detailed discussion of events during the Salinas presidency with references to past trends and patterns.

1243. Schmidt, Samuel. *The Deterioration of the Mexican Presidency: The Years of Luis Echeverría*. Edited and translated by Dan A. Cothran. Tucson, AZ: University of Arizona Press, 1991. 222 p. Bibl., index. ISBN 0816512533.

This is a critique of the Mexican political system between 1970–1976. The Mexican presidency, despite a seventy-year period when it remained virtually unchanged, has been experiencing a transformation toward a more democratic, multiparty system.

1244. Smith, Clint E. *Inevitable Partnership: Understanding Mexico-U.S. Relations*. Boul-

der, CO: Lynne Rienner Publishers, 2000. 241 p. Bibl., ill., index. ISBN 1555878970.

This summary of Mexican political history introduces contemporary issues that affect the bilateral relationship.

1245. Tangeman, Michael. *Mexico at the Crossroads: Politics, the Church, and the Poor*. Maryknoll, NY: Orbis Books, 1995. 138 p. Bibl., ill., index. ISBN 1570750181.

This work explores the tensions between progressive and conservative forces within the church as it becomes involved in political developments. (OP)

1246. Vázquez Gómez, Juana. *Dictionary of Mexican Rulers, 1325–1997*. Westport, CT: Greenwood Press, 1997. 191 p. Bibl., index. ISBN 0313300496.

This dictionary provides biographical sketches of those who held or shared the chief executive authority of the nation from pre–Columbian times to the present.

1247. Weintraub, Sidney. *A Marriage of Convenience: Relations Between Mexico and the United States*. New York: Oxford University Press, 1990. 270 p. Bibl., index. ISBN 019506125X.

This work confronts and explains controversial political and economic issues concerning U.S.-Mexican relations and makes policy recommendations.

Nicaragua

1248. Barrios de Chamorro, Violeta, with Sonia Cruz de Baltodano, and Guido Fernández. *Dreams of the Heart: The Autobiography of President Violeta Barrios de Chamorro of Nicaragua*. New York: Simon & Schuster, 1996. 352 p. Ill., index. ISBN 0684810557.

President Chamorro details her family's opposition to the Somoza dictatorship that ended in 1979. Her eventual disagreement with Sandinista policies led her to become president of Nicaragua.

1249. Benjamin, Alan. *Nicaragua: Dynamics of an Unfinished Revolution.* 1st ed. San Francisco: Walnut Pub. Co., 1989. 176 p. ISBN 0929405021.

This examines the internal political dynamics of the Nicaraguan revolution and focuses on the impact of U.S. policy toward the Sandinista government.

1250. Bermann, Karl. *Under the Big Stick: Nicaragua and the United States since 1848.* Boston: South End Press, 1986. 339 p. Bibl., ill., index. ISBN 0896083241.

This is an analysis of the 140-year relationship between Nicaragua and the U.S. from the Nicaraguan perspective.

1251. Burns, E. Bradford. *At War in Nicaragua: The Reagan Doctrine and the Politics of Nostalgia.* 1st ed. New York: Harper & Row, 1987. 211 p. Bibl., ill., index. ISBN 0060550740.

This work provides a historical and geographic analysis of Nicaragua's political situation in the 1980s with a summary of U.S. policy. (OP)

1252. Catholic Institute for International Relations. *Nicaragua: The Right to Survive.* Croton-on-Hudson, NY: North River Press, 1987. 135 p. Bibl., ill., index. ISBN 0884270742.

This report of human rights in Nicaragua is based on documents of organizations that monitor these issues.

1253. Close, David. *Nicaragua: The Chamorro Years.* Boulder, CO: Lynne Rienner Publishers, 1999. 243 p. Bibl., index. ISBN 1555876439.

This thematic and chronological study of the Chamorros presidency examines how constitutional democracies (including the Chamorro and Sandinista regimes) deal with the legacy of authoritarianism.

1254. Collinson, Helen et al., eds. *Women and Revolution in Nicaragua.* Atlantic Highlands, NJ: Zed Books, 1990. 207 p. Bibl., ill., index. ISBN 0862329345.

This examines political and social changes that influenced Nicaraguan women in the late 1980s.

1255. Dematteis, Lou, and Chris Vail. *Nicaragua, a Decade of Revolution.* 1st ed. New York: W.W. Norton, 1991. 168 p. Ill. ISBN 0393029654.

This traces the activities of the Sandinistas and the U.S.-supported Contras from the overthrow of Somoza in 1979 to the election of Violeta Chamorro to the presidency in 1990.

1256. Hale, Charles R. *Resistance and Contradiction: Miskitu Indians and the Nicaraguan State, 1894–1987.* Stanford, CA: Stanford University Press, 1994. 296 p. Bibl., index. ISBN 0804722552.

This work exposes the differences between Sandinista government policy and the Miskitu's historical efforts towards self-determination and autonomy.

1257. Hodges, Donald Clark. *Intellectual Foundations of the Nicaraguan Revolution.* 1st ed. Austin, TX: University of Texas Press, 1986. 378 p. Bibl., index. ISBN 0292738382.

This is an assessment of the Nicaragua-based liberation movement that was influenced by Sandino's philosophy. (OP)

1258. Kinzer, Stephen. *Blood of Brothers: Life and War in Nicaragua.* New York: Putnam, 1991. 450 p. Bibl., ill., index. ISBN 0399135944.

This work examines Sandino's anti–U.S. campaign in 1927–1933 and how these activities contributed to the eventual overthrow of Somoza in 1979. The Nicaraguan situation in the late twentieth century is presented within the context of other Central American conflicts. (OP)

1259. Kirk, John M. *Politics and the Catholic Church in Nicaragua.* Gainesville, FL: University of Florida Press, 1992. 246 p. Bibl., ill., index. ISBN 0813011388.

This historical overview of Nicaraguan church-state relations includes the Church's active participation in the Sandinista regime.

1260. Pezzullo, Lawrence, and Ralph Pezzullo. *At the Fall of Somoza.* Pittsburgh, PA: University of Pittsburgh Press, 1994. 303 p.

Bibl., ill., index. (Pitt Latin American series.) ISBN 0822937565.

This is a chronicle of the final days of Somoza's government in 1979 including U.S. actions as the Sandinistas approached Managua.

1261. Prevost, Gary, and Harry E. Vanden, eds. *The Undermining of the Sandinista Revolution.* New York: St. Martin's Press, 1997. 226 p. Bibl., ill., index. ISBN 0312161123.

This is an assessment of why the revolution failed and whether successful Sandinista policies (agrarian reform, social policy, autonomy of ethnic groups, etc.) were undone by the Chamorro government, U.S. policy, and the International Monetary Fund.

1262. Sklar, Holly. *Washington's War on Nicaragua.* Boston: South End Press, 1988. 472 p. Bibl., index. ISBN 0896082962.

This work analyzes U.S. policy toward Sandinista Nicaragua from an historical perspective.

1263. Walker, Thomas W., ed. *Nicaragua Without Illusions: Regime Transition and Structural Adjustment in the 1990s.* Wilmington, DE: SR Books, 1997. 332 p. (Latin American silhouettes.) ISBN 0842025782.

This volume traces political changes in post–Sandinista Nicaragua. The first part deals with the impact of internationalization on domestic structures while the second examines political adjustments in legal and institutional frameworks that continue to be affected by the revolutionary legacy.

1264. Walter, Knut. *The Regime of Anastasio Somoza, 1936–1956.* Chapel Hill, NC: University of North Carolina Press, 1993. 303 p. Bibl., ill., index. ISBN 0807821063.

This study follows Somoza's successful rise to power through his control of the military and ability to gain and maintain support from the two major political parties.

1265. Wright, Bruce E. *Theory in the Practice of the Nicaraguan Revolution.* Athens, OH: Ohio University Center for International Studies, 1995. 272 p. Bibl., index.

(Monographs in international studies. Latin America series; 24.) ISBN 0896801853 pbk.

Along with an examination of Nicaraguan political events since 1979, this work examines the unique revolutionary theory, rooted in political pluralism, of Nicaragua's Sandinista government.

Panama

1266. Buckley, Kevin. *Panama: The Whole Story.* New York: Simon & Schuster, 1991. 304 p. ISBN 067172794X.

This work traces Manuel Noriega's rise to power and his connections to the U.S. government. (OP)

1267. Conniff, Michael L. *Panama and the United States: The Forced Alliance.* Athens, GA: University of Georgia Press, 1992. 201 p. Bibl., ill., index. (The United States and the Americas.) ISBN 0820313599.

This volume explores the two-centuries long alliance between the U.S. and Panama.

1268. Major, John. *Prize Possession: The United States and the Panama Canal, 1903–1979.* New York: Cambridge University Press, 1993. 432 p. Bibl., ill., index. ISBN 0521433061.

This presents the history of the Panama Canal including U.S. administration of the zone, the Panamanian government, and U.S. intervention in its politics.

1269. Noriega, Manuel Antonio, and Peter Eisner. *America's Prisoner: The Memoirs of Manuel Noriega.* 1st ed. New York: Random House, 1997. 293 p. ISBN 0679432272.

This memoir reveals a controversial portrait of U.S. policy towards Panama including its invasion in December 1989 and the trial of the Panamanian leader in the U.S.

1270. Pearcy, Thomas L. *We Answer Only to God: Politics and the Military in Panama, 1903–1947.* 1st ed. Albuquerque, NM: University of New Mexico Press, 1998. 232 p. Bibl., ill., index. ISBN 082631841X.

This work examines the role of the military and national police in the evolution of Panamanian politics during the first half of the twentieth century.

Peru

1271. Crabtree, John. *Peru Under García: An Opportunity Lost.* Pittsburgh, PA: University of Pittsburgh Press, 1992. 236 p. Bibl., ill., index. (Pitt Latin American series.) ISBN 082291168X.

This is an assessment of the García presidency, 1985–1990, within the context of modern Peruvian history. (OP)

1272. Graham, Carol. *Peru's APRA: Parties, Politics, and the Elusive Quest for Democracy.* Boulder, CO: L. Rienner Publishers, 1992. 267 p. Bibl., ill., index. ISBN 1555873065.

This analyzes the populist political party and its contemporary leadership.

1273. Palmer, David Scott, ed. *The Shining Path of Peru.* 2nd ed. New York: St. Martin's Press, 1994. 270 p. Bibl., ill., index. ISBN 031210619X.

Fifteen Shining Path scholars analyze the roots of the strongest contemporary communist insurgency in Peru, the role of its leader, ties to drug traffickers, and historical context.

1274. Pike, Fredrick B. *The Politics of the Miraculous in Peru: Haya de la Torre and the Spiritualist Tradition.* Lincoln, NE: University of Nebraska Press, 1986. 391 p. Bibl., ill., index. ISBN 0803236727.

This is a political biography of Haya de la Torre, founder of APRA, and the influence of this party on Peruvian and Latin American affairs. (OP)

1275. Saba, Raúl P. *Political Development and Democracy in Peru.* Boulder, CO: Westview Press, 1987. 180 p. Bibl., index. (Westview special studies on Latin America and the Caribbean.) ISBN 0813374359.

This work surveys Peruvian politics from the early 1960s through 1987. (OP)

1276. St. John, Ronald Bruce. *The Foreign Policy of Peru.* Boulder, CO: L. Rienner Publishers, 1992. 269 p. Bibl., index. ISBN 1555873049.

This chronicles the interplay of Peruvian domestic and foreign political history since its nineteenth century independence. (OP)

1277. Stern, Steve J., ed. *Shining and Other Paths: War and Society in Peru, 1980–1995.* Durham, NC: Duke University Press, 1998. 534 p. Bibl., ill., index. (Latin America otherwise.) ISBN 0822322013.

This comprehensive analysis of *Sendero Luminoso*, one of the most violent terrorist movements of the hemisphere, includes a discussion of its revolutionary struggle and defeat, and political and cultural legacy.

1278. Tulchin, Joseph S., and Gary Bland, eds. *Peru in Crisis: Dictatorship or Democracy?* Boulder, CO: L. Rienner Publishers, 1994. 208 p. Bibl., index. (Woodrow Wilson Center current studies on Latin America.) ISBN 1555815432 pbk.

This work examines Peru's troubled and complex political situation including Fujimori's controversial policies; *Sendero Luminoso*'s guerrilla war; drug trafficking; and U.S.-Peru policy. (OP)

1279. Vargas Llosa, Alvaro. *The Madness of Things Peruvian: Democracy Under Siege.* New Brunswick, NJ: Transaction Publishers, 1994. 173 p. Bibl., index. ISBN 1560001143.

This comprehensive review of recent Peruvian politics also presents a historical analysis of Peru and Latin America.

Puerto Rico

1280. Fernández, Ronald. *The Disenchanted Island: Puerto Rico and the United States in the Twentieth Century.* 2nd ed. Westport, CT: Praeger, 1996. 278 p. Bibl., index. ISBN 0275952266.

This is a historical examination of the island's political evolution and its relationship with the U.S. from 1898 through the current suppression of its independence movement.

1281. López, Alfredo. *Dona Licha's Island: Modern Colonialism in Puerto Rico.* Boston: South End Press, 1987. 178 p. ISBN 0896082571 pbk.

This work examines Puerto Rico's current economic and political situation, relations with the U.S., and Puerto Rican independence efforts.

1282. Meléndez, Edgardo. *Puerto Rico's Statehood Movement.* New York: Greenwood Press, 1988. 194 p. Bibl., index. (Contributions in political science; 220.) ISBN 0313261318.

This historiography of Puerto Rico's annexation movement examines commonwealth and independence alternatives in their socioeconomic and political contexts.

1283. Perusse, Roland I. *The United States and Puerto Rico: Decolonization Options and Prospects.* Lanham, MD: University Press of America, 1988. 177 p. Bibl., index. ISBN 081916657X.

This work analyzes Puerto Rico's future status.

Suriname

1284. Dew, Edward M. *The Trouble in Suriname, 1975–1993.* Westport, CT: Praeger, 1994. 243 p. Bibl., ill., index. ISBN 027594834X.

This examines the initial efforts of the former Dutch colony to develop its own political culture.

Uruguay

1285. Gillespie, Charles. *Negotiating Democracy: Politicians and Generals in Uruguay.* New York: Cambridge University Press, 1992. 264 p. Bibl., index. (Cambridge Latin American studies; 72.) ISBN 0521401526.

This volume studies the key role of the political parties in restoring democracy in Uruguay.

Venezuela

1286. Coronil, Fernando. *The Magical State: Nature, Money, and Modernity in Venezuela.* Chicago: University of Chicago Press, 1997. 447 p. Bibl., ill., index. ISBN 0226116018.

This work examines the evolution and formation of the Venezuelan state in the twentieth century from its early authoritarian days to the consolidation of its petroleum economy.

1287. Ewell, Judith. *Venezuela and the United States: From Monroe's Hemisphere to Petroleum's Empire.* Athens, GA: University of Georgia Press, 1996. 267 p. Bibl., index. (The United States and the Americas.) ISBN 0820317829.

This is an assessment of the role oil has played in Venezuela's relations with the U.S.

1288. Hellinger, Daniel. *Venezuela: Tarnished Democracy.* Boulder, CO: Westview Press, 1991. 236 p. Ill., index. (Westview profiles. Nations of contemporary Latin America.) ISBN 0813307007.

This analyzes Venezuelan democracy and its two-party system. (OP)

1289. Martz, John D., and David J. Myers, eds. *Venezuela: The Democratic Experience.* Rev. ed. New York: Praeger, 1986. 489 p. Bibl., ill. ISBN 0030034647.

This is an examination of the evolution of Venezuelan democracy, its governmental structures and functions, and the growing strength of the dominant political parties within the context of declining oil revenues.

SOCIOLOGY

This section includes works about sports; ethnicity and race; gender and sexuality; social change and history; violence; and migration.

Due to the extensive coverage of social issues, the section begins with general works then is subdivided by these subtopics: "Gender and Sexuality," and "Race and Ethnicity." The section is subdivided by geographic regions and countries.

Latin America

1290. Arbena, Joseph. *Sport and Society in Latin America: Diffusion, Dependency, and the Rise of Mass Culture.* New York: Greenwood Press, 1988. 162 p. (Contributions to the study of popular culture; 20.) ISBN 0313247749.

Bicycling, baseball, soccer, popular sports in several Latin America countries, are examined from socioeconomic and political perspectives. (OP)

1291. Beezley, William, and Linda Curcio-Nagy, eds. *Latin American Popular Culture: An Introduction.* Wilmington, DE: SR Books, 2000. 255 p. Bibl., index. ISBN 0842027106.

A funeral and popular medicine are analyzed as examples of cultural events or activities that define national identity and social awareness.

1292. Domínguez, Jorge I., ed. *Social Movements in Latin America: The Experience of Peasants, Workers, Women, the Urban Poor, and the Middle Sectors.* New York: Garland, 1994. 384 p. Bibl., ill. (Essays on Mexico, Central and South America; 4.) ISBN 0815314884.

This volume provides a summary of scholarly debates by Latin American experts in the realm of social movements.

1293. Eckstein, Susan, ed. *Power and Popular Protest: Latin American Social Movements.* Index. Berkeley, CA: University of California Press, 1989. 342 p. ISBN 0520062175.

These articles present a comprehensive view of the cause and consequences of social protest movements in contemporary Latin America.

1294. Escobar, Arturo, and Sonia E. Alvarez, eds. *The Making of Social Movements in Latin America: Identity, Strategy, and Democracy.* Boulder, CO: Westview Press, 1992. 383 p. (Series in political economy and economic development in Latin America.) ISBN 081331206X.

This analyzes the great diversity of social movements such as peasantry, gay activists, women, church groups, and ecologists, and examines strategies the groups employ to further their agendas as they interact with evolving sociopolitical realities.

1295. Morrison, Andrew R., and María Loreto Biehl, eds. *Too Close to Home: Domestic Violence in the Americas.* Washington, DC: Inter-American Development Bank, 1999. 206 p. Bibl., ill. ISBN 188693844X.

This work presents the work of psychologists, doctors, economists, and other experts on the chronic problem of domestic violence in the region.

1296. Oleksak, Michael M., and Mary Adams Oleksak. *Béisbol: Latin Americans and the Grand Old Game.* 1st ed. Grand Rapids, MI: Masters Press, 1995. 303 p. Bibl., ill., index. ISBN 0940279355.

This is an analysis of the role of athletes from Cuba, Venezuela, Panama, Nicaragua, the Dominican Republic, and Puerto Rico who have played big-league baseball. (OP)

1297. Rosenberg, Tina. *Children of Cain: Violence and the Violent in Latin America.* New York: Morrow, 1991. 394 p. Bibl. ISBN 0688084656.

This cruel portrait of violence in the region also includes the voices of those who perpetrate it and are its victims.

1298. Rowe, William, and Vivian Schelling. *Memory and Modernity: Popular Culture in Latin America.* New York: Verso, 1991. 243 p. Bibl., ill., index. (Critical studies in Latin American culture.) ISBN 0860913228.

Popular Catholicism, carnival, soccer, and national independence are the examples described in this analysis of the resistance of local and indigenous forms of behavior and customs against the intrusion of Western culture. (OP)

1299. Stavans, Ilan. *The Riddle of Cantinflas: Essays on Hispanic Popular Culture.* 1st ed. Albuquerque, NM: University of New Mexico Press, 1998. 157 p. Ill., index. ISBN 0826318606.

These essays explore Latin American cultural expression through popular culture icons such as Cantinflas, Comandante Marcos of the Chiapas uprising, José Guadalupe Posada, the graphic artist of the Mexican revolution, among others.

Gender and Sexuality

1300. Balderston, Daniel, and Donna J. Guy, eds. *Sex and Sexuality in Latin America.* New York: New York University Press, 1997. 288 p. Bibl., index. ISBN 0814712894.

These essays present a growing body of literature that examines sexual behavior from anthropological, historical, literary, and cultural perspectives.

1301. Jaquette, Jane S. *The Women's Movement in Latin America: Participation and Democracy.* 2nd ed. Boulder, CO: Westview Press, 1994. 257 p. Bibl., index. (Thematic studies in Latin America.) ISBN 0813384869.

This is an analysis of the history and development of women's political participation in Brazil, Argentina, Uruguay, Chile, Peru, Nicaragua, and Mexico during the last twenty-five years.

1302. Lavrin, Asunción, ed. *Sexuality and Marriage in Colonial Latin America.* Lincoln, NE: University of Nebraska Press, 1992. 349 p. Bibl., ill., index. (Latin American studies series.) ISBN 080327940X.

These essays reconstruct the personal and private lives of colonial Latin Americans.

1303. Melhuus, Marit, and Kristi A. Stolen, eds. *Machos, Mistresses, Madonnas: Contesting the Power of Latin American Gender Imagery.* New York: Verso, 1996. 272 p. Index. (Critical studies in Latin American and Iberian cultures.) ISBN 1859848052.

This work examines Latin American sexual identities and stereotypical societal roles, in particular, those defined by Catholic traditions.

1304. Miller, Francesca. *Latin American Women and the Search for Social Justice.* Hanover, NH: University Press of New England, 1991. 324 p. Ill., index. ISBN 0874515572.

This volume traces the social history of women in the Caribbean, Central, and South America from the conquest to the present.

1305. Murray, Stephen O. *Latin American Male Homosexualities.* 1st ed. Albuquerque, NM: University of New Mexico Press, 1995. 304 p. Bibl. ISBN 0826316468.

This sociocultural analysis of male homosexuality in contemporary Brazil and Costa Rica includes one chapter about pre–Columbian and colonial Mexico.

1306. Nash, June et al. *Women and Change in Latin America.* South Hadley, MA: Bergin & Garvey Publishers, 1986. 372 p. Bibl., ill., index. ISBN 0897890698.

This is a survey of research about Latin American women whose powerlessness has resulted in the development of successful strategies to overcome their limited opportunities.

1307. Randall, Margaret. *Gathering Rage: The Failure of Twentieth Century Revolutions to Develop a Feminist Agenda.* New York: Monthly Review Press, 1992. 192 p. Bibl. ISBN 085345860X.

This work exposes the failure of the Cuban and Nicaraguan revolutions to create truly egalitarian societies in which both women and men can participate fully in the political process.

1308. Randall, Margaret. *Our Voices, Our Lives: Stories of Women from Central America and the Caribbean.* Monroe, ME: Common Courage Press, 1995. 213 p. Bibl., ill., index. ISBN 1567510477.

These essays present the life stories of women from the Dominican Republic, Belize, Guatemala, and Nicaragua.

1309. Socolow, Susan Migden. *The Women of Colonial Latin America.* New York: Cambridge University Press, 2000. 237 p. Bibl., ill., index. (New approaches to the Americas.) ISBN 0521470528.

This volume examines gender, race, and class issues and their effect on women's lives throughout the pre–Columbian and colonial periods.

1310. Stephen, Lynn. *Women and Social Movements in Latin America: Power from Below.* 1st ed. Austin, TX: University of Texas Press, 1997. 332 p. Bibl., ill., index. ISBN 0292777167.

This work studies the changing role of Latin American women during the 1970–80s. During this period women organized to fight their oppression but encountered resistance due to their defiance of the established social order.

1311. Stoner, K. Lynn. *Latinas of the Americas: A Source Book.* New York: Garland, 1989. 692 p. Bibl., index. (Garland reference library of social science; 363.) ISBN 0824083361.

This survey and bibliography includes short essays about education, feminist studies, demography, history, political, and social issues. (OP)

Race and Ethnicity

1312. Davis, Darién J., ed. *Slavery and Beyond: The African Impact on Latin America and the Caribbean.* Wilmington, DE: SR Books, 1995. 301 p. (Jaguar books on Latin America; 5.) ISBN 0824024859.

These essays explore the regional and cultural factors of west Africans in Latin America from colonial times to the present.

1313. Domínguez, Jorge I., ed. *Race and Ethnicity in Latin America.* New York: Garland, 1994. 371 p. Bibl., ill. (Essays on Mexico, Central and South America; 7.) ISBN 0815314914.

Volume seven of this series provides a summary of scholarly debates by Latin American experts in race and ethnic issues. Particular emphasis is placed on Afro- and Indo-American societies and the relation-

ship between social class and race/ethnic matters.

1314. Elkin, Judith Laikin. *The Jews of Latin America.* Rev. ed. New York: Holmes & Meier, 1997. 339 p. Bibl., ill., index. ISBN 0841913684.

This is a comprehensive view of the Jewish communities in Central and South America through the 1990s.

1315. Graham, Richard, ed. *The Idea of Race in Latin America, 1870–1940.* Austin, TX: University of Texas Press, 1990. 135 p. Bibl., ill., index. (Critical reflections on Latin America series.) ISBN 0292738560.

This presents historical, political, and intellectual perspectives about race matters in Brazil, Argentina, Cuba, and Mexico.

1316. Jackson, Robert H. *Race, Caste, and Status: Indians in Colonial Spanish America.* Albuquerque, NM: University of New Mexico Press, 1999. 151 p. Bibl., index. ISBN 0826321089.

This analyzes the creation of the Indian status focusing on a community in colonial Bolivia and nineteenth century northwestern Mexico.

1317. Klein, Herbert S. *African Slavery in Latin America and the Caribbean.* Rep. ed. New York: Oxford University Press, 1988. 311 p. Bibl., ill., index. ISBN 019503838X.

This comparative introduction about the history of slavery in Spanish, Portuguese, and French former colonies covers adaptation, rebellion, and emancipation.

1318. Klich, Ignacio, and Jeffrey Lesser, eds. *Arab and Jewish Immigrants in Latin America: Images and Realities.* Portland, OR: F. Cass, 1998. 263 p. Bibl., index. ISBN 0714648736.

This comparative study examines Jewish and Arab immigration to several South, Central American, Caribbean countries, and Mexico in the nineteenth and twentieth centuries.

1319. Sheinin, David, and Lois B. Barr, eds. *The Jewish Diaspora in Latin America: New Studies on History and Literature.* New York:

Garland, 1996. 302 p. Bibl., index. (Latin American studies; 8.) ISBN 0815322836.

This is an examination of the Jewish experience in Latin America as depicted in literature and historical studies.

Brazil

1320. Andrews, George Reid. *Blacks & Whites in São Paulo, Brazil, 1888–1988.* Madison, WI: University of Wisconsin Press, 1992. 369 p. Bibl., ill., index. ISBN 0299131009.

This study examines race relations in Brazil's largest city within sociocultural and historical contexts.

1321. Freyre, Gilberto. *The Masters and the Slaves = Casa-Grande & Senzala: A Study in the Development of Brazilian Civilization.* 2nd English-lang. ed. rev. Translated by Samuel Putnam. Berkeley, CA: University of California Press, 1986. 537 p. Bibl., ill., index. ISBN 0520056655 pbk.

This interdisciplinary analysis of Brazilian social issues was written by Brazil's most influential cultural historian.

1322. Hahner, June Edith. *Emancipating the Female Sex: The Struggle for Women's Rights in Brazil, 1850–1940.* Durham, NC: Duke University Press, 1990. 301 p. Bibl., ill., index. ISBN 0822310511.

This study of the women's movement in Brazil from mid-nineteenth century to the 1930s focuses on urban, upper, and middle-class women.

1323. Hecht, Tobias. *At Home in the Street: Street Children of Northeast Brazil.* New York: Cambridge University Press, 1998. 267 p. Bibl., index. ISBN 0521591325.

This work provides disturbing details of the life of a street child in Northeast Brazil. These children endure a constant struggle for survival and often are the victims of violence.

1324. Lesser, Jeff. *Welcoming the Undesirables: Brazil and the Jewish Question.* Berkeley, CA: University of California Press, 1995. 280 p. Bibl., ill., index. ISBN 0520084128.

This volume examines Brazilian attitudes towards Jews and the impact of prevailing perceptions on the country's Jewish community.

1325. Levine, Robert M., and José Carlos Sebe Bom Meihy. *The Life and Death of Carolina Maria de Jesus.* 1st ed. Albuquerque, NM: University of New Mexico Press, 1995. 162 p. Ill., index. (Diálogos.) ISBN 0826316476.

This biography of a Brazilian slum dweller who became a celebrity after fleeing the countryside in search of a better life in São Paulo also presents political, social, and cultural aspects of her life.

1326. Linger, Daniel Touro. *Dangerous Encounters: Meanings of Violence in a Brazilian City.* Stanford, CA: Stanford University Press, 1995. 289 p. Bibl., index. ISBN 0804725896.

This is a study of the role violence in the lives of ordinary citizens during Carnival and face-to-face fights in Northeast Brazil.

1327. Mattoso, Katia M. de Queiros. *To Be a Slave in Brazil, 1550–1888.* Translated by Arthur Goldhammer. New Brunswick, NJ: Rutgers University Press, 1986. 250 p. Bibl., index. ISBN 0813511542.

This work traces the psychological trajectory of Brazilian slaves for more than three hundred years.

1328. Nascimento, Abdias do, and Elisa Larkin Nascimento. *Africans in Brazil: A Pan-African Perspective.* Trenton, NJ: Africa World Press, 1993. 218 p. Bibl., index. ISBN 0865432384.

This autobiography relates the author's struggles against discrimination in a country that promotes the myth of racial equality and tolerance.

1329. Parker, Richard G. *Beneath the Equator: Cultures of Ddesire, Male Homosexuality, and Emerging Gay Communities in Brazil.* New York: Routledge, 1999. 288 p. Bibl., ill., index. ISBN 0415916208.

This is an analysis of the evolution of metropolitan Brazil's contemporary gay life style.

1330. Ribeiro, Darcy. *The Brazilian People: The Formation and Meaning of Brazil.* Translated by Gregory Rabassa. Gainesville, FL: University Press of Florida, 2000. 332 p. Bibl. ISBN 0813017777.

This presents a summary of Ribeiro's classic work that focuses on race relations and the Brazilian power structure.

1331. Schwartz, Stuart B. *Slaves, Peasants, and Rebels: Reconsidering Brazilian Slavery.* Chicago: University of Illinois Press, 1996. 174 p. Bibl., ill., index. (Blacks in the New World.) ISBN 0252065492 pbk.

This historiographic introduction to slavery in Brazil also discusses its social and economic dimensions.

Caribbean Area

1332. Acosta-Belén, Edna. *The Puerto Rican Woman: Perspectives on Culture, History, and Society.* 2nd ed. New York: Praeger, 1986. 212 p. Bibl., ill., index. ISBN 0275921336.

This provides an overview of the Puerto Rican woman from cultural, historical, socioeconomic, and interdisciplinary perspectives. (OP)

1333. Beckles, Hilary, and Verene Shepherd, eds. *Caribbean Slave Society and Economy: A Student Reader.* New York: New Press, 1991. 480 p. Bibl., ill. ISBN 1565840860.

This is an introduction to the main themes of Caribbean slavery including patterns and forms of socioeconomic activity as it molded the region's slave societies.

1334. Klein, Alan M. *Sugarball: The American Game, the Dominican Dream.* New Haven, CT: Yale University Press, 1991. 179 p. Index. ISBN 0300048734.

This historical account of baseball in the Dominican Republic examines the sport within its social and cultural contexts.

1335. Levine, Barry B. *The Caribbean Exodus.* New York: Praeger, 1987. 293 p. Bibl., index. ISBN 0275921832.

These essays focus on migration from the Caribbean to the U.S. and Europe due to rising expectations and lack of opportunities.

1336. Momsen, Janet Henshall, ed. *Women and Change in the Caribbean: A Pan–Caribbean Perspective.* Bloomington, IN: Indiana University Press, 1996. 308 p. Bibl., ill., index. ISBN 0253338972.

This is a discussion of socioeconomic aspects of women's lives in the contemporary British, Dutch, French, and Hispanic Caribbean.

1337. Morrissey, Marietta. *Slave Women in the New World: Gender Stratification in the Caribbean.* Lawrence, KS: University Press of Kansas, 1989. 202 p. Bibl., ill., index. (Studies in historical social change.) ISBN 0700603948.

This examines gender stratification of Caribbean women slaves who were oppressed by slavery and by the patriarchy. (OP)

1338. Ramírez, Rafael L. *What It Means to Be a Man: Reflections on Puerto Rican Masculinity.* Translated by Rosa E. Casper. New Brunswick, NJ: Rutgers University Press, 1999. 139 p. Bibl., index. ISBN 0813526604.

This study explores issues of power, masculinity, and sexism among men in Puerto Rico.

1339. Richardson, Ronald Kent. *Moral Imperium: Afro-Caribbeans and the Transformation of British Rule, 1776–1838.* New York: Greenwood Press, 1987. 211 p. Bibl., index. (Contributions in comparative colonial studies; no. 22.) ISBN 0313247242.

This volume examines slavery and the importance of ideals and self-interest in the emancipation movement.

1340. Singh, Kelvin. *Race and Class Struggles in a Colonial State: Trinidad, 1917–1945.* Calgary, Alberta: University of Calgary Press, 1994. 284 p. Bibl., index. ISBN 1895176433.

This is an analysis of the complex relations of Trinidad and Tobago's multiethnic, multicultural, and multiracial society through 1945. (OP)

1341. Yelvington, Kevin A., ed. *Trinidad Ethnicity.* Knoxville, TN: University of

Tennessee Press, 1993. 296 p. Bibl., ill., index. ISBN 0870497790.

This work examines Trinidadian ethnicity from multidisciplinary perspectives. It seeks to explain how the diverse groups strive to define a Trinidadian identity.

Central America

1342. Chomsky, Aviva. *West Indian Workers and the United Fruit Company in Costa Rica, 1870–1940.* Baton Rouge, LA: Louisiana State University Press, 1996. 302 p. Bibl., ill., index. ISBN 0807119792.

This is a social history of African-Caribbean banana plantation workers in Costa Rica. It discusses their organization efforts to protect their culture and interests due to their mistreatment by United Fruit and the Costa Rican banana growers.

1343. Golden, Renny. *The Hour of the Poor, the Hour of Women: Salvadoran Women Speak.* New York: Crossroad, 1991. 207 p. Bibl., ill., index. ISBN 0824510887.

This is a description of the daily lives of Salvadoran women who struggle to preserve their families and communities. (OP)

1344. Lancaster, Roger N. *Life Is Hard: Machismo, Danger, and the Intimacy of Power in Nicaragua.* Berkeley, CA: University of California Press, 1994. 340 p. ISBN 0520089294 pbk.

This analyzes Nicaraguan power structure through machismo, homosexuality, and violence against women.

1345. Randall, Margaret. *Sandino's Daughters Revisited: Feminism in Nicaragua.* New Brunswick, NJ: Rutgers University Press, 1994. 311 p. Bibl., ill. ISBN 081352024X.

In a critical examination of the male-dominated Sandinista leadership, twelve Nicaraguan women discuss the relationship between feminism and socialist revolution.

1346. Thomson, Marilyn. *Women of El Salvador: The Price of Freedom.* Philadelphia: Institute for the Study of Human Issues,

1986. 165 p. Bibl., ill. (ISHI publications.) ISBN 0897270711.

Salvadoran women refugees discuss their organized responses to government intimidation. (OP)

Cuba

1347. Brock, Lisa, and Digna Castañeda Fuertes, eds. *Between Race and Empire: African-Americans and Cubans Before the Cuban Revolution.* Philadelphia: Temple University Press, 1998. 298 p. Bibl., ill., index. ISBN 1556395860.

This examines the intellectual, cultural, and social relations between African-American communities in the U.S. and Cuba before the 1959 revolution.

1348. González Echevarría, Roberto. *The Pride of Havana: A History of Cuban Baseball.* New York: Oxford University Press, 1999. 464 p. Bibl., ill., index. ISBN 0195069919.

This is a cultural history of Cuban baseball from 1860 through the twentieth century.

1349. Leiner, Marvin. *Sexual Politics in Cuba: Machismo, Homosexuality, and AIDS.* Boulder, CO: Westview Press, 1994. 184 p. (Series in political economy and economic development in Latin America.) ISBN 0813386543.

Despite Cuba's universal health care and sexual education programs, this study presents Cuban society's pervasive machismo and homophobia during the past forty years. (OP)

1350. Levine, Robert M. *Tropical Diaspora: The Jewish Experience in Cuba.* Gainesville, FL: University of Florida Press, 1993. 398 p. Bibl., ill., index. ISBN 081301218X.

This is a survey of the cultural, economic, and political life of Cuba's Jewish community from 1881 to the present.

1351. Pérez Sarduy, Pedro, and Jean Stubbs, eds. *Afro-Cuban Voices: On Race and Iden-*

tity in Contemporary Cuba. Gainesville, FL: University Press of Florida, 2000. 200 p. Bibl. ISBN 0813017351.

This collection of Afro-Cuban voices represents many geographical regions, generations, socioeconomic, and political perspectives. They discuss the challenges non-whites face in Cuban society before and after the Cuban revolution.

1352. Stoner, K. Lynn. *From the House to the Streets: The Cuban Woman's Movement for Legal Reform, 1898–1940.* Durham, NC: Duke University Press, 1991. 242 p. Bibl., ill., index. ISBN 0822311313.

This examines the careers of several Cuban feminists and their successes in getting family and gender goals incorporated in the constitution of 1940.

Mexico

1353. Beezley, William, H. et al., eds. *Rituals of Rule, Rituals of Resistance: Public Celebrations and Popular Culture in Mexico.* Wilmington, DE: SR Books, 1994. 374 p. Bibl., ill. (Latin American silhouettes.) ISBN 0842024166.

These essays explore Mexican social and political culture as expressed through objects, places, and activities from the colonial period through the 1970s.

1354. Carrier, Joseph. *De los Otros: Intimacy and Homosexuality Among Mexican men.* New York: Columbia University Press, 1995. 231 p. (Between men—between women.) ISBN 0231096925.

This is a groundbreaking study about male homosexual behavior in northwestern Mexico.

1355. Franco, Jean. *Plotting Women: Gender and Representation in Mexico.* New York: Columbia University Press, 1991. 235 p. Bibl., ill., index. (Gender and culture.) ISBN 0231064233.

Mexican women's struggle to become part of the male-dominated world from the

seventeenth century through the present is the focus of this volume.

1356. Reavis, Dick J. *Conversations with Moctezuma: Ancient Shadows Over Modern Life in Mexico.* 1st ed. New York: Morrow, 1990. 296 p. Ill. ISBN 0688079997.

This is an interpretation of the Mexican national character in terms of its fatalism, emphasis on family, and resistance to the West's credo of personal success. (OP)

1357. Soto, Shirlene Ann. *Emergence of the Modern Mexican Woman: Her Participation in Revolution and Struggle for Equality, 1910–1940.* Denver, CO: Arden Press, 1990. 199 p. Bibl., ill., index. (Women and modern revolution series.) ISBN 0912869119.

This analyzes the participation of women in the Mexican revolution and women's rights movement during the 1910 to 1940 period.

1358. Tuñón Pablos, Julia. *Women in Mexico: A Past Unveiled.* 1st U Texas Press ed. Translated by A. Hynds. Austin, TX: University of Texas Press, 1999. 144 p. Bibl., index. (Translations from Latin America series.) ISBN 0292781601.

This examines the role of Mexican women from pre–Columbian times to the 1980s through various female archetypes such as La Malinche, La Virgen de Guadalupe, and Sor Juana Inés de la Cruz.

1359. Weckmann, Luis. *The Medieval Heritage of Mexico.* Translated by Frances M. López-Morillas. New York: Fordham University Press, 1992. 692 p. Bibl., index. ISBN 0823213242.

This work studies the lasting and contemporary social significance of medieval ideas, customs, and practices introduced by Spain.

South America

1360. Blanchard, Peter. *Slavery & Abolition in Early Republican Peru.* Wilmington, DE: SR Books, 1992. 247 p. (Latin American silhouettes.) ISBN 084202400X.

This in-depth study of African slavery in Peru between 1821–1855 relies on archival and published sources.

1361. Cadena, Marisol de la. *Indigenous Mestizos: The Politics of Race and Culture in Cuzco, 1919–1991.* Durham, NC: Duke University Press, 2000. 408 p. Bibl., ill., index. (Latin America otherwise.) ISBN 0822323850.

This is an assessment of race, ethnicity, culture, and social class in twentieth century Peru within the context of the development of the modern state.

1362. Wade, Peter. *Blackness and Race Mixture: The Dynamics of Racial Identity in Colombia.* Baltimore, MD: Johns Hopkins University Press, 1993. 415 p. Bibl., ill., index. (Johns Hopkins studies in Atlantic history and culture.) ISBN 0801844584.

This study discusses the complexity of discrimination against African-Colombians and includes background information about the development of black culture in the mostly mestizo nation.

1363. Wright, Winthrop R. *Café con Leche: Race, Class, and National Image in Venezuela.* 1st ed. Austin, TX: University of Texas Press, 1993. 167 p. Bibl., ill., index. ISBN 0292790805.

This assesses attitudes towards blacks in Venezuela and challenges a commonly held view that social mobility has been more fluid in this country compared with other Latin American nations. (OP)

VI

Science and Technology

GENERAL WORKS

This section includes natural history, flora and fauna, minerals, health and medicine, and evolutionary theory. The section is subdivided by geographic regions.

Latin America

1364. Cook, Noble David, and George W. Lovell, eds. *Secret Judgments of God: Old World Disease in Colonial Spanish America.* 1st ed. Norman, OK: University of Oklahoma Press, 1992. 285 p. Bibl., ill., index. (The Civilization of the American Indian series.) ISBN 0806123729.

These papers from the 46th International Congress of Americanists (1988) summarize the historical ramifications of disease in the Americas including pre–Columbian pathogens of the Andean region. (OP)

1365. Crump, Martha L. *In Search of the Golden Frog.* Chicago: University of Chicago Press, 2000. 299 p. Bibl., ill., index. ISBN 0226121984.

This work is a travel and research chronicle by an experienced Central and South American tropics herpetologist.

1366. Eisenberg, John Frederick. *Mammals of the Neotropics.* Chicago: University of

Chicago Press, 1989–1999. 3 vols. Bibl., ill., index. ISBN 0226-

Contents: v. 1 (-195392): the Northern neotropics: Panama, Colombia, Venezuela, Guyana, Suriname, French Guiana; V. 2 (-706818): the Southern Cone: Chile, Argentina, Uruguay, Paraguay; V. 3 (-195414): the Central neotropics: Ecuador, Peru, Bolivia, Brazil.

1367. Emmons, Louise. *Neotropical Rainforest Mammals: A Field Guide.* 2nd ed. Chicago: University of Chicago Press, 1997. 307 p. Bibl., ill., index. ISBN 0226207196.

This directory of mammals from Central and South America contains information about their size and markings, geographic range, conservation status, local names, and references to the scientific literature.

1368. Hogue, Charles Leonard. *Latin American Insects and Entomology.* Berkeley, CA: University of California Press, 1993. 536 p. Ill., index. ISBN 0520078497.

This is an introduction to the common insects and related terrestrial arthropods of the region.

1369. Kricher, John C. *A Neotropical Companion: An Introduction to the Animals, Plants, and Ecosystems of the New World Tropics.* 2nd ed. rev. and expd. Princeton, NJ:

Princeton University Press, 1997. 451 p. Bibl., ill., index. ISBN 0691044333.

This volume introduces naturalists and conservationists to the complex ecosystems of the Central and South American tropics including birds, mammals, plants, and insects.

1370. Lang, James. *Inside Development in Latin America: A Report from the Dominican Republic, Colombia, and Brazil.* Chapel Hill, NC: University of North Carolina Press, 1988. 307 p. Ill., index. ISBN 0807817538.

This work compares public health care programs in the Dominican Republic, Colombia, and Brazil. (OP)

1371. Peritore, N. Patrick, and Ana K. Galve-Peritore, eds. *Biotechnology in Latin America: Politics, Impacts, and Risks.* Wilmington, DE: SR Books, 1995. 229 p. Bibl., ill., index. (Latin American silhouettes.) ISBN 084202557X.

Complex issues such as intellectual property, economic and political relations between Latin American and other governments, between research centers and companies, are among the complex issues examined concerning the region's biotechnology industry.

1372. Reddish, Paul. *Spirits of the Jaguar: The Natural History and Ancient Civilizations of the Caribbean and Central America.* London, England: BBC Books, 1996. 224 p. Bibl., ill., index. ISBN 0563387432.

This companion volume to the PBS series traces the natural history of the area including human occupation and impact, animal life, and physical geography. Excellent color photographs illustrate the text.

1373. Stillwaggon, Eileen. *Stunted Lives, Stagnant Economies: Poverty, Disease, and Underdevelopment.* New Brunswick, NJ: Rutgers University Press, 1998. 342 p. Bibl., ill., index. ISBN 0813524938.

This work examines the extreme circumstances endured by Latin America's poor (substandard housing and sanitation, unsafe water, no health care, poor nutrition, environmental hazards) in the context of developing economies.

Amazon Region

1374. Davis, Wade. *One River: Explorations and Discoveries in the Amazon Rain Forest.* New York: Simon & Schuster, 1996. 537 p. Bibl., ill., index. ISBN 0684808862.

The rapidly disappearing biological and cultural resources of the Amazon rainforest are the focus of this chronicle of exploration tales. The author and his mentor, R. Evans Schultes, seek to identify spiritual and medicinal properties of plants in the rainforest.

1375. Duke, James A., and Rodolfo Vásquez. *Amazonian Ethnobotanical Dictionary.* Boca Raton, FL: CRC Press, 1994. 215 p. Bibl., index. ISBN 0849336643.

This dictionary includes detailed information about medicinal plants of the Amazon rainforest.

1376. Schultes, Richard Evans, and Robert F. Raffauf. *The Healing Forest: Medicinal and Toxic Plants of the Northwest Amazonia.* Portland, OR: Dioscorides Press, 1990. 484 p. Bibl., ill., index. (Historical, ethno- & economic botany series; 2.) ISBN 0931146143.

Almost 1,500 plant species and variants of northwest Amazonia are described before they vanish.

Caribbean Area

1377. Farmer, Paul. *AIDS and Accusation: Haiti and the Geography of Blame.* Berkeley, CA: University of California Press, 1992. 338 p. Bibl., index. (Comparative studies of health systems and medical care.) ISBN 0520077016.

This is an account of the HIV epidemic in Haiti and the clinical experience of AIDS in a small village.

1378. Feinsilver, Julie Margot. *Healing the Masses: Cuban Health Politics at Home and*

Abroad. Berkeley, CA: University of California Press, 1993. 307 p. Bibl., index. ISBN 0520082184.

This volume describes and analyzes the Cuban health care system and its role in international health promotion.

1379. Wauer, Roland H. *A Birder's West Indies: An Island-by-Island Tour.* 1st ed. Austin, TX: University of Texas Press, 1996. 238 p. Bibl., ill., index. (The Corrie Herring Hooks series; 30.) ISBN 0292791011.

This guidebook describes bird habitat and ecological status for each island and includes basic tourist information.

Central America

1380. Campbell, Jonathan A. *Amphibians and Reptiles of Northern Guatemala, the Yucatán, and Belize.* Norman, OK: University of Oklahoma Press, 1998. 380 p. Bibl., ill., index. (Animal natural history series; 4.) ISBN 0806130644.

This herpetology identification guide of the Petén region of northern Central America includes historical, vegetation, and environmental information.

1381. DeVries, Philip J. *The Butterflies of Costa Rica and Their Natural History.* Princeton, NJ: Princeton University Press, 1987–1997. 2 vols. Bibl., ill., index. ISBN 06910-

This two-volume set describes the natural history, life cycle, mimicry, and ecology of nearly 750 species. Vol. 1: (-84203); Vol. 2: (-28893).

1382. Dressler, Robert L. *Field Guide to the Orchids of Costa Rica and Panama.* Ithaca, NY: Comstock Pub. Associates, 1994. 374 p. Ill. ISBN 0801425824.

This well-illustrated guide describes most of the orchid species of the region.

1383. Howell, Steve N. G., and Sophie Webb. *A Guide to the Birds of Mexico and Northern Central America.* New York: Oxford University Press, 1995. 851 p. Bibl., ill., index. ISBN 0198540124.

This text includes color plates and range maps.

1384. Panczner, William D. *Minerals of Mexico.* New York: Van Nostrand Reinhold, 1987. 459 p. Bibl., ill. ISBN 0442272855.

This catalog of more than 600 minerals includes a description of their localities. (OP)

1385. Reid, Fiona. *A Field Guide to the Mammals of Central America & Southeast Mexico.* New York: Oxford University Press, 1997. 334 p. Bibl., ill., index. ISBN 0195064003.

This field guide covers mammals of all habitats of Central America and southern Mexico. Excellent illustrations including the tracks of large and small bat species accompany the text.

1386. Rosa, Carlos Leonardo de la. *A Guide to the Carnivores of Central America: Natural History, Ecology, and Conservation.* 1st ed. Austin, TX: University of Texas Press, 2000. 244 p. Bibl., ill., index. ISBN 0292716044.

This source presents the four indigenous families of carnivores and the individual species that live in the region.

1387. Stiles, F. Gary, and Alexander F. Skutch. *A Guide to the Birds of Costa Rica.* Ithaca, NY: Comstock Pub. Associates, 1989. 511 p. Bibl., ill., index. ISBN 0801422876.

This guide lists brief descriptions of seventy birding localities, their geography, climate, habitats, and conservation.

1388. Wallace, David Rains. *The Monkey's Bridge: Mysteries of Evolution in Central America.* San Francisco: Sierra Club Books, 1997. 277 p. Bibl., index. ISBN 0871565862.

This is a survey of the natural history, evolution, and scientific expeditions of the biological diversity of the region.

1389. Wiard, Leon A. *An Introduction to the Orchids of Mexico.* Ithaca, NY: Comstock Pub. Associates, 1987. 239 p. Bibl., ill., index. ISBN 080141833X.

This is an alphabetical list and description of 154 native Mexican orchid species. (OP)

1390. Young, Allen M. *The Chocolate Tree: A Natural History of Cacao.* Washington, DC:

Smithsonian Institution Press, 1994. 200 p. Bibl., ill., index. (Smithsonian nature books.) ISBN 1560983574.

This work presents the natural history of cacao, its transformation into a cultivated crop of ancient and modern peoples, and its ecological connections to the Mesoamerican rainforest.

South America

1391. Castro, Isabel C., and Antonia Phillips. *A Guide to the Birds of the Galápagos Islands.* Princeton, NJ: Princeton University Press, 1996. 144 p. Bibl., ill., index. ISBN 0691012253.

This field guide identifies resident, migrant, and vagrant birds on the islands and includes some information about habitat, conservation, and island flora and fauna.

1392. Hilty, Steven L., and William L. Brown. *A Guide to the Birds of Colombia.* Princeton, NJ: Princeton University Press, 1986. 836 p. Bibl., ill., index. ISBN 0691083711.

This guide includes information about bird topography, climate, vegetation, and habitat.

1393. McQueen, James, and Barbara McQueen. *Orchids of Brazil.* Portland, OR: Timber Press, 1993. 200 p. Ill., index. (The World of orchids.) ISBN 088192248X pbk.

This volume presents an alphabetical listing of Brazilian species including information about Brazil's geography and climate, history of orchid botany, conservation efforts, growing methods, and orchid taxonomy. (OP)

1394. Ridgely, Robert S., and Guy Tudor. *The Birds of South America.* 1st ed. Austin, TX: University of Texas Press, 1989–1994. 2 vols. Bibl., ill., index. ISBN 02927-

Bird habitat, biogeography, migration, and conservation are covered in this two-volume set. V. 1 (-07568): The oscine passerines contains more than 750 species; V. 2

(-70634): The suboscine passerines contains more than 1,000 species.

1395. Sick, Helmut. *Birds in Brazil: a natural history.* Translated by William Belton. Princeton, NJ: Princeton University Press, 1993. 703 p. Bibl., ill., index. ISBN 0691085692.

This work, originally published in Portuguese as *Ornitologia brasileira* (1985), presents a history of ornithology in Brazil, and includes conservation, biogeography, and speciation information.

1396. Steadman, David W., and Steven Zousmer. *Galápagos: Discovery on Darwin's Islands.* Washington, DC: Smithsonian Institution Press, 1988. 207 p. Bibl., ill. ISBN 0874748828.

This field guide of evolutionary theory includes biographical notes about Darwin and summary of human exploitation of the Galapagos Islands. (OP)

1397. Wheatley, Nigel. *Where to Watch Birds in South America.* Princeton, NJ: Princeton University Press, 1995. 431 p. Ill., index. ISBN 069104337X.

This compact site guide reviews each country's prime natural areas for bird watching.

ENVIRONMENTAL SCIENCES

This section includes the effects of land use and resource development on the environment, environmental policy, pollution, ecology, and conservation. The section is subdivided by regions and countries.

Latin America

1398. Collinson, Helen, ed. *Green Guerrillas: Environmental Conflicts and Initiatives in Latin America and the Caribbean; a Reader.* London, England: Latin America Bureau, 1996. 250 p. Index. ISBN 0853459800.

This reader focuses on environmental management successes and solutions from government policy and grassroots perspectives.

1399. Hopkins, Jack W. *Policymaking for Conservation in Latin America: National Parks, Reserves, and the Environment.* Westport, CT: Praeger, 1995. 216 p. Bibl., index. ISBN 0275953491.

This is a history of conservation development and national parks systems in Argentina, Chile, and Costa Rica. The socioeconomic, political, and environmental background for these conservation policies is also presented.

1400. Murray, Douglas L. *Cultivating Crisis: The Human Cost of Pesticides in Latin America.* 1st ed. Austin, TX: University of Texas Press, 1994. 177 p. Bibl., ill., index. ISBN 0292751680.

This study addresses the complex ecological, economic, and public health effects of the extensive use of synthetic pesticides in the region.

1401. Place, Susan E., ed. *Tropical Rainforests: Latin American Nature and Society in Transition.* Wilmington, DE: Scholarly Resources, 1993. 229 p. Bibl., ill. (Jaguar books on Latin America; 2.) ISBN 0842024239.

This survey presents various issues concerning the vanishing rainforests. Among the topics discussed are how the forests are perceived, why they are being destroyed, why they should be saved, and alternative development options.

1402. Schumann, Debra A., and William L. Partridge, eds. *The Human Ecology of Tropical Land Settlement in Latin America.* Boulder, CO: Westview Press, 1989. 470 p. Bibl., ill., index. (Westview special studies on Latin America and the Caribbean.) ISBN 0813372674.

This volume describes general and specific case studies about socioeconomic and environmental consequences of new land settlement and conversion of tropical forest to agriculture. (OP)

Amazon Region

1403. Almeida, Anna Luiza Ozorio de. *The Colonization of the Amazon.* 1st ed. Austin, TX: University of Texas Press. 1992. 371 p. Bibl., ill., index. (Translations from Latin America series.) ISBN 0292711468.

The physical, demographic, institutional, and economic dimensions of organized settlement are discussed in the context of deforestation of the Amazon basin.

1404. Colby, Gerard, with Charlotte Dennett. *Thy Will Be Done: The Conquest of the Amazon: Nelson Rockefeller and Evangelism in the Age of Oil.* 1st ed. New York: Harper Collins, 1995. 960 p. Bibl., ill., index. ISBN 0060167645.

This is an exposé of the devastating impact of missionaries (sponsored by the Rockefellers and the U.S. government) in the destruction of the Amazon rainforest and its cultures. (OP)

1405. Cowell, Adrian. *The Decade of Destruction: The Crusade to Save the Amazon Rain Forest.* 1st ed. New York: H. Holt, 1990. 215 p. Bibl., ill. ISBN 0805014942.

This work details the destruction of the area beginning in the 1950s and provides evidence of international and national interests that have contributed to its rapid exploitation. (OP)

1406. Dickinson, Robert E., ed. *The Geophysiology of Amazonia: Vegetation and Climate Interactions.* New York: Wiley for the United Nations University, 1987. 526 p. Bibl., ill., index. (Wiley series in climate and the biosphere.) ISBN 0471845116.

This collection of papers describes the diverse physiology of the Amazon basin.

1407. Goulding, Michael, Nigel J. H. Smith, and Dennis J. Mahar. *Floods of Fortune: Ecology and Economy Along the Amazon.* New York: Columbia University Press, 1996. 193 p. Bibl., ill., index. ISBN 0231104200.

This is a historical and contemporary overview of how humans use the Amazon River and its products.

1408. Harcourt, Caroline S., and Jeffrey A. Sayer, eds. *The Conservation Atlas of Tropical Forests: The Americas.* New York: Simon & Schuster, 1996. 1 atlas (335 p). Bibl., ill., index. ISBN 01334008868.

This is a country-by-country description of conservation, colonization, deforestion, and biodiversity of the Amazon.

1409. Jordan, Carl F., ed. *Amazonian Rain Forests: Ecosystem Disturbance and Recovery: Case Studies of Ecosystem Dynamics under a Spectrum of Land Use-Intensities.* New York: Springer-Verlag, 1987. 133 p. Bibl., ill., index. (Ecological studies; V. 60.) ISBN 0387963979.

This work contains an introduction and seven case histories of human activities that impact the land in Amazonia.

1410. Margolis, Mac. *The Last New World: The Conquest of the Amazon Frontier.* 1st ed. New York: WW Norton, 1992. 367 p. Ill., index. ISBN 0393033791.

This volume examines social, economic, and ecological issues of the Amazon basin in their historical and contemporary contexts. (OP)

1411. Smith, Nigel J. H. *The Enchanted Amazon Rain Forest: Stories from a Vanishing World.* Gainesville, FL: University Press of Florida, 1996. 194 p. Bibl., ill., index. ISBN 0813013771.

This collection of folkloric tales about daily life in the Amazon rainforest also includes information about rainforest ecology, its history, and social structure.

1412. Stone, Roger D. *Dreams of Amazonia.* New York: Penguin Books, 1993. 203 p. Bibl., ill., index. ISBN 0140174303.

This compact history traces human activity in the Amazon basin from the European conquest to the present. (OP)

1413. Tidwell, Mike. *Amazon Stranger.* New York: Lyons & Buford, Publishers, 1996. 215 p. ISBN 1558214062.

This is a description of the ecological damage caused by oil exploration and exploitation in the Ecuadorian Amazon where the Cofan people live. It also tells the story of Randy Borman, son of missionary American parents, who has organized the Cofan to oppose further encroachment by the oil companies.

Brazil

1414. Banks, Vic. *The Pantanal: Brazil's Forgotten Wilderness.* San Francisco: Sierra Club Books, 1991. 254 p. Ill., index. ISBN 0871567911.

This is a description of the Paraguay River flood plain that supports a variety of wildlife but is also being destroyed by illegal hunters, miners, commercial fishermen, and agrochemicals. (OP)

1415. Dean, Warren. *Brazil and the Struggle for Rubber: A Study in Environmental History.* New York: Cambridge University Press, 1987. 234 p. Bibl., ill., index. (Studies in environment and history.) ISBN 0521334772.

This is a study of rubber tapping from an environmental history perspective.

1416. Dean, Warren. *With Broadax and Firebrand: The Destruction of the Brazilian Atlantic Forest.* Berkeley, CA: University of California Press, 1995. 482 p. Bibl., ill., index. ISBN 0520087755.

This is an environmental history of human intrusions in the Brazilian Atlantic forest.

1417. Foresta, Ronald A. *Amazon Conservation in the Age of Development: The Limits of Providence.* Gainesville: University Press of Florida, 1991. 366 p. Bibl., ill., index. ISBN 0813010926.

Stressing the conflict between economic development policies and environmental activists, this work examines Brazilian environmental history and nature preservation during the 1970s through the mid–1980s.

1418. Hall, Anthony L. *Sustaining Amazonia: Grassroots Action for Productive Conservation.* New York: Manchester University Press, 1998. 269 p. Bibl., ill., index. (Issues in environmental politics.) ISBN 071904698X.

This work presents several examples of noteworthy conservation activities by indigenous peoples in the Brazilian Amazon. Subsistence fishing, agriculture, and rubber tapping are among the industries that have successfully conserved natural resources and developed accountable local institutions.

1419. Le Breton, Binka. *Voices from the Amazon.* West Hartford, CT: Kumarian Press, 1993. 151 p. Bibl., ill., index. (Kumarian Press books for a world that works.) ISBN 1565490215.

These interviews with people from the western states of Acre and Rondônia in Brazil express concerns with Amazon basin development and includes suggestions for sustainable solutions.

1420. Revkin, Andrew. *The Burning Season: The Murder of Chico Mendes and the Fight for the Amazon Rain Forest.* Boston: Houghton Mifflin, 1990. 317 p. Bibl., ill. ISBN 039552394X.

This work presents information about the Brazilian rainforest, its development and conservation, and union history that includes details of the conflict between rubber tappers and landowners that ultimately led to the murder of the union leader.

1421. Schmink, Marianne, and Charles H. Wood. *Contested Frontiers in Amazonia.* New York: Columbia University Press, 1992. 387 p. Bibl., ill., index. ISBN 0231076606.

This is an interdisciplinary case study of the Brazilian state of Pará and the process of change with a summary of the environmental effects of development policy during the past twenty years.

Caribbean Area

1422. Díaz-Briquets, Sergio, and Jorge Pérez-López. *Conquering Nature: The Environmental Legacy of Socialism in Cuba.* Pittsburgh, PA: University of Pittsburgh Press, 2000. 328 p. Bibl., index. (Pitt Latin American series.) ISBN 082294118X.

This volume examines environmental trends and issues in the socialist state, their socioeconomic and legal backdrop, as well as the effect of the Soviet Union's collapse.

Central America

1423. Faber, Daniel J. *Environment Under Fire: Imperialism and the Ecological Crisis in Central America.* New York: Monthly Review Press, 1993. 301 p. Bibl., ill., index. ISBN 0853458391.

This is an analysis of the roots of Central America's current social and ecological crisis, including the significant role played by U.S. economic policies.

1424. Leonard, H. Jeffrey. *Natural Resources and Economic Development in Central America: A Regional Environmental Profile.* New Brunswick, NJ: Transaction Books, 1987. 279 p. Ill., index. ISBN 0887387225.

This examines the link between the region's natural resources, its burgeoning population, and socioeconomic and political implications. (OP)

1425. McDade, Lucinda A. *La Selva: Ecology and Natural History of a Neotropical Rain Forest.* Chicago: University of Chicago Press, 1994. 486 p. Bibl., ill., index. ISBN 0226039501.

This is a description of La Selva Biological station in Costa Rica. Part I: Abiotic aspects; Part II: Plant communities; Part III: Animals; Part IV: Plant-animal interactions; and Part V: La Selva human environment.

1426. Primack, Richard B. et al., eds. *Timber, Tourists, and Temples: Conservation and Development in the Maya Forest of Belize, Guatemala, and Mexico.* Washington, DC: Island Press, 1998. 426 p. Bibl., ill., index. ISBN.

This recounts multiple efforts to establish sustainable forestry in Central America within different social and political structures. Among the many challenges are how to maintain a balance between current community needs while also addressing long-term development goals.

1427. Stonich, Susan C. *"I Am Destroying the Land!": The Political Ecology of Poverty and Environmental Destruction in Honduras.* Boulder, CO: Westview Press, 1993. 191 p. Bibl., ill. (Conflict and social change series.) ISBN 0813386497.

This is an account of the adverse consequences of Honduran capitalist agriculture in human and environmental terms. (OP)

1428. Wallace, David Rains. *The Quetzal and the Macaw: The Story of Costa Rica's National Parks.* San Francisco: Sierra Club Books, 1992. 222 p. Bibl., ill., index. ISBN 0871565854.

This describes Costa Rica's successful land protection policy with implications for other developing countries and tropical regions. (OP)

Mexico

1429. Gore, Robert H. *The Gulf of Mexico: A Treasury of Resources in the American Mediterranean.* Sarasota, FL: Pineapple Press, 1992. 384 p. Bibl., ill., index. ISBN 1561640107.

This is an environmental and natural resource study of the regions surrounding the Gulf of Mexico.

1430. Simon, Joel. *Endangered Mexico: An Environment on the Edge.* San Francisco: Sierra Club Books, 1997. 275 p. Bibl., index. ISBN 0871563517.

This is a balanced examination of the socioeconomic, historical, cultural, and political background to Mexico's environmental problems.

1431. Simonian, Lane. *Defending the Land of the Jaguar: A History of Conservation in Mexico.* 1st ed. Austin, TX: University of Texas Press, 1995. 326 p. Bibl., ill., index. ISBN 029277690X.

Resource protection in Mexico always has been a pragmatic and utilitarian discussion

that contrasts markedly with that of its northern neighbor. This work is a point of departure for Mexican environmental studies.

South America

1432. Colchester, Marcus. *Guyana, Fragile Frontier: Loggers, Miners and Forest Peoples.* Kingston, Jamaica: Ian Randle Publishers, 1997. 171 p. Bibl., ill., index. ISBN 9768123222.

This is an examination of Guyana's current focus on development of interior resources that interest multinational companies. It considers the significant impact of timber and mining extraction activities on Amerindian populations as these development activities expand.

1433. Kane, Joe. *Savages.* 1st ed. New York: Knopf, 1995. 273 p. Ill. ISBN 0679411917.

This is an account of cultural destruction and environmental devastation caused by oil companies that operate in the Amazon region of Ecuador where the Huaorani nomadic warriors live.

FOODS AND COOKERY

This section includes works about diverse traditional cooking and ingredients in one alphabetical list.

1434. Botafogo, Dolores. *The Art of Brazilian Cookery: A Culinary Journey Through Brazil.* Reprint ed. New York: Hippocrene Books, 1993. 240 p. Ill. (Hippocrene international cookbook classics.) ISBN 0781801303 pbk.

This provides a solid introduction to Brazilian cooking traditions with adaptations for U.S. cooks

1435. Creen, Linette. *A Taste of Cuba: Recipes from the Cuban-American Community.* New York: Dutton, 1991. 322 p. Ill., index. ISBN 0525249702.

This cookbook provides a variety of authentic Cuban recipes adapted for the U.S. kitchen.

1436. Foster, Nelson, and Linda S. Cordell, eds. *Chilies to Chocolate: Food the Americas Gave the World.* Tucson, AZ: University of Arizona Press, 1992. 191 p. Bibl., index. ISBN 0816513015.

This collection of essays combines elements of natural and social history with American contributions to global food systems.

1437. Kennedy, Diana. *The Art of Mexican Cooking: Traditional Mexican Cooking for Aficionados.* New York: Bantam Books, 1989. 526 p. Ill., index. ISBN 0553057065.

One of the foremost authorities on Mexican cooking provides authentic recipes of the country's traditional and popular foods.

1438. Marks, Copeland. *False Tongues and Sunday Bread: A Guatemalan and Mayan Cookbook.* New York: Donald Fine, 1993. 416 p. Ill. ISBN 155611379X.

These recipes from highland Guatemala are characterized by tangy and acidic flavors instead of the spicy hot of the lowlands.

1439. Novas, Himilce, and Rosemary Silva. *Latin American Cooking Across the U.S.A.* 1st ed. New York: Knopf, 1997. 331 p. Ill., index. (Knopf cooks American.) ISBN 0679444084.

The cooking traditions and recipes from twenty-six Latin American countries are presented in this cookbook. The cultural context of the dishes and products are also included.

1440. Ortiz, Elisabeth Lambert. *A Taste of Latin America: Recipes and Stories.* 1st Am. ed. New York: Interlink Books, 1999. 121 p. Ill., index. ISBN 1566562872.

This book offers a variety of recipes of Latin America's rich food culture representing indigenous, Spanish, Portuguese, and African influences. Samples of Latin American prose and poetry accompany the cookbook.

1441. Pilcher, Jeffrey M. *Que Vivan los Tamales!: Food and the Making of Mexican Identity.* Albuquerque, NM: University of New Mexico Press, 1998. 234 p. Bibl., ill., index. (Diálogos.) ISBN 082631872X.

This work explores the intimate connection between national identity and Mexican food habits.

1442. Rojas-Lombardi, Felipe. *The Art of South American Cooking.* 1st ed. New York: HarperCollins Pub., 1991. 504 p. ISBN 0060164255.

Peru's most famous chef in the U.S. presents outstanding examples of South American specialties in this cookbook.

1443. Spieler, Marlena. *Flavors of Mexico: Fresh, Simple Twists on Classic Regional Dishes.* 1st Galahad ed. New York: Galahad Books, 1995. 311 p. Bibl., index. ISBN 0883658895.

This cookbook includes hundreds of recipes and variations of Mexican traditional, peasant cuisine, mostly unfamiliar to U.S. audiences.

1444. Trilling, Susana. *Seasons of My Heart: A Culinary Journey Through Oaxaca, Mexico.* 1st ed. New York: Ballantine Books, 1999. 369 p. Bibl., ill., index. ISBN 0345425960.

This is the companion volume to the popular PBS television series.

1445. Van Waerebeek-González, Ruth. *The Chilean Kitchen: Authentic, Homestyle Foods, Regional Wines, and Culinary Traditions of Chile.* 1st ed. New York: HPBooks, 1999. 324 p. Index. ISBN 1557883076.

This is an introduction to Chile's culinary traditions.

1446. Waldo, Myra. *The art of South American cookery.* New York: Hippocrene Books, 1996. 266 p. Ill. index. (Hippocrene international cookbook series.) ISBN 078180485X pbk.

These recipes represent Spanish, Portuguese, Indian, and African influences with adaptations for U.S. users.

Index

References are to entry numbers.

147